D1287512

A Practical Guide to Needs Assessment

Third Edition

ABOUT THE AMERICAN SOCIETY FOR TRAINING & DEVELOPMENT

The American Society for Training & Development (ASTD) is the world's largest professional association dedicated to the training and development field. In more than 100 countries, ASTD's members work in organizations of all sizes, in the private and public sectors, as independent consultants, and as suppliers. Members connect locally in 130 U.S. chapters and with 30 international partners.

ASTD started in 1943 and in recent years has widened the profession's focus to align learning and performance to organizational results and is a sought-after voice on critical public policy issues. For more information, visit www.astd.org.

A Practical Guide to Needs Assessment

Third Edition

Catherine M. Sleezer

Darlene F. Russ-Eft

Kavita Gupta

WILEY

Copyright © 2014 by John Wiley & Sons, Inc. All Rights Reserved.
Published by Wiley
One Montgomery Street, Suite 1200, San Francisco, CA 94104-4594
www.wiley.com

Cover Design by Wiley
Cover art by Hero Images | Getty

No part of this publication may be reproduced, stored in a retrieval system, or transmitted in any form or
by any means, electronic, mechanical, photocopying, recording, scanning, or otherwise, except as permitted
under Section 107 or 108 of the 1976 United States Copyright Act, without either the prior written permission of the Publisher, or authorization through payment of the appropriate per-copy fee to the Copyright
Clearance Center, Inc., 222 Rosewood Drive, Danvers, MA 01923, 978-750-8400, fax 978-646-8600, or
on the web at www.copyright.com. Requests to the Publisher for permission should be addressed to the
Permissions Department, John Wiley & Sons, Inc., 111 River Street, Hoboken, NJ 07030, 201-748-6011,
fax 201-748-6008, or online at http://www.wiley.com/go/permissions.

Limit of Liability/Disclaimer of Warranty: While the publisher and authors have used their best efforts in
preparing this book, they make no representations or warranties with respect to the accuracy or completeness
of the contents of this book and specifically disclaim any implied warranties of merchantability or fitness for
a particular purpose. No warranty may be created or extended by sales representatives or written sales materials. The advice and strategies contained herein may not be suitable for your situation. You should consult
with a professional where appropriate. Neither the publisher nor authors shall be liable for any loss of profit
or any other commercial damages, including but not limited to special, incidental, consequential, or other
damages. Readers should be aware that Internet websites offered as citations and/or sources for further information may have changed or disappeared between the time this was written and when it is read.

For additional copies/bulk purchases of this book in the U.S. please contact 800–274–4434.

Wiley books and products are available through most bookstores. To contact Wiley directly call our Wiley
publishes in a variety of print and electronic formats and by print-on-demand. Some material included
with standard print versions of this book may not be included in e-books or in print-on-demand. If this
book refers to media such as a CD or DVD that is not included in the version you purchased, you may
download this material at http://booksupport.wiley.com. For more information about Wiley products,
visit www.wiley.com. Customer Care Department within the U.S. at 800-274-4434, outside the U.S. at
317-572-3985, fax 317-572-4002, or visit www.wiley.com

For more information about Wiley products, visit www.wiley.com.

Library of Congress Cataloging-in-Publication Data

CIP data is available on file at the Library of Congress.

ISBN 978-1-118-45789-4 (hbk); 9781118458112 (ebk); 9781118458082 (ebk)

Printed in the United States of America
HB Printing   10 9 8 7 6 5 4 3 2 1

Contents

List of Figures

List of Needs Assessment Toolkit Forms

The following forms from Section Four of this book also are available at www.wiley.com/go/needs3e, password: professional.

The Instructor's Manual for the third edition of *A Practical Guide to Needs Assessment* is available free online to qualified college and university instructors. To download a printable copy of the manual, please visit: www.wiley.com/college/gupta3e

Preface

Ignorance of all things is an evil neither terrible nor excessive, nor yet the greatest of all; but great cleverness and much learning, if they be accompanied by a bad training, are a much greater misfortune.

Plato

When I wrote the first edition of this book in 1999, I had no idea that it would sustain such a long run and continue to retain its initial focus fifteen years later. Back in the day, needs assessment was in its nascent stages and the majority of books on the subject focused mostly on theory rather than practice. By cutting to the chase, the simplicity of the first edition, with its toolkit, provided just the formula that human resource development (HRD) professionals needed to carry out on-the-job needs assessments. In the second edition, Sleezer and Russ-Eft built on the success of the first edition by using their vast experience as scholarly practitioners and prominent leaders in the field to add depth and breadth to the book.

In today's online, global world, technology will more than likely play an important role in your needs assessment. This updated edition reflects this recent trend by providing access to online links from vendors who may have already developed the tool or process that you are looking for, an online toolkit that you can customize easily and resources from professional associations.

The book also brings a global perspective that encapsulates needs assessments for corporations, communities, and educational institutions worldwide, including schools and universities. It offers practical guidance for managers and for the professionals in such fields as human resource development, human performance technology, and instructional design. It also offers expert advice for community and international development leaders; board, committee, and volunteer leaders of non-profit organizations; government officials, and master's and doctoral students pursuing this subject.

It is estimated that the business world spends over $60 billion on training in the United States alone. Worldwide, this figure is more than double that. But it is a recognized fact that most organizations operate on lean budgets, careful about how training dollars are spent. Thus, it is even more imperative than before that needs assessments pinpoint the root cause of performance problems and offer solutions that are cost-effective.

A doctor might prescribe medication in response to a simple problem, but the diagnosis of a complex health problem might warrant the need for additional lab tests, x-rays, or a referral to a specialist. In the same fashion, developing a master training plan that reflects new policy changes for city social workers, where employee productivity is low and complaints about poor management are high, may call for a multi-pronged approach. This may require a job and task analysis, competency study, or strategic needs assessment to examine the problems before a game plan can be created.

This new edition focuses precisely on the fact that organizational and human performance needs are increasingly becoming more interwoven. For those of you who may be faced with these intricacies, a new chapter on how to navigate and implement a complex needs assessment has been added (Chapter Eight).

New, real-life case studies showcase these mid-size to large-scale needs assessments in various contexts. In one instance, a complex needs assessment is used to help an executive determine why his team is missing its performance goals. Another case examines how an organizational culture survey developed by an external agency gauges the culture change of a company transitioning from one CEO to another over a six-year period. A third case study shows how the three-step complex needs assessment process is used to craft a strategic training plan for a government agency that involved a multi-state review of federal, state, and local requirements and regulations on safety and health needs.

Additional new case studies in Chapter Eleven also provide frameworks for understanding how an assessment for an Asia-Pacific-based corporate university was conducted and how an informal needs assessment to establish the challenges faced by senior officers across a broad range of public and private sector industries was leveraged.

This third edition covers everything from the basics to advanced strategies for managing a needs assessment with in-house or external clients in an organization or community. It also offers an overview of how needs assessment has evolved from the days of vestibule training to the savvy online performance support tools that are used today. With its smorgasbord of needs assessment tools, tips, and examples from the real world, I hope that this new all-in-one edition will help you learn, plan, and execute your initiatives successfully.

Kavita Gupta
September 2013

Acknowledgments

THIS THIRD EDITION OF *A Practical Guide to Needs Assessment* contains material from the earlier editions of the book as well as new information, tools, and resources. We want to acknowledge all the needs assessment instructors, researchers, and practitioners whose contributions are included in this edition.

We especially thank those who provided feedback on the previous editions, including what worked and should remain the same and also what was missing or could be improved. We took the feedback seriously and worked hard to make this edition even more helpful than the previous ones.

We also want to thank the expert practitioners who offered new case studies. These include Kelly Hannum, Emily Hoole, Cathy McCullough, Brenda Nickel, Rebecca Roehm, Shari Stein, Dave Torres, and Thomas Wood. These case studies yield first-hand insights into how needs assessments are conducted in the real world.

Thanks to the staff at Wiley, including Matthew Davis, Ryan Noll, and Dawn Kilgore, who delivered amazing assistance every step of the way. The best words to describe working with these experts who are exceptionally skilled in collaborating and teamwork are "fun," "easy," and "rewarding."

This edition was greatly enriched by the thinking and editing skills that Deane B. Gradous contributed. Thanks also to Oregon State University and Baker Hughes for their support. A special thanks to our spouses, Jim Sleezer, Jack Eft, and Rahul Gupta, who continue to give us their patience, understanding, and encouragement.

Catherine (Cathy) M. Sleezer

Darlene F. Russ-Eft

Kavita Gupta

Introduction

NEEDS ASSESSMENT IS AN important step in the performance improvement business. It precedes the design and development of human resource development (HRD), human performance technology (HPT), and community-building initiatives. Needs assessment is a process for examining and framing people-related problems, performance improvement opportunities, and organization-related or community-related problems and potential solutions. It might be initiated in response to a problem or opportunity, or it might be used in ongoing learning initiatives, performance improvement efforts, and organization or community development work.

A needs assessment can focus on one or more individuals, on people within units or teams, on people across job functions, on a business, a government agency, or an entire community or community group. It can also focus on the people-related problems and improvement opportunities that are an ordinary part of interorganizational, national, and international education, development, and performance improvement efforts.

Tip

Organizations are comprised of people working together to accomplish something, so throughout this book we refer to government agencies, businesses, communities, community groups, inter-organizational groups, and so forth as *organizations*. Also, we use the term *community development* to include efforts that focus on building strong local communities and as well as international efforts that focus more globally.

Needs assessments rely on "insider" information about a situation. Whether we work as internal or external consultants on a needs assessment with partners who have insider information about a situation, we do so to diagnose the needs accurately and to provide practical solutions to address the needs. In some cases, however, we lack the knowledge, skills, or tools to conduct an effective assessment or we are confused about which approach to use, given the wide array of choices.

PURPOSE OF THE BOOK

This book bridges the gap between needs assessment theory and practice. The world has changed greatly since 2007 when the second edition of *A Practical Guide to Needs Assessment* was published. The footprints of individual and organizational behaviors can now be captured in real time via technology for all to see, and this archival information can be displayed in various formats, including text, voice recordings, photographs, and videos.

Organizations are now flatter, more geographically dispersed, and matrixed—and they have cross-site coordination. This results in issues related to cultural differences and to technology-enhanced communications. Furthermore, with the cross-site coordination, more people are involved in making decisions. Seldom does one person have sole decision authority for a project.

Furthermore, computer technology has enabled many organizations to move from using a "one-size-fits-all" approach to taking advantage of the snowflake effect (Hodgins, 2009a) in which products and services are tailored to the unique attributes and needs of individuals and groups. Hodgins describes the snowflake effect:

Just the right CONTENT, to
Just the right PERSON, at
Just the right TIME, on
Just the right DEVICE, in
Just the right CONTEXT, in
Just the right WAY.. (Hodgins, 2009 b, Slide 8)

As an example of the snowflake effect, consider television programming. In the past, the programs on a few television channels were accessed by many individuals. Today each individual can pick and choose the sources of news and programming from among the many available television channels or an individual can bypass television altogether and download favorite programs from other sources, such as the web or radio. Also, consider the options that automobile companies now offer each individual to design a new car. The customer can select the car's exterior color, the upholstery pattern, and, of course, the payment plan. Finally, consider the impact of the snowflake effect on instructional design. The traditional process of developing training using a systematic process and input from experts is challenged by learners who use search engines and online networks to create, with a few clicks on the keypad, their own snowflake effects for learning. Moreover, learners can use the user ratings posted on websites to guide their decisions.

As these examples highlight, many organizations are trying to understand the individual's experience (one person at a time) so they can tailor products and services to meet the unique needs of individual customers, employees, and other stakeholders. In this environment, it should not be surprising that businesses are driving greater efficiencies in their processes. Other types of organizations, including communities, not-for-profit organizations, and interorganizational committees that also compete for resources, have adapted business labels and business processes. For example, many communities now have strategic plans and managers who make the business decisions that enable the communities to access and efficiently use the resources that are required for continued existence and growth.

Advances in computer technology continue to drive changes in how individuals work, learn, and live their lives. Examples of such changes include online banking, computer-aided engineering, and self-checkout registers at stores. Individuals who want to keep up with these changes often cannot wait for formal training. For example, a hungry person with a cart of produce who faces a self-checkout terminal for the first time usually can manage to complete the grocery purchase using the learning-by-doing approach. As this example highlights, learning new ways of doing things is an inherent part of completing tasks—and completing tasks contributes to individual learning.

Individual performance also has changed. Over 33 percent of individuals worldwide now are connected to the Internet (Miniwatts Marketing Group, 2012). Performance now often involves connecting with others virtually, interacting with ever larger networks of people, and managing and analyzing greater amounts of information.

The networked capabilities of cell phones, tablets, laptops, and computers alters how individuals learn. Individuals increasingly turn to the Internet, where with a few key strokes they can compare the information and misinformation that are available online from multiple sources. They can access information nuggets quickly to inform their specific learning or performance needs. In such situations, the person who posted the information may be unknown, and the facts may be intermingled with the fiction. Learning can also occur via massive open online learning courses (MOOCs), where one instructor runs a course for thousands of learners.

Each of these changes affects the practice of needs assessment. Seasoned practitioners recognize that conducting needs assessments today involves networking with more people in more places, working with more data, completing this work more quickly, and negotiating more effectively to meet the specific needs of individuals and groups. Conducting needs assessments today also involves separating fact from fiction, synthesizing various kinds of data (such as photographs, database information, interviews), and sharing the results with decision-makers and those who have a stake in the needs assessment (the stakeholders) in ways that allow them to quickly access and execute on the insights that they can use.

To address these changes in the learning and performance environment, this third edition of *A Practical Guide to Needs Assessment* has updated content, new cases, and expanded instructor materials. However, we continue to focus on practitioner needs and provide practitioners with how-to answers to fundamental questions, such as How is a needs assessment conducted? and What are the steps in a competency-based needs assessment? We also provide recommendations that are based on sound research and theory.

Over the years, scores of practitioners have expressed their frustration at the lack of resources that describe needs assessment in practitioner terms. This book, which was initially published in 1999, was a response to this frustration, and it provided a resource for the professionals who were responsible for assessing workplace and community needs for training, learning, organization development, and performance improvement. It served as a resource for practitioners in human performance technology, human resource management, professional development, education, community development, international development, human resource development, leadership development, education, instructional design, management, social services, and adult education.

For this edition, we asked experts who use the book to suggest improvements, and we sincerely appreciate their feedback. Throughout this edition, you will see ideas, cases, and exercises contributed by these professionals who are on the front line of needs assessment.

The third edition also contains the following updates:

- A summary of recent advances in our knowledge about learning, training, and performance that you can use to quickly prepare for client meetings

- An overview of eight world views (or structures of thinking) that are used by individuals, organizations, and societies. Each world view offers a unique understanding about how the world operates, who makes decisions, and what rules govern a society. The analyst's, client's, and stakeholders' world views influence the needs assessment

- Additional information on techniques for analyzing qualitative and quantitative data

- A discussion of some tools offered by vendors to assess individual, group, and organizational needs and competencies

- A new chapter that describes the complex needs assessment approach

- The use of workforce surveys in assessing organizational needs

- Cases and examples that include for-profit, non-profit, governmental agencies, and community organizations
- New Toolkit forms
- Expanded materials for instructors who use this book as a text for courses at the undergraduate or graduate level

Expert tips and case studies appear throughout the book, marked with the following icons:

This icon marks an expert tip that can save you time, money, and frustration.

This icon marks a short case that demonstrates an aspect of needs assessment.

AUDIENCE FOR THE BOOK

This book is intended for practitioners who are looking for systematic approaches to conducting needs assessments as the basis for the following types of initiatives:

- Introducing a training, development, or change program or initiative
- Designing a training, development, or change program or initiative
- Assessing the development needs of a workforce
- Improving individual, group, organization, or interorganization performance
- Providing community, regional, national, and international development interventions

The book's straightforward approach is designed to keep you on target with your initiative. Its no-frills style allows you to reach the heart of the subject matter quickly and apply the principles right away.

The book is also for educators and students who want to learn more about practical approaches to needs assessment. A supplemental Instructor Manual with exercises, assessment materials, and discussion questions for each chapter is available for this edition [www.wiley.com/college/gupta3e].

Finally, the book is appropriate for community leaders, managers and small-business owners, family-owned businesses, and heads of small- or medium-sized organizations, including those who perform needs assessment only on an occasional basis.

SCOPE OF THE BOOK

The book lays the foundation for sound needs assessment practice through initial grounding in the whats and whys of the process. This foundation is followed by the how-tos of needs assessment. The book includes the following elements:

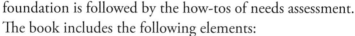

- A framework for understanding needs assessment and the reasons for doing one

- Needs assessment models and theories

- Information on how to collect and analyze data

- Step-by-step strategies for launching and implementing five needs assessment approaches

- Information on managing needs assessments

- Information on professional ethical guidelines

- Resources for accessing additional information

- A Toolkit containing templates, worksheets, and resources that you can customize for immediate use, both in hard copy and via a link that can be downloaded from the web

- A glossary to facilitate the use of a common language among needs assessment practitioners

HOW THE BOOK IS ORGANIZED

The book has four sections, as shown in Figure I.1.

Part One (Chapters One through Three) begins with a bird's-eye view of needs assessment. Use the information on what needs assessment is, on the well-known models and theories of needs assessment, and on the how-tos of data collection and analysis to frame your project and to enhance your credibility with stakeholders and clients.

Chapter One defines needs assessment and describes its key features. It also describes some challenges to assessing needs within complex systems, and it contains a matrix that compares the five needs assessment approaches that are described in the book.

Chapter Two describes practical needs assessment ideas and models. It also identifies some thought leaders in the field and provides a summary of key advances over time in our knowledge about learning, training, and performance. Being able to reference these works and thought leaders can increase your credibility with clients and other stakeholders.

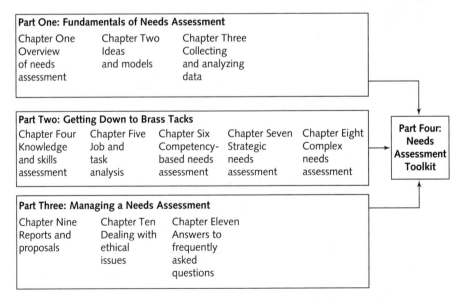

FIGURE I.1 *Overview of Book Contents*

This chapter also provides an overview of eight structures of thinking, which can be thought of as value or belief systems, that are used by individuals, organizations, and societies.

Chapter Three describes strategies for gathering and analyzing data. It offers guidelines for conducting interviews, focus groups, and observations. It also presents things to consider when reviewing written records and developing surveys. In addition, the chapter discusses how to analyze your needs assessment data.

Part Two (Chapters Four through Eight) describes five approaches to needs assessment that can contribute greatly to your success. Each approach is described in a separate chapter that includes when to use the approach, its benefits, its drawbacks, and its critical success factors. Where appropriate, time-saving tips are offered. Key steps are explained and corresponding forms and worksheets in the Toolkit section are referenced.

Chapter Four is the first in the series of how-to chapters. It details steps for doing a conventional needs assessment to identify the knowledge and skill needs for training.

Chapter Five explains the steps for performing a job and task analysis and for formulating a training plan based on the resulting information. It also shows how to write effective job and task statements.

Chapter Six explains how to conduct a competency-based assessment. The steps for developing competencies using behavioral interviews are presented, and a competency dictionary and competency model are described.

Chapter Seven shows how to link performance problems and performance needs to the business strategy of an organization. Porter's (1980) five-forces model for analyzing the external environment is explained, and guidelines for using process maps are provided.

Chapter Eight describes the complex needs assessment approach. Using this approach can require combining knowledge from the other needs assessment approaches, applying extensive expertise from other subject areas (such as knowledge of safety regulations or organization development)—and most importantly using innovation.

Part Three (Chapters Nine through Eleven) describes strategies for managing a needs assessment. It includes ideas for writing proposals and reporting results, strategies for dealing with the ethical issues that can arise when implementing a needs assessment, and answers to frequently asked questions.

Chapter Nine explains how to write proposals and reports. It also describes how to use these documents to keep a needs assessment effort on track.

Chapter Ten describes ethical issues that may arise when conducting a needs assessment. It also provides insights and ethical guidelines for addressing such issues.

Chapter Eleven presents answers to frequently asked questions; for example, what to do about the client who does not pay or how to handle project creep. It presents practical strategies for addressing these issues.

Part Four contains the Needs Assessment Toolkit. It includes templates, worksheets, and assessments that can be replicated and either used as they are or customized. You can also access the Needs Assessment Toolkit online at www.wiley.com/go/needs3e, download the templates, worksheets, and resources, and customize them for your situation.

HOW TO USE THE BOOK

This book includes basic information for those who have little prior knowledge about needs assessment, as well as more sophisticated information for experienced practitioners who are facing complex needs assessment situations. If you fall into the first category, consider reviewing all the chapters first. You can then use the information immediately or assimilate it and use it at a later date. For instance, if you want to conduct a job and task analysis for technicians right away, then consult Chapter Five. You can also use the corresponding Toolkit templates. At a later date you may want to perform a competency study for first-line supervisors. The guidelines outlined in Chapter Six, as well as the corresponding Toolkit forms, which provide templates and worksheets that can give you a head start on this type of assessment.

If you have prior knowledge or experience with needs assessment, skim Part One. Then focus on those chapters in Part Two that provide more in-depth information.

If you are involved in a complex needs assessment or run into problems while conducting a needs assessment, check out the models and theories in Chapter Two and the ideas for managing a needs assessment in Chapters Nine, Ten, and Eleven.

Throughout the book, we share web pages that can help you quickly access information. However, the information on such sites can change quickly. If you find that a web page is no longer available, we suggest that you conduct a quick search of the organization's website or use the web to search for another site. For a quick reference guide to the chapters, see Figure I.2.

NEEDS ASSESSMENT TOOLKIT

The Needs Assessment Toolkit, Section Four of this book, contains more than twenty-five templates, resources, and worksheets that you can use and customize for your needs assessments. Each Toolkit form was designed to be used in conjunction with this third edition of *A Practical Guide to Needs Assessment*. Microsoft® Word templates can be downloaded, customized for your situation, and used for multiple projects.

To	Consult
Review the book's contents.	Introduction
Learn the definition of needs assessment, some challenges to assessing needs within complex systems, and the differences among the five approaches to needs assessment that are described in this book.	Chapter One
Learn about practical needs assessment ideas, models, and thought leaders in the field. Learn how our understanding of learning, training and performance changed over time and how world views influence needs assessments.	Chapter Two
Determine which data-collection methods to use in a needs assessment and how to analyze the data.	Chapter Three
Link performance problems or performance needs to the business strategy of an organization.	Chapter Seven
Identify training needs.	Chapters One, Two, Three, Four
Identify knowledge, skills, and abilities needed for a specific job or task. Develop a job description. Develop a job training plan.	Chapters One, Two, Three, Five
Identify competencies for effective performance. Build success profiles, particularly for supervisory or managerial jobs. Assess gaps in proficiency levels and formulate training or performance management systems.	Chapters One, Two, Three, Six
Develop a long-term performance improvement plan for an organization.	Chapters One, Two, Three, Seven
Assess gaps in performance that focus on non-training or systemic issues	Chapters One, Two, Four, Five, Six, Seven, Eight
Write a needs assessment proposal or create in-process and final reports.	Chapter Nine
Troubleshoot your needs assessment.	Chapters Two, Three, Nine, Ten, Eleven

FIGURE I.2 *Quick Reference Guide to Chapters*

I

Fundamentals of Needs Assessment

ONE Overview of Needs Assessment

PURPOSE

This chapter will enable you to accomplish the following:

- Describe what a needs assessment is.
- Identify the purposes and characteristics of a needs assessment.
- Define key terms.
- Learn how the definitions of needs assessment, sources of data, and data-collection and analysis strategies can be combined to create a needs assessment.
- Describe five approaches to needs assessment.

OVERVIEW

Most experts agree that human learning, training, and performance-improvement initiatives should begin with a needs assessment. This chapter sorts through the confusing collection of ideas about what a needs assessment really is and what the best ways to conduct one are.

As you read the following examples of typical requests that should lead to needs assessments, think about their similarities and differences:

- *"The vice president is ready to start his personal development program. How should he proceed?"*

- *"Team production is down! The engineers say the technician team is struggling with the new process. The team disagrees. Can you give them all training or something?"*

- *"We need to update the curriculum in our graduate program. What should the new curriculum include?"*

- *"Two major employers are moving out of our community. What actions should we take to keep employers here and to entice other employers to move to this community?"*

- *"What issues are of greatest concern to the communities in this region?"*

- *"Which workforce development initiatives should we invest in to make our country more competitive in the global marketplace?"*

- *"Next year our plant will continue the projects in Six Sigma quality and culture change. We also will implement new manufacturing procedures, install new equipment, and introduce new product lines. If employees try to make all these changes at once, productivity will fall. Where do you recommend we start? How can these efforts be integrated?"*

These requests probably sound familiar to most human resource development (HRD), human performance technology (HPT), instructional design (ID), community development, and international development professionals. Let's consider the similarities in the requests first and then their differences. Along the way, we will discuss the characteristics of needs assessment and define some key terms.

SIMILARITIES AMONG NEEDS ASSESSMENT REQUESTS

First, did you identify *dissatisfaction with the current situation* and *desire for change* as similarities among the requests? Each request implies that a gap or discrepancy exists between what is and what could or should be. A learning or performance gap between the current condition and the desired condition is called a need (see Figure 1.1).

Needs assessment is a process for figuring out how to close a learning or performance gap. It involves determining what the important needs are and how to address them. The process includes comparing the current condition to the desired condition, defining the problem or problems, understanding the behaviors and mechanisms that contribute to the current condition, determining if and how specific behaviors and mechanisms can be changed to produce the desired condition, developing solution strategies, and building support for action.

Second, did you notice the similar aims for the requests? They all focus on *addressing current issues* or on *specifying future learning or performance needs*. Needs assessment requests are typically aimed at the following situations:

- Solving a current problem
- Avoiding a past or current problem
- Creating or taking advantage of a future opportunity
- Providing learning, development, or growth

Third, did you notice that the requests *imply a solution that requires training, learning, performance improvement, community development, international development, or a combination of these*? Needs assessment is a diagnostic process that relies on data collection and analysis,

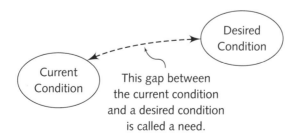

FIGURE 1.1 *Definition of a Need*

collaboration, and negotiation to identify and understand gaps in learning and performance and to determine future actions. Examples of actions that could be implemented as the result of a needs assessment include offering improved incentives, providing better information, engaging the appropriate people, enhancing the work design, supplying essential tools or technology, and implementing training or learning programs.

Fourth, did you also recognize that the requests are alike in including *little evidence* and *few clues* about whether taking the requested action will likely improve learning, development, or performance? Important details about the situation and the expected course of action are unknown to both those who request a needs assessment and those who receive such requests.

Similar to the sample requests at the beginning of this section, most requests that lead to needs assessments include fuzzy goals, incompatible beliefs, flawed assumptions, and large leaps in logic. In addition, they contain *little diagnostic information* about the specific behaviors or mechanisms that produced the current condition, about what particular changes could create the desired condition, or about what support may be required from other people or groups. Assessing needs in such situations before jumping in with solutions greatly increases the likelihood of success and avoids costly mistakes.

Tip Throwing resources at problems or opportunities is like throwing a chocolate pie at the wall and hoping some of it will stick: the action is more likely to create a mess than an improvement; furthermore, it is a waste of good resources.

Finally, did you notice that all the sample requests include *challenging questions*? The right answers to these questions cannot be found in a book or on the Internet. Indeed, such questions do not have one right answer. Using quick, commonsense solutions or throwing resources at such situations seldom work well either.

Instead, the requests for learning, training, development, and performance improvement initiatives must be evaluated and the "merit, worth, or value" (Scriven, 1991, p. 139) of the various options must be analyzed. Thus, needs assessment is a type of evaluation.

The Systems Model of Evaluation (Preskill & Russ-Eft, 2003; Russ-Eft & Preskill, 2005, 2009) identifies various factors for one organization that affect the success and the outcomes of an evaluation, including a needs assessment (see Figure 1.2). Factors in the needs assessment or

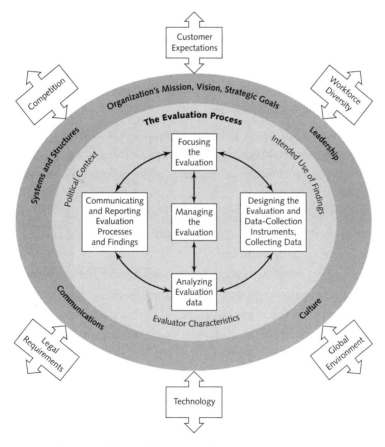

FIGURE 1.2 *A Systems Model of Evaluation*

Reprinted with permission from Sage, appearing in Russ-Eft, D., and Preskill, H. (2005). In search of the Holy Grail: ROI evaluation in HRD. *Advances in Developing Human Resources, 7,* 71–85.

evaluation project itself (such as the approach to managing the project) are shown in the model's inner circle; factors within the organization (such as the organization's mission, vision, and strategic goals) are shown in the model's outer circle; and factors that are outside the organization (such as customer expectations) are shown in the shapes that encircle the ring of organizational factors. Thus, many factors can influence how the challenging questions raised by a needs assessment are answered.

We have considered the similarities among the requests that lead to needs assessments. Next, we consider their differences.

DIFFERENCES AMONG REQUESTS THAT LEAD TO NEEDS ASSESSMENT

First, did you notice that the requests represent *different definitions of need*? Stufflebeam (1985) identified four useful definitions of need: discrepancy, democratic, diagnostic, and analytic. To explore these definitions, let's examine how needs could be determined for one example presented at the beginning of this chapter: "We need to update the curriculum in our undergraduate program. What should the new curriculum include?"

Discrepancy needs are based on the differences between the current and the ideal or the expected performance. Using a discrepancy definition of the needs, faculty members could compare their undergraduate curriculum with an ideal undergraduate curriculum, such as the one offered by a top-rated university program or endorsed by a professional association. The faculty members could also compare the number of outstanding alumni from their program and an ideal program using pre-determined criteria.

Democratic needs are based on what most people prefer or select and are determined by majority rule. Using a democratic definition of needs, faculty members could examine student choices. Because students vote with their feet, course enrollment in elective courses could serve as a measure of students' preference. Data on student preferences for elective courses could also be collected by surveying or interviewing students about their favorite electives.

If the faculty members believed that students enrolled in courses based on the instructor rather than the course title, they could use a democratic assessment to measure the enrollments for each faculty member over a period of time. Similarly, if faculty members assume that students prefer to avoid early morning courses, they could review several years of course schedules and the records showing the enrollments in electives.

Analytic needs are determined by intuition, insight, expert consideration, or enlightenment. Using an analytic definition of need, faculty members could identify the curricular changes that would improve the department's performance based on the insights of internal or external consultants or a program review committee.

Diagnostic needs are defined through causal analysis and research. Using diagnostic needs, faculty members could research the program's contributions to the job skills of recent graduates. Such analysis could provide insight into how each course contributes to the graduates' success in securing and keeping a job.

As the example above highlights, needs assessments are greatly influenced by the definition of need (i.e., discrepancy, democratic, analytic, or diagnostic), the sources of data, and the approach by which the data are collected. Needs assessments are also influenced by how the data are analyzed. In the curriculum example, some data could be analyzed using numerical rating scales, and other data could be analyzed using themes. Concept mapping could be used to visually show the relationships among the collected data (Watkins, Meiers, & Visser, 2012), or scenarios could be created. In addition, stories could be told.

Our curriculum example does not list all the data sources, data collection, or analysis options available to the faculty members—or, indeed, to anyone who conducts a needs assessment. However, it is sufficient to illustrate that the definition of need, the sources of data, and the choices about data collection and analysis influence the needs assessment process and outcomes. The analyst, sometimes with the help of a needs assessment committee, plans which definition of need is used, how needs assessment data will be collected and analyzed, and which data sources will be used. Most needs assessments rely on multiple sources of data, multiple kinds of data and more than one kind of data analysis.

Of course, the data sources and the data collection and analysis methods should reflect serious consideration of the political situation and the kinds of information that will have credibility for the decision maker(s). For instance, in our extended curriculum example above, some choices might be more appropriate if faculty members feel political pressure to justify the curricular changes to the college president and board. However, other less costly choices might be appropriate for a cohesive faculty group seeking to understand the situation before using their own authority to make changes.

Second, did you notice that the sample requests target *different levels of learning, development, and performance*? Needs assessment can be used to diagnose the learning and performance needs of individuals, teams, functional units, and whole organizations. They can also be used to diagnose the people-related issues of interorganizational groups, communities, countries, and even international efforts.

Third, did you notice that the requests focus on *various aspects of learning and performance*? Learning is the act of gaining knowledge or skills. It can exist in the individual, and it can reside in an organization's systems, databases, technologies, and culture. Training supports individual learning (that is, a gain in knowledge and skills) through specialized instruction and practice. The terms *knowledge* and *skill* have different meanings:

- *Knowledge:* The body of facts about a subject matter and the understanding that a person acquires through study or experience

- *Skill:* Knowledge that one proficiently applies in appropriate situations

The goalie in Figure 1.3 may have in-depth knowledge of soccer rules and the various plays allowed in the game. His role on the team is to prevent the ball from going into the net and allowing the opposing team to score. The picture shows that he has failed to block several balls.

Performance includes accomplishments, the processes that result in accomplishments, and the capacity for future performance. Let us consider each of these aspects of performance for our soccer goalie:

- *Accomplishment:* The major accomplishment desired for the goalie during the game is to save the goal by preventing the ball from going into the net.

- *Process:* To save the goal, the goalie integrates his knowledge of how to play the position with such skills as deflecting the ball and falling on it. His knowledge and skills interact with other factors (such as the defensive skills of his teammates) to affect how well he carries out the process of playing goalie.

- *Capacity:* The goalie's capacity for performance includes his bundle of skills and resources that can be applied to future play. They indicate his abilities to apply his mental, physical, and social skills to add value to the team.

FIGURE 1.3 *Soccer Player Who Knows Game's Rules but Lacks Game's Skills*

The goalie's accomplishments, processes, and capacity could affect the team's accomplishments (for example, the number of games won), their processes (such as the strategies the team uses while playing the game), and their capacity (that is, the team's bundle of skills and resources that can be applied to future play).

Some people see learning and performance as separate activities. We see them as interconnected. As seen in the example of the goalie, learning in the form of knowledge and skills can affect performance and vice versa. Although learning is not directly observable, many behaviors that create performance can be observed. Thus, changes in behavior often are used to infer that learning has occurred. For example, if our goalie observed a new technique, practiced the technique, and in subsequent games effectively used that technique, we could infer that learning had occurred.

This section has described the similarities and differences among sample requests that lead to needs assessments and in the process described the characteristics of needs assessments and defined some key terms. Next we focus on the benefits of needs assessment.

BENEFITS OF A NEEDS ASSESSMENT

A needs assessment frames the problems or opportunities of interest and builds relationships among the people and groups who have a stake in the issue. It also can provide the foundation for planning and action to improve learning, training, development, and performance. More specifically, a needs assessment can align resources with strategy, build relationships among those who have a stake in the situation, clarify problems or opportunities, set goals for future action, and provide data, insights, or justification for decision making. A needs assessment can also identify leverage points and resources for making changes, establish objectives for initiatives, prioritize actions, determine who must be involved for the HRD, HPT, or development efforts to be successful, and provide baseline data for later evaluation of results.

Equally important, a needs assessment can build support for HRD, HPT, community development, and international development efforts. The processes of using accurate data and negotiating among differing points of view can engage and mobilize decision-makers and others who have a stake in the situation. By sharing their knowledge, insights, and resources, those who are closest to the situation contribute to creating solutions that are practical, credible, and appropriate for the situation.

Given all of these benefits, it is obvious why so many training, learning, community and international development, and performance improvement models advocate systematic needs assessment: it ensures that interventions are relevant and address the needs.

FIVE APPROACHES TO NEEDS ASSESSMENT

Needs assessments are particularly important to professionals in such fields as HRD, HPT, and community and international development, who must align their work with strategic, individual, organizational, or community needs. In today's competitive climate, improving learning, training, and performance is emphasized more than ever before.

At the same time, individuals, organizations, and communities guard their resources. Today's decision-makers want HRD, HPT and community development initiatives to focus on their critical priorities and to drop the non-value-added work. Needs assessments can provide such a focus, but politics will affect how needs assessments are actually conducted.

Consider the situation facing Ruth Duple, the new manager of learning and organization development for an international firm that manufactures computer equipment. The firm's management team recently speculated that poor supervisory performance was causing quality problems, increased turnover, and missed production deadlines. They handed the problem to Ruth. When she reviewed this new challenge, Ruth realized that she did not know how the poor supervisory performance related to the organization's strategic goals, the cause or causes of the problems, or the management team's vision for supervisory performance.

> **Tip**
>
> Some people focus on the problems in a situation, while others recognize that the same problems present opportunities for improvement.

To aid her thinking, Ruth sketched a simplified systems diagram of her firm (see Figure 1.4). The large circle represents the firm. Note that it is bordered with dashed lines to acknowledge that changes from outside the firm (such as government regulations, politics, competition, and availability of raw materials) can affect the firm, and that changes from inside the firm (such as increased wages) can affect the larger environment. Inputs to the firm's performance system include the employees, tools, and raw materials (such as sound and video cards).

Within the firm, each gray box represents a distinct unit or department that contributes to the production process. Of course, the firm actually has many more units than are shown in Figure 1.4. Employees in each unit use work processes (shown by the darker gray horizontal boxes) to convert materials and other inputs into unit outputs. The outputs of one unit become the inputs for other units. When all the production processes are complete, the firm's output—computer equipment—is loaded on trucks for shipment to customers.

The employees in each unit report to a supervisor who in turn reports to a manager. The managers and some other executives report to the firm's CEO.

For the sake of simplicity, Ruth did not include in her sketch the collaborative efforts that span units; the feedback that supervisors receive from internal and external customers and from managers; the firm's structure, politics, and culture; or the external community. However, her sketch does provide a focus for thinking about the needs assessment.

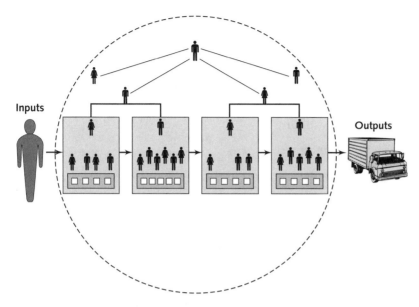

FIGURE 1.4 *Ruth's Sketch of a Simplified Systems Diagram*

As an experienced HRD professional, Ruth knows many needs assessment models, each with its own jargon and unique steps. She also has reflected on how the four definitions of need could fit her situation, the many ways to collect and analyze data, and the sources of data for her situation.

Ruth also is familiar with the needs assessment study by Mathews, Ueno, Kekale, Repka, Pereira, and Silva (2001). It focused on organizations in the United Kingdom, Finland, and Portugal that were implementing quality management practices, such as ISO 9001:2000. The study ranked the importance of the following elements to assessing training needs within an organization:

- Senior management decisions
- Supervisors' opinions
- Skills inventory
- Employee surveys

- Analysis of projected business or service plans
- Customer opinions
- Training audits
- Requests from work groups
- External consultant
- Advisory committee

The study found that senior management decisions and supervisors' opinions received much higher rankings than the other elements, indicating the importance of the senior management and supervisors in determining training needs. The authors recommended that objective and formal methods of assessing needs be more widely adopted. This study highlights that, while management and supervisor perspectives are important, using objective data and formal methods could ensure broader support for addressing quality management practices.

Ruth's firm must address its quality problems, increased turnover, and missed production deadlines to remain competitive in today's marketplace. Given the importance of these issues, Ruth decided to use a formal needs assessment approach to gain more knowledge about the gap between actual and desired supervisory performance and to figure out how to close it. She considered five needs assessment approaches.

The first approach, *knowledge and skills assessment*, focuses on the knowledge and skill needs that may exist. If such needs do exist, they can be addressed with training. Ruth could survey the supervisors themselves to obtain a list of their knowledge and skill needs or she could talk to managers. Then Ruth could implement training programs that address the needs. This approach to needs assessment is described in Chapter Four.

The second approach, *job and task analysis*, focuses on information about the scope, responsibilities, and tasks of particular job functions. Because Ruth knows that supervisors regularly mishandle performance reviews, she could implement a job and task analysis to gather specific information about how this supervisory job task should be conducted in the firm. Ruth could use this needs assessment approach to prioritize the knowledge, skills, and other improvements that are required to close the gap between the way the performance reviews are conducted and the way they should be conducted. This approach to needs assessment is described in Chapter Five.

The third approach, *competency-based needs assessment*, focuses on determining the competencies needed for specific job functions. Competencies are the knowledge, skills, attitudes, values, motivations, and beliefs that people must have to be successful in a job. Ruth knows that successful supervisors are those whose teams continually outperform other teams and who have higher employee retention rates. Ruth could use this needs assessment approach to identify specific behaviors that are exhibited by successful supervisors and not exhibited by less successful supervisors. This approach to needs assessment is described in Chapter Six.

The fourth approach, *strategic needs assessment*, focuses on learning and performance gaps within the context of an organization's business strategy. Ruth could use this needs assessment approach to learn how supervisors do and do not contribute to the unit's and the firm's strategic goals and about the work mechanisms that contribute to their current performance. She could also consider factors in the firm's external and internal environments. Ruth could use the information she gathers to map the desired work processes and outcomes, to develop supervisory training, and to address non-training issues. This approach to needs assessment is described in Chapter Seven.

The fifth approach, a *complex needs assessment*, is used when applying a single approach alone, such as a knowledge and skills assessment, a job and task assessment, competency needs assessment, or a strategic needs assessment, is insufficient for assessing the needs. For example, complex needs assessments are appropriate for assessing needs at the operational level of an organization that is facing many non-training and systemic issues. Conducting a complex needs assessment can require the analyst to combine components from the other approaches to needs assessment, apply expertise from other subject areas (such as knowledge of safety regulations or organization development)—and, most importantly, to innovate.

Figure 1.5 is a graph of the relative time and effort required to complete each approach to needs assessment. The approaches in the lower portion of the chart are less time- and effort-intensive. Figure 1.6 summarizes the approaches presented in Figure 1.5, starting with the lower-most approach, describing when to use each approach and its advantages and disadvantages.

Regardless of which approach you decide to use, consider the realities of conducting needs assessments in the workplace or community. First, time will always be a critical factor, as most clients or sponsors will be more concerned about implementing the actual improvement than about spending time analyzing needs. Second, line managers may be reluctant to release personnel to participate in interviews or focus groups, especially if operations will be affected. Third, needs assessments are political. Individuals hold differing and sometimes conflicting opinions, and they use power and influence to achieve their own ends. Therefore, a needs assessment usually involves negotiating cooperation among people to achieve a common task. For this reason, a needs assessment committee can provide important support for a needs assessment. Often individual advisory committee members serve as liaisons with groups who have important stakes in the outcomes of the needs assessment.

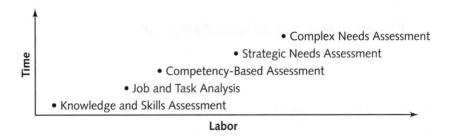

FIGURE 1.5 *Comparison of Time and Effort Required for the Needs Assessment Approaches*

Approach	Purpose	When to Use	Advantages	Disadvantages
Knowledge and Skills Assessment	Identify the knowledge and skills required to perform a job	Implement new technology Identify training needs Develop a training plan	Ensures training is linked to the learner's needs Easiest to implement	Has a limited focus
Job and Task Analysis	Determine responsibilities and tasks necessary to perform a job	Develop new job descriptions or revise existing position profiles Identify task listings for new or redesigned job functions: knowledge, skills, abilities, and standards Develop consistent training requirements, especially for technical and specialized jobs	Stimulates interest Defines skill requirements for entry-level versus mid-level positions Identifies additional knowledge, skills, and abilities to move across or upward within a job function	Does not take into account the external factors that may affect job performance Is time-consuming Is costly in time and personnel resources Assumes that the work is static Assumes that there is one best way to perform the work
Competency-Based Needs Assessment	Identify knowledge, skills, and attitudes for superior job performance	Identify competencies that are required for jobs Measure proficiency levels of people Develop standardized training Develop performance management systems (recruiting, hiring, promoting, or career planning)	Determines qualities that distinguish average from superior performance Provides information about current and future predictors or job performance	Is time-consuming Requires high involvement of many people within an organization Is costly Requires good project management system for large projects

FIGURE 1.6 *Matrix of Needs Assessment Approaches*

Approach	Purpose	When to Use	Advantages	Disadvantages
Strategic Needs Assessment	Examine existing performance problems (reactive) or address new and future performance needs (proactive) within the context of the organization's or the community's business strategy Develop long-term performance improvement plan	Link performance improvement needs to business strategy of the organization or community Identify performance improvement opportunities at various levels (such as individual, process, and organizational)	Develops long-term solutions to existing performance problems or new performance needs Solves problems that affect core business processes Eliminates non-value-added activities	Is time-consuming Is costly in time and personnel resources Requires that a business strategy exist
Complex Needs Assessment	Assess situations that include non-training or systemic needs as well as training needs; assess needs that are complex, require innovation or one or more bodies of expertise beyond needs assessment (e.g., safety, organization development) level	Because this approach is more complex than the other four approaches, use it when the other approaches are insufficient or when components of the other approaches must be combined	Provides flexibility	Is time-consuming Requires the analyst to innovate Is costly May require the creation of needs assessment processes and forms

FIGURE 1.6 *Matrix of Needs Assessment Approaches* (continued)

After considering all her options for this needs assessment including the five approaches described above, Ruth concluded that this could be a high-stakes needs assessment both for the firm and for her career. Because of the project's importance, Ruth decided to review the needs assessment ideas and models presented in the next chapter before selecting a needs assessment approach.

CONCLUSION

Needs assessment requires carefully analyzing a situation and building support for action. It involves considering all the various kinds of data that could inform the decisions and actions, the potential sources for the data, and choices among data analysis method to determine what will best provide a foundation for the learning, training, development, or performance improvement initiative.

Regardless of which needs assessment approach you choose to implement, the message is simple: needs assessments set the direction for learning, training, development, and performance improvement initiatives. The next chapter describes some practical ideas and models that can contribute greatly to a successful needs assessment.

TWO   Ideas and Models That Guide Practice

PURPOSE

This chapter will enable you to accomplish the following:

- Recognize the difference between needs and wants.

- Identify different kinds of needs.

- Recognize different kinds of assessments.

- Recognize the thought leaders in the needs assessment field.

- Understand how the world views that clients and other stakeholders use influence needs assessment.

- Consider the recent changes in our understanding of performance, learning, and training.

RELATED TOOLKIT JOB AIDS

The following job aids for use with the material in this chapter are available in the Needs Assessment Toolkit, Section Four of this book.

- Tools and Strategies for Assessing Systems
- Advances Over Time in Knowledge About Learning, Training, and Performance

OVERVIEW

Why should you take the time to learn about needs assessment ideas and models? Because they can make your job easier and add great value to your needs assessment! Today's learning and performance improvement situations are complex. Moreover, HRD, HPT, and development initiatives are key drivers of growth, transformation, and productivity for individuals, organizations, communities, and countries. In this high-stakes environment, knowing needs assessment ideas and models that provide the language and insights for success is simply smart practice.

You also should know the names of the thought leaders who contributed significantly to our current understanding of needs assessment, for example, Thomas Gilbert, Joe Harless, Roger Kaufman, Robert Mager, Allison Rossett, Geary Rummler, and Richard Swanson. As you read this chapter and other chapters in this book, watch for their names.

The ideas and models presented in this chapter can be used in conjunction with the approaches to needs assessment described in Chapters Four, Five, Six, Seven, and Eight. The ideas and models are grouped into three categories based on use: (1) prioritizing needs, (2) measuring performance, and (3) finding the causes of problems. During initial meetings with the client or decision-makers to contract a needs assessment, be prepared, if asked, to discuss needs assessment ideas, models, and thought leaders. Most decision-makers carefully select the analyst who conducts their assessment, and they often rely on informal discussions of these topics to select practitioners who have appropriate, in-depth knowledge.

Tip Informal discussions about the needs assessment can reveal an analyst's areas of expertise and also his or her level of truthfulness. Decision-makers seldom expect the analyst to know *every* idea, model, and thought leader who is mentioned. They do, however, expect some knowledge of the major contributors to the field and they do expect honesty from the analyst in describing his or her level of knowledge.

PRIORITIZING NEEDS

Most individuals, teams, organizations, communities, and countries have more *wants* and *needs* than available resources to address them. Use the information in this section to quickly separate needs from wants, distinguish among various kinds of need, and consider the kind of analysis that a project requires.

A want is something the client would like to have even though it does not contribute to a long-term learning or performance goal. By contrast, a need, when addressed, contributes to achieving the desired learning or performance goal by closing the gaps between the current condition and the desired condition. Thus, important questions for any proposed needs assessment are, *Whose needs will the project address?* and *What kind of needs will the project address?*

Because needs assessments are implemented in complex systems, a change in one level or element of the system can affect other levels and elements. For example, a needs assessment within an organization can produce results that contribute to the larger shared society (Guerra-Lopez & Kaufman, 2013; Kaufman, 2005). However, practitioners should carefully consider the focus for a needs assessment before starting any project. Four kinds of needs that you are likely to see in practice and that warrant a needs assessment are as follows:

- *Strategic needs:* These are gaps between current and desired conditions that focus on the long-term organizational goals. Closing these gaps is critical for the long-term success of the entity.

- *Operational or tactical needs:* These are gaps between the current and desired conditions that must be addressed in the short term in order to achieve an operational or tactical initiative. Addressing these needs can change how the organization's work is accomplished.

- *Individual performance needs:* These are gaps between current and desired conditions relative to a person's accomplishments, behaviors, or capacity for performance. An individual sometimes closes such gaps to meet personal goals or to meet strategic or operational business goals.

- *Learning needs:* These are gaps in knowledge and skill between the current and desired conditions. Most needs assessment experts agree that individuals have learning needs. In addition, growing bodies of literature describe the learning needs of teams and organizations.

Other kinds of needs may involve various groups (such as specific teams or departments, organizational units, community groups, or national groups) and different foci (such as sales performance or community collaboration and development).

When determining which needs to address first, keep in mind that interventions will be perceived as valuable only if they contribute to reducing the need by providing a solution. Usually the strategic or operational business needs are assessed for an entity before other kinds of needs are assessed. The ultimate goal of interventions in private-sector organizations is usually increased profitability (which is achieved through reduced costs and time, improved quality, or increased revenues), and the goal of interventions in public-sector organizations is usually fuller achievement of the mission or the funding goals.

The kind of need and the context influence the type of analysis that should be conducted:

- *Business analysis:* To identify an organization's strategic or operational goals, clarify that they are appropriate, and determine how to measure them.

- *Performance analysis:* To identify the capacity and processes for producing accomplishments, to ensure that performance requirements and changes are linked to organizational strategic or operational goals, and to ensure that performers have the support they need to achieve the goals.

- *Cause analysis:* To identify the specific reasons for performance gaps.

- *Training needs assessment:* To identify the performance gaps that can be addressed with training solutions. This type of analysis is usually conducted for providers of training solutions. It identifies the training and the non-training components that must be addressed to close performance gaps.

When determining which needs to address first, also consider how your clients and stakeholders view the world. Figure 2.1 shows eight world views, which can be thought of as value or belief systems, that are used by individuals, organizations, and societies. Each world view has a unique structure of thinking about how the world operates, who should make decisions, and what rules govern society (Beck & Cowan, 2006).

As you review this figure, start at the bottom and progress to the top. Notice that the world views become increasingly complex as you move up the figure. That's because new ways of thinking emerge as individuals, organizations, and societies develop; the new ways build on the old ways. Circumstances determine which world views are likely to be acceptable and justifiable. For example, an individual who learned that she had a life-threatening illness could change from viewing the world as containing many opportunities to viewing it through a survivalist lens.

When reviewing Figure 2.1, compare your world view, the client's world view, and the stakeholders' world view. Are they congruent? Also consider how decisions are made in those world views and the related language that could be important when discussing the needs assessment and prioritizing needs.

	World View	Reasonable Actions	Applications to the World of Work
The Global Viewer	Part of a global, ecological order	Everything is connected; an individual is both distinct and part of a larger whole	Work is meaningful, and everything connects to everything else
The Choice Seeker	Comprised of natural systems and forms	See life as a mixture of natural hierarchies, systems and flows; view competency as more important than rank, power, or status	People enjoy doing work that fits who they are
The Involver	An egalitarian order where everyone shares the environment	Care about inner peace, other people, and use consensus to make decisions	Getting along and being accepted is important; more can be accomplished by consensus than by competition
The Achiever	Containing many opportunities	Take enterprising actions that benefit you; focus on results and self-reliance	Achieving materialistic rewards and making things better for oneself are important
The Loyalist	An absolute order	Support the absolute order with laws, regulations, and discipline that control individuals for the good of the group	People should be told what to do and the right way to do it
The Loner	Jungle-like with predators and threats	Use power, aggression, and cunning to dominate and exploit others; take care of yourself, and enjoy yourself now without guilt	Strong leaders give rewards and meet workers' basic needs
The Tribesperson	Mysterious and frightening	Join a tribe for protection, live by the tribe's rules, and show allegiance to the tribe and the tribe's leaders	Employees are fully committed to the organization, and the organization takes care of them
The Survivalist	A state of nature	Rely on instincts and habits to do whatever is needed to stay alive	Do whatever is needed to stay alive

FIGURE 2.1 *World Views and Reasonable Actions Based on Each View, Plus Applications to the World of Work*

CASE

The board of a non-profit professional organization included members who viewed the world through the involver lens, the achiever lens, the loyalist lens, and the loner lens. Assessing needs was difficult in this group. The *involvers* advocated addressing the needs that everyone agreed could best benefit the organization. The *achievers* focused on needs that would give the organization more visibility and status in the profession and bring in more financial resources. The *loyalist* was adamant that the exact process that was previously used to determine the organization's needs be replicated, and the *loners* finessed discussions to assess organizational needs that would benefit them personally. Determining how to assess the organization's needs in this situation involved understanding each individual's world view and extensive, ongoing negotiation.

MEASURING PERFORMANCE

Some people claim that it is impossible to measure performance precisely or to establish its values. They are correct. Other people claim that not all HRD, HPT, and development initiatives are designed to produce economic value. They are also correct.

We find, however, that most people rely on less-than-perfect measures to make decisions and that they do indeed place economic values on learning and performance when making such decisions as selecting products to use, choosing strategies for accomplishing tasks, assigning people to participate in projects, and selecting needs to address. One key to making better decisions is to share the expectations, criteria, and formulas for measuring and valuing performance.

Gilbert's (1978) Behavior Engineering Model (BEM) is the classic model for measuring performance. It describes the relationships among behaviors, accomplishments, and performance. Behaviors are what people do, accomplishments are their outputs, and individual performance includes both behaviors and accomplishments. Consider the following three examples:

- In a restaurant, three waiters serve meals.
- In a garage, ten mechanics repair autos.
- In a clinic, twenty physicians treat patients.

The accomplishments in these examples are the served meals, repaired autos, and treated patients. The behaviors are the specific actions taken by the individuals who served meals, repaired autos, and treated patients. According to the BEM, an individual's performance reflects both valued accomplishments and the costs of their behaviors.

Tip

When assessing performance, first look at the desired condition and identify and measure the accomplishments that contribute to reaching it. Then analyze the behaviors that lead to the accomplishment.

To measure performance efficiently among the individuals in a group, try this Gilbert (1978) strategy:

1. Compare the accomplishments of typical and outstanding performers.

2. Identify patterns in their accomplishments. (For example, have the typical and outstanding performers reached the same levels of accomplishment? What are the differences in their processes or approaches?)

3. Find the specific behaviors that contribute to the differences in processes or approaches.

When typical and outstanding performers work in the same environment, their differences in accomplishments are often the result of small differences in their behaviors. The following case shows a real-life example of such differences.

CASE

A needs assessment at a call center for a provider of telephone services relied on comparing typical and outstanding performance. The call center's mission was to increase the satisfaction and retention of those customers who called with complaints. A strategic goal was to address 99 percent of all customer complaints effectively and efficiently. However, the employees who recorded customer complaints often mis-recorded the addresses and phone numbers, making it difficult and costly for technicians to follow up with customers.

Measuring and comparing the accomplishments of employees who worked the call lines revealed that one outstanding employee had a far higher level of accomplishment than the other employees as measured by the number of customer complaints that were accurately and quickly entered into the call center's database.

Further investigation revealed that the outstanding employee used different behaviors than the typical employees. For example, when a customer called in a complaint, the outstanding employee asked about his or her contact information and typed changes into the call center database at about seventy words per minute. She also repeated the contact information back to customers while entering it into the database, thus ensuring accuracy. By comparison, typical employees usually had to hunt and peck to locate the correct keys for entering data, and they did not repeat back to the customer the changes they had entered into the database.

The call center supervisor knew that the average number of missed service calls due to this issue was fifteen per week and the average costs for technicians who drove around but could not find the customer was $110 (wages and transportation). To calculate the annual cost of poor performance, the supervisor multiplied fifteen by $110 times fifty-two weeks per year to get $85,800. These costs were so high that the supervisor did not even bother calculating the average worth of dissatisfied customers who chose a new telephone company when technicians did not solve their problems.

Instead, he improved unit performance by using a two-pronged intervention that (a) provided training on keyboarding skills to employees who needed them and (b) changed the work design so that everyone who answered customer complaints repeated changes in contact information while entering them into the computer. The total cost for these changes was around $5,000.

Today, performance improvements are typically measured using *return-on-investment* (ROI). This formula compares the investment in a program with its return.

$$\text{ROI} = (\text{Gain from Investment} - \text{Cost of Investment})/ \text{Cost of Investment}$$

For example, to calculate the ROI for a program with a $85,800 benefit and a $5,000 cost for the investment, first calculate that $85,800 minus $5,000 equals $80,800 (the gain from the investment). Then divide $80,800 by $5,000. This equals 16.16. For each $1 invested, the return is a little more than $16. To calculate ROI as a percentage, multiple 16.16 by 100 to obtain 1,616 percent.

Tip

When measuring accomplishments, such soft measures as improved teamwork or innovation can be converted into hard numbers by considering exactly how the accomplishment affects mission-critical work. Resources that offer specific strategies for completing such conversions include *Forecasting the Financial Benefits of HRD*, by Swanson and Gradous (1990), and *Measuring Return on Investment (ROI) Basics*, by Phillips and Phillips (2005).

DIAGNOSING THE CAUSES OF POOR PERFORMANCE

Learning and performance needs may be only vaguely understood when they first come to our attention. Moreover, as Harless (1970) often observed, organizations—when confronted with problems—tend to look for solutions even before the problem is fully defined or alternate courses of action have been considered. Harless recommended front-end analysis for uncovering the root causes of performance problems prior to looking for solutions. We now examine the root causes of individual, organizational, and systems problems.

Individual Performance Problems

When individuals do not perform as expected, organizations often train them or remove them. Mager and Pipe (1984) differentiated between performance problems that result from a skill deficiency and those that result from other causes (such as lack of motivation or obstacles to performing). There is little point to providing individuals with knowledge and skills if the lack of performance is caused by low motivation or obstacles to performing (such as lack of resources).

Gilbert (1978) identified six barriers to performance for individuals. Figure 2.2 shows the six variables and sample questions for identifying whether a variable is a barrier. The traditional assumption is that if an individual performer would simply change, improvement would result (for example, "if he were not so lazy," or "if she had the drive to do the work," or "if they just had the knowledge and skills. . ."). However, performance problems more often result from a lack of support in the work environment (for example, bad data, worn-out tools, or poor incentives).

For instance, the expensive software purchased by a school system to improve student reading skills received little use even though the teachers in the system had received training on how to use the software. The expected performance did not appear until the school superintendent dialogued with teachers about how using the software could improve student learning, supplied sufficient computers, and provided feedback on the level of the software use in each classroom.

Barriers to Performance	Sample Question About the Barrier
1. Data	Does the individual have sufficient and reliable information (such as purpose and expectations for the job and feedback on performance) to guide performance?
2. Tools	Does the individual have all the resources needed to perform the work?
3. Incentives	Are the financial and non-financial incentives adequate and based on performance?
4. Knowledge	Is lack of knowledge (or skill) contributing to the problem?
5. Capacity	Do the individual's physical, emotional, and intellectual abilities match the job requirements?
6. Motives	Does the person have the appropriate motives to perform this work well?

FIGURE 2.2 *Barriers to Performance and Sample Questions*

Organizational Performance Problems

Diagnosing an organization's problems is complex. Here we review two models that can aid you in this process.

The Organizational Elements Model

In the Organizational Elements Model (OEM), needs assessment and strategic planning are used to link and define an organization's desired external and internal results (Guerra-Lopez & Kaufman, 2013; Kaufman, 1992, 2005). Elements in the OEM include the following:

- *Inputs:* The resources an organization uses
- *Processes:* The internal ways, means, methods, activities, and procedures an organization uses to achieve desired results
- *Products:* The results produced within an organization
- *Outputs:* The end results delivered outside an organization
- *Outcomes:* The effects or payoffs for clients and society

You can use the OEM to compare the current situation and the desired situation across all five elements, thus obtaining information about the organization (the inputs, process, and products), the external clients (the outputs), and the societal context (the outcomes).

Improving Performance: Managing the White Space on the Organizational Chart

With the publication of their book *Improving Performance* in 1995, Rummler and Brache revolutionized the practice of needs assessment in organizations. Instead of referring to a traditional organizational chart with its departmental silos, they described an organization as a system with such components as inputs, a processing system, outputs, markets, and shareholders.

They also showed how to depict the interrelationships between departments. Figure 2.3 compares a traditional view and a systems view of an organization. Needs assessment practitioners who understand the systems view of an organization can move beyond focusing on activities that occur within departmental silos to focusing on activities that occur across departments.

Rummler and Brache also described the importance of diagnosing performance needs that occur at three levels: the organization, the processes, and the individual jobs and performers. Because the three levels are interdependent and critical to the whole system's optimal performance, a failure of any one level can affect the ability of the organization to perform optimally. Today most needs assessment practitioners recognize that organizations are systems comprised of subsystems. Moreover, many practitioners and decision makers refer to the three levels of performance that were first identified by Rummler and Brache.

Tip

Most people who use systems thinking in their work acknowledge that no single systemic tool depicts the whole truth about a situation.

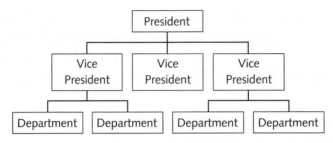

Traditional View of an Organization

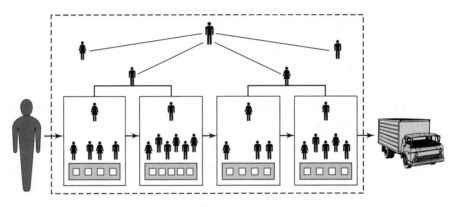

Systems View of an Organization

FIGURE 2.3 *Comparison of the Traditional and Systems Views of an Organization*

Diagnosing Systems

Our knowledge about how to analyze complex systems has improved greatly in recent years. Eoyang (2004) presented strategies and tools for assessing the patterns that occur within systems:

1. Surface structures are patterns visible to anyone in the organization and easily measured (for example, lagging sales, interpersonal conflict, and client dissatisfaction).

2. Evident deep structures are patterns that are partially or totally invisible but easily measured (for example, the beliefs shared by members of the organization about its mission).

3. Subtle deep structures are patterns that are invisible and not easily measured (for example, data points concerning quality issues that occur at different places and are distributed across time).

You can use this information when planning a needs assessment. Surface structures are usually easier to diagnose than evident deep structure, and subtle deep structures can be very difficult to diagnose.

Toolkit Form 2.1 shows assessment tools and strategies for each of the three categories. You can use it to become more intentional in imagining multiple options for each type of system pattern.

Advances Over Time in Knowledge About Learning, Training, and Performance

When planning a needs assessment, clients and stakeholders often refer to models, theories, and ideas that were popular at earlier times in history. Moreover, they often have incomplete understandings of how learning or performance could be viewed, and they are looking to the analyst to provide this insight.

You can prepare for your initial meeting with a client by skimming Toolkit Form 2.2 to review how ideas about learning, training, and performance have changed over time. Pay special attention to the italicized jargon so you are in the know if a client mentions one of these terms.

CONCLUSION

The ideas and models described in this chapter can be used with the five needs assessment approaches presented in this book. Select the ones that best fit your situation to cut through the complexities in your situation. The next chapter describes strategies for collecting and analyzing data.

THREE

Strategies for Collecting and Analyzing Data

PURPOSE

This chapter will enable you to do the following:

- Prepare for and conduct individual interviews.
- Conduct focus groups.
- Make observations.
- Develop and use surveys.
- Gather data from documents and artifacts.
- Collect data from photos and videos.
- Identify strategies for analyzing data.
- Review options for organizing data for decision making.

OVERVIEW

The results of a needs assessment reflect the methods that were used to collect the data and also the methods that were used to analyze those data. Thus, data collection and analysis are cornerstone skills for any needs assessment project. Separating fact from fiction in today's information-rich and complex environment requires analysts to pay careful attention to these processes. The analyst works with the client and/or needs assessment committee to determine the data collection and analysis methods. Depending on the needs assessment, the data that are collected may be quantitative (relies on numbers), qualitative (relies on words, pictures, and so forth), or a combination of quantitative and qualitative data.

Most needs assessments use multiple data-collection methods. To identify the training needs of plant personnel, you could choose to conduct interviews and review job descriptions and quality records. To measure the proficiency levels of the office staff for a volunteer organization, you could choose to conduct a survey and observe them at work. This material in this chapter will help you decide which methods are most appropriate for your situation and provide guidelines for using the methods. It also describes how to analyze the data after they have been collected to produce accurate and useable results. While you can hire experts who specialize in data collection and analysis methods (such as statistics and survey design), most methods are straightforward to learn.

DATA-COLLECTION METHODS

The data-collection methods discussed in this chapter are interviews, focus groups, surveys, observations, archival records, photographs and videos. Additional methods, such as the nominal group technique, action research, and Dacum (developing a curriculum) are beyond the scope of this chapter. For real-life applications of these latter data-gathering techniques, consult *In Action: Conducting Needs Assessment* (Phillips & Holton, 1995). Although using many different approaches may seem tempting, be sure to target your data collection to reflect the purpose of the needs assessment. Also, be sure to obtain feedback from the client and the needs assessment committee to assure that the data-collection and analysis approaches are appropriate for the situation.

Interviews

Some people assume that interviews are one of the easiest tools for gathering information about learning and performance needs. A brief discussion with customer service associates could uncover reasons why phone calls are not being handled properly. An in-depth discussion with senior management could clarify perspectives on strategic training issues. However, such interviews can be challenging; a certain amount of knowledge and skills are involved in conducting informative interviews.

Types of Interviews

Interviews can be conducted in person, by phone, or by computer. The greatest benefit of one-on-one, in-person interviews is the human interaction that occurs. In-person interviews allow the interviewer to observe the respondent's facial expressions and other nonverbal cues.

Phone interviews are useful when people in remote locations cannot be accessed easily. They are also useful when people do not have the time and resources to travel to meet in person. Because most people will refuse to participate in long phone interviews, phone interviews are typically scheduled to last no longer than thirty minutes. Such time limitations clearly reduce the amount of information that can be gathered. Therefore, a phone interview is not the optimal choice when extensive discussion is likely, anticipated, or desired.

Computer-aided telephone interviewing can be useful in some situations; the text can appear on the interviewer's computer screen along with the response options, and the interviewer can enter the respondent's answers.

Computer-supported interviews can be a good choice when people are comfortable using technology, such as online cameras and videoconferencing. With these aids, as with in-person interviews, the interviewer can observe nonverbal cues and, as with phone interviews, people do not have to travel to meet in person. Even without visual technology, computer-supported interviews also can be a good choice when:

- The interview involves parties who are available virtually but not co-located,

- The interview involves sharing some documents, such as the project brochures or timelines, and

- The participants are experienced in using the technology.

Whether conducting interviews in person, by phone, or with computer technology, it is useful to remember the following tips:

- Use a moderate tone.

- Enunciate clearly.

- Speak slowly.

- Keep the discussion focused.

- Probe for additional responses to your questions.

Interview Approaches

Interviews can be structured (or scripted), unstructured, or semi-structured. In structured interviews, a list of objectives and a corresponding list of questions guide the interview process. In unstructured interviews, questions are not listed in advance. Rather, a list of objectives and topics to be covered guide the interview. In semi-structured interviews, a list of objectives with corresponding questions initially guide the interview and the interviewer spontaneously asks supplemental questions to explore further areas of interest.

In structured or scripted interviews, the interview dialogue and the questions, and in some cases the responses to closed-ended questions, are written out and practiced in advance. Scripts are useful when multiple interviewers are involved in the data-collection process and when using computer-aided interviewing. A script can be combined with a protocol that details all data-collection procedures (for example, initial contact procedures, interview follow-up procedures, and the confidentiality agreement). Scripted interviews help to ensure accuracy and consistency of the interview process. They may, however, inhibit spontaneity. Figure 3.1 shows a sample interview protocol, the script, and the sample questions.

Keys to a successful interview include preparing for it, developing questions, and actually conducting the interview at the scheduled time and place. Some people develop the interview script before developing questions and some people develop questions first. Figures 3.2, 3.3, and 3.4 present some helpful hints for each of these tasks.

Protocol

These interviews are conducted as part of a strategic needs assessment that focuses on customer perceptions of a manufacturing division. The performance improvement specialist will conduct interviews during the next week with all the direct reports of the vice president of manufacturing. The administrative assistant will schedule the interviews. All interview responses will be grouped for reporting and, therefore, individual responses will remain confidential. The interview script and sample questions will guide the activity; as issues surface, additional questions may be asked. The collected data will be analyzed by identifying themes, and the themes will be reported to the vice president of manufacturing.

Interview Script

Thank you for meeting with me. The purpose of this interview is to discuss the recent customer survey and to get your views for the strategic needs assessment. I am interviewing all of the direct reports of the vice president of manufacturing. Your responses to questions will be confidential. I will group the responses from all the interviews before reporting the results to the vice president of manufacturing. No individual responses will be identified. I have a list of questions to get us started, and there may be other questions as we talk. Would you like to see the list of questions?

Sample Questions

1. What do you think about the recent customer survey?
2. What changes in our production process do you think we should make to address our weaknesses and improve our strengths?
3. What other factors outside the organization could lead to changes in our production process? [Follow-up: What could the changes look like?]
4. What other factors inside the organization could lead to changes in our production process? [Follow-up: What could the changes look like?]
5. What are the barriers to making efficient and effective changes in the production process?
6. What are the supports for making efficient and effective changes in the production process?
7. In thinking about our future production process, what additional information should be considered?
8. Do you have any additional thoughts or questions about the customer survey?
9. Thank you for meeting with me to discuss the strategic needs for the production area. If I think of additional questions later or need clarification on a question, may I call you?

FIGURE 3.1 *Sample Interview Protocol, Script, and Questions*

1. Familiarize yourself with technical and industry and/or organization or community-specific terms.
2. Obtain background information about the problem or issue of concern if possible.
3. Establish the purpose, expected outcomes, and objectives for the interview.
4. Determine whether the interview will be conducted in person, by phone, or online.
5. Identify a comfortable and private location for conducting a one-on-one, in-person interview.
6. Decide how information will be recorded. Handwritten notes? Typing responses into computer? Use a recording?
7. Test the equipment that will be used.
8. Develop an interview protocol if multiple interviewers will be involved.
9. Notify interviewees and their managers or supervisors of the interviews.
10. Send a letter of introduction to each interviewee that states who authorized the interview and the objectives of the interview:
    a. Explain why he or she was selected.
    b. Specify whether confidentiality will be maintained.
    c. Explain how the results will be used.
    d. Specify a time when you will call to schedule an interview appointment.
11. Call the interviewee to schedule the interview.
12. Allow twenty to thirty minutes between interviews to document the results.
13. Allow flexibility in scheduling to accommodate those working in shifts.

FIGURE 3.2 *Hints for Preparing for an Interview*

1. Place easy-to-answer, open-ended questions at the beginning. This can help the interviewee to begin talking and can help to develop trust and rapport.
2. Place important questions near the beginning of the interview.
3. Place controversial or sensitive questions, including demographic questions, at the end.
4. Specify the amount of time to be spent on each question.
5. Ensure that each question matches a stated objective.
6. Sequence questions from general to specific.
7. Sequence and cluster questions in a logical order.
8. Ensure that questions are clear, concise, and jargon-free.
9. Be sure that questions are appropriate for the skill and experience levels of the target audience.
10. Provide adequate space between questions to record information.
11. Pilot-test interview questions.
12. Make appropriate revisions to the questions based on the pilot test.

FIGURE 3.3 *Hints for Developing Interview Questions*

1. Begin with a few rapport-building questions.
2. Obtain permission to record the interview.
3. Avoid adhering rigidly to the question sequence, unless using a structured or computer-aided interview. If not a structured interview, be flexible, but ensure that all questions have been covered by the end. If they have not been, schedule a follow-up phone or online interview.
4. Give all participants an equal amount of time to respond to each question.
5. Clarify responses when necessary.
6. Ask for concrete examples to support statements.
7. Separate facts from opinions, if possible.
8. Maintain a neutral attitude.
9. Avoid discussing results with other interviewees.
10. Ask whether interviewees have additional questions or comments at the end.
11. Offer appreciation for participation.
12. Summarize key points.
13. Ask whether interviewees can be contacted again if necessary.

FIGURE 3.4 *Hints for Conducting an Interview*

Focus Groups

In the focus group interview method, people who have something in common are brought together and asked their opinions and ideas about a specific topic. Most focus groups are made up of five to eight people. Unlike an individual interview, the focus group interview involves not just asking questions but managing the group dynamics as well.

To be effective, focus groups require skilled facilitators. Krueger and Casey (2000) noted that a facilitator must be mentally prepared, familiar with such techniques as the five-second pause and probing for more information, and able to show positive regard and empathy for participants. As Schwarz (1995) pointed out, focus group facilitators must keep in mind that they are not content experts, mediators, arbitrators, or judges. Schwarz's suggestions for facilitators included the following:

- Accept responses in a nonjudgmental manner.

- Avoid making decisions or comments about a group's work.

- Encourage an atmosphere of openness and mutual respect.

The work of conducting needs assessments via focus groups involves three phases: prepare, conduct, and report.

Prepare

Preparing for a focus group involves several activities. First, the facilitator becomes familiar with the purpose of the focus group and its expected outcomes, the topic of interest, and any specific terminology or jargon that is likely to be used. Second, the facilitator develops and pilot-tests a list of questions that will encourage focus group participants to disclose information on the topic. In a few cases, the facilitator creates a short survey for use at the beginning of the focus group session. Such a document can help to orient participants to the topic and can provide a filler task for those who arrive early. During this preparing stage, the facilitator identifies a time and arranges a specific location for the focus group meeting. The facilitator also determines whether the focus group will be conducted in person, via telephone, or via computer. Note that a face-to-face meeting or a videoconference allows you to view the participants' non-verbal communication.

Next, the facilitator selects and recruits members of the target population to participate in the focus group. Finally, the facilitator gathers resources for the session (for example, note paper, name tags, and flip-chart paper). In most cases, the facilitator also arranges refreshments for the participants.

Conduct

At the beginning of a session, the facilitator introduces himself or herself, identifies the purpose of the session, describes the facilitator role, establishes the objectives, reviews the agenda, and sets the ground rules. In some cases, a colleague can act as a recorder for the session; the facilitator should introduce this person and his or her role.

During the session, the facilitator must balance the following tasks:

• Lead and facilitate the discussion.

• Encourage participation.

- Manage those who dominate the discussion.

- Record participants' responses.

- Ensure that the recorder (if used) is functioning (or have the colleague who is acting as recorder do this).

- Keep track of time so that the session ends as scheduled.

Report

The last phase in administering a focus group consists of two steps: analyzing data and preparing a report. The analysis of focus group data must be systematic, because all the reported findings must be supported by data (Krueger & Casey, 2000). Figure 3.5 shows various types of reports.

Chapter Eight contains additional information on how to report needs assessment results.

- Narrative reports are written, about fifteen to thirty pages long, and include quotations.
- Top-line reports are written and often used for interim reports that are given to the client within several days of the focus group; they are several pages long and provide bullet points of information relevant to the purpose of the focus group.
- Bulleted reports are written and outline a narrative report using words and phrases that convey the report's meaning.
- Oral reports are shared via the spoken word, tell the audience why the focus group was important, present findings, and allow the audience to respond to the results and ask questions.
- Electronic reports, which may be integrated into other types of reports, can rely on Internet, data storage devices, WinSCP (or Windows Secure CoPY), a dropbox, or digital recording device.

FIGURE 3.5 *Various Types of Focus Group Reports*

Surveys

Although many believe that a survey is a quick way to gather responses, developing a good survey that addresses the issues of concern is extremely difficult and time consuming. Following a systematic process helps to ensure that the objectives and desired results are achieved. The phases involved in surveying needs are as follows:

- Prepare the survey.
- Design the survey.
- Develop questions.
- Write instructions.
- Write the cover letter or email.
- Pilot-test and revise. (Note that, depending on the importance of the survey, the pilot testing and revision may require several rounds.)
- Conduct the survey and follow-up.

Prepare

Critical tasks during the preparatory phase include: (a) establish the goals for this data-collection effort and (b) become familiar with the situation and typical expressions. Before constructing a survey, it is useful to familiarize yourself with difficult terms. If necessary, consider using a subject-matter expert or an internal team member to translate technical jargon into simpler language.

You may also want to observe people in their work environments or review written reports. Observations can provide useful information about how people perform their job tasks, and conducting a few interviews can help to surface items for the survey. Previous surveys and reports can provide figures, indices, or trends that help in framing specific questions. They may also provide question items that you can use in your survey.

Many commercially available surveys that can be administered quickly online are now available. Figure 3.6 lists some examples. Many survey vendors provide analysts with ready-to-use reports that specify the gaps between the current and the ideal situation and ways to address the gaps.

The list below provides a starting point for finding commercially available online needs assessment surveys. Of course, these are not the only vendors who offer assessment tools. You can identify additional vendors by entering the topic of focus in your Internet browser (e.g., supervisor assessment, leadership assessment, and so forth). Remember, vendors' surveys usually are based on specific theories and models of learning and performance, so be prepared to understand this background before purchasing or using the instrument.

- DiSC® assesses individual personality and behavioral styles, the team profile, or the workplace profile.
- Myers-Briggs Type Indicator® (MBTI) assesses individuals, teams, and such organizational needs as team building, conflict management, and leadership.
- BarON EQ-I® assesses emotional intelligence for individuals and teams.
- PDI Ninth House's Leadership Assessments identify needs for development for first-level leaders to C-suite leaders.
- Lominger's Voices 360 assess needs for individual and team development.
- Wilson Learning's Sales Navigator, Sales Leader Navigator, and Leader Navigator uses 360 feedback to identify strengths and development opportunities.
- Center for Creative Leadership assesses team and organizational climate (creativity and innovation). They also offer leadership assessments.
- Blessing White's High-Performance Culture Scan™ uses an online employee survey and interviews with leaders to measure the alignment of leaders and business practices with the espoused organizational values.
- Dimensions of the Learning Organization Questionnaire (DLOQ) measures organizational learning.
- CEB Valtera offers a tool to build consensus on organizational priorities and to improve productivity on the activities that build competitive advantage

FIGURE 3.6 *Examples of Commercially Available Surveys for Assessing Needs*

At this point, decide whether a previously designed or commercially available survey can be used or modified or whether to design a new survey that targets the specific situation. The first two options may save you money, but may not address the specific issues in your situation.

Design the Survey

When designing a survey, consider the following factors:

- *The number of people involved.* If the group to be surveyed is large, use mostly closed-ended questions that can be recorded and analyzed easily by computer. (More detail about closed-ended questions is provided later in this chapter.) If qualitative information is required, decide whether to include open-ended questions or conduct separate interviews or focus groups to collect the required information.

- *How the data will be collected.* Survey data can be collected using paper forms, or you can collect data by posting the survey online using an organization's intranet or the Internet. A web-based survey allows respondents to access the survey and respond when it is convenient for them. Furthermore, the data can be immediately captured in a database for easy analysis. For community surveys, determine whether an online survey will reach all your target group; you should verify, in advance, the target group's level of computer access and use.

- *How the data will be analyzed.* Responses to online surveys are often analyzed with easy-to-use web-based software. Responses to paper instruments can be analyzed by hand counting answers, or the surveys can be electronically scanned. Surveys that will be electronically scanned may require special predesigned "bubble" forms. In such cases, consider using the services of an internal market research department or an external agency to provide assistance in instrument design. Universities with data-processing departments may provide such services for a nominal fee.

- *Whether color schemes will be used.* Robinson and Robinson (1989) suggested using a color-coding system if a large number of paper surveys will be sent to different sources. This technique facilitates the data-analysis process by allowing completed surveys to be categorized by group for later analysis. If color papers are used, be sure they are pastel so that the print can be easily read.

- *Whether individual survey responses will be confidential or anonymous.* Confidentiality means that individual respondents can be identified by the analyst, but individual responses will not be shared. Anonymous means that there is no record of the respondents' identity. If you elect to use an anonymous survey, note that the follow-up with non-respondents cannot be targeted because the specific respondents cannot be identified.

- *How the data will be grouped for reporting.* More options exist for survey reporting today, because many organizations rely on a human resource information system (HRIS) that includes a database of employee information, such as supervisor name, performance ratings, demographic data, salary, attendance, and so forth. Using the HRIS individual identifier when administering a survey allows the survey results to be easily grouped for reporting. Also, the survey results and HRIS data can be used together to analyze data. For example, the survey ratings given by high performers can be compared to the survey ratings given by low performers. Many online tools and services are available for creating surveys and collecting survey data. To find free tools and services, search the Internet using the words "free online survey."

Develop Questions

Nothing is more frustrating than sending out five hundred surveys only to find out later that 60 percent of the respondents misinterpreted a question. When developing survey questions, it is crucial to follow a few basic guidelines.

Avoid complexity. Frame questions to be answered easily. Avoid asking questions that require extensive calculations. For example, "How many sales calls do you make in a year?" requires respondents to compute an annual figure based on their weekly or monthly totals. Similar information could be elicited by an easier question, "How many sales calls do you make per week?" or alternatively, "How many sales calls do you make in a typical work day?"

Word questions carefully. Questions must be clear and easy to understand. Here are a few guidelines to follow when wording questions:

- Use simple words.

- Avoid leading questions, such as, "Do you feel that offering this well-tested management training program will improve your managerial skills?"

- Avoid negatively phrased questions, such as, "Did you not receive the computer training?"

Sequence questions. The order in which questions appear is important. Begin a survey with a few simple and interesting questions. Potentially sensitive questions should be presented later. In most cases, place demographic questions at the end of the survey. Also, avoid clustering similar items together as well as labeling sections. Such clustering and labeling can create "halo" effects, which occur when the rating on an item affects the rating on another item.

Limit the amount of information gathered in one question. Requests for multiple pieces of information should always be divided into separate questions. For example, "Is this task challenging and rewarding?" asks for two pieces of information. In many cases, respondents will either overlook the second portion of the question entirely or just not answer it. A more effective way to gather the same information is to ask two questions, "Is this task challenging?" and "Is this task rewarding?"

Determine the type of questions. There are different types of questions. Two basic types are open-ended questions and closed-ended questions.

Open-ended questions require respondents to answer in their own words. Asking open-ended questions may elicit in-depth responses. For example, an open-ended question could be, "What do you see as the mission of this organization?"

Asking open-ended or fill-in-the-blank questions is relatively easy. However, you should think carefully about using such questions in a survey because analyzing the various responses, especially with large numbers of respondents, requires more time and effort than analyzing closed-ended questions.

Tip We learned the hard way to limit responses for open-ended question to a specific number of characters (e.g., 50, 100, or 500). Without such limits, the time required to review lengthy open-ended responses is enormous—and, moreover, such responses often contain unfocused information.

Closed-ended questions, in contrast to open-ended questions, allow respondents to choose from defined options. An advantage to asking closed-ended questions is that they facilitate data entry and analysis. A disadvantage of asking closed-ended questions is that respondents cannot elaborate on their answers. There are several types of closed-ended questions:

- Two choice
- Multiple choice
- Scales of various kinds

Two-choice questions (for example, yes/no or true/false) are asked when an answer can be either one thing or the other, and the responses are mutually exclusive. For example:

Q. Everyone has access to the organization's mission statement.

_____ True
_____ False

Note that even with two-choice questions you must decide whether to provide other options, such as "don't know" or "not applicable."

Multiple-choice questions usually include a list of four or more options from which respondents select one or more responses. For example:

Q. With which of the following departments do you work most closely? (Check only one.)

_____ a. Accounting
_____ b. Information Services
_____ c. Human Resources
_____ d. Marketing
_____ e. Operations

A fill-in-the-blank option may be included. The preceding example could offer an additional choice:

_____ f. Other, please specify: _____

Scales of various kinds. Two types of scales commonly used in surveys are the Likert-type scale and the interval scale.

Survey items that ask respondents to rate values and attitudes use Likert-type scales (Likert, 1932). When using such scales, it is usually best to assign the most positive value at the higher end of the scale (Paul & Bracken, 1995). Two examples follow:

Q. Recreation program volunteers should receive monthly safety training. (Check one of the following.)

1 = Strongly disagree
2 = Disagree
3 = Somewhat agree
4 = Agree
5 = Strongly agree

Q. How skilled are your co-workers in troubleshooting the new computer equipment? (Check one of the following.)

1 = Very low skilled
2 = Low skilled
3 = Average skilled
4 = Highly skilled
5 = Very highly skilled

Survey items that collect numeric information from or about respondents use *interval scales.* These scales are also useful for obtaining information about a range of possibilities. For example:

Q. How many loans do you close in a week? (Select one.)

_____ a.   Under 25
_____ b.   25–35
_____ c.   36–45
_____ d.   46–55
_____ e.   Over 55

Note that a common mistake when creating interval scales is to provide options that overlap. Such a mistake would appear if we were to present the following options for the previous question:

Q. How many loans do you close in a week? (Circle only one.)

```
_____  a.   Under 25
_____  b.   25–35
_____  c.   35–45
_____  d.   45–55
_____  e.   55 and over
```

[The respondent would have difficulty answering if the number of loans equaled 35, 45, or 55.]

Figure 3.7 summarizes when to use each type of question.

Type of Question	When to Use the Question
Open-Ended or Fill-in-the-Blank	Obtain qualitative information
	Capture respondents' own words
	Probe for more information
	Seek more information as a follow-up to a closed-ended question
Closed-Ended	Obtain quantitative information
Two-Choice	Obtain opposite or mutually exclusive answers
Multiple Choice	Obtain one response from a list of choices (with instruction to "check only one")
	Obtain multiple responses from a list of choices (with instruction to "check as many as apply")
	Obtain responses with no rank order
	Obtain certain demographic data
Likert Scale	Obtain ratings (possibly leading to a rank order)
Interval Scale	Obtain interval-level data
	Obtain certain demographic data

FIGURE 3.7 *Types of Questions and When to Use Them*

Tip

Use the same scale for all the survey items that will be compared. In the example below, individual responses are summarized for each survey item. Notice that the ratings for the first three items can be quickly compared, but the fourth item uses a different scale. Rewarding team performance is the lowest rated of the first three items, but we do not know how satisfaction with salary really compares. Did you also notice that considering both scales required considerable concentration? Avoid this problem by using the same rating scale for all survey items.

		Agree	Neither agree nor disagree	Disagree	
1	My manager respects me	40	5	15	
2	I enjoy my work	35	6	19	
3	My team is rewarded based on performance	5	15	40	
		Very Satisfied	Satisfied	Dissat-isfied	Very Dissatisfied
4	How satisfied are you with your salary?	4	16	20	20

Write Instructions

The fourth phase in preparing surveys involves writing explicit instructions that specify how respondents should complete the form. Explain whether they should circle items, use check marks, fill in the "bubble," or write comments. Indicate whether survey items require only one response or multiple responses. State the amount of time required to complete the survey and the date by which the completed survey is due. For an emailed or a paper-based survey, list to whom or to what address the survey should be returned.

Write the Cover Letter/Email

Another critical phase in implementing surveys is preparing the cover letter/email that explains why the person is being asked to complete the survey and how he or she (or the organization or community) will benefit from it. To improve the response rate, ask a recognized person (such as the president of the organization or the mayor of the city) to endorse the survey with his or her signature. State whether the information that is gathered will be kept confidential.

Pilot-Test

After a survey has been designed, it is usually a good idea to pilot-test it. A pilot test can identify problems in construction or physical layout; it can also answer the following questions:

- Are the instructions clear and concise?

- Can respondents understand the questions easily?

- Can respondents answer the questions easily?

- Do respondents have enough space to record their comments?

- Do the questions elicit responses that address the survey purpose?

- How long does it take respondents to complete the survey?

The process of pilot-testing consists of several steps. If diverse groups will be surveyed, select a few people from each group. In a private meeting room, distribute the form and ask respondents to complete it while you are in the room. Observe the respondents' reactions closely and watch their faces for reactions that may indicate confusion or frustration. In addition, ask respondents to document anything they found confusing. After the survey questions are answered, ask respondents to describe their understanding of each question, discuss the reasons for their responses, and identify any problems.

Later, summarize the results of the pilot test. Tabulate the pilot-test survey responses to see whether there will be any problems with data analysis. Also analyze pilot-test data to determine whether the analyses and the results address the purpose of the survey, the survey questions, and the issues of concern.

After an initial pilot test, make appropriate changes to the form and conduct a second pilot test. If the group size for the survey is more than two hundred people, use ten to twenty respondents in the pilot test (Callahan, 1985).

Conduct the Survey and Follow-Up

Upon completion of the pilot test, the survey is ready to launch. If a paper survey is used, print it on high-quality paper. If an online survey is used, send the link to the web survey. Be sure to frequently monitor the incoming responses. If you encounter non-respondents—a situation that is very likely—be prepared to follow up (Dillman, 2000; Dillman, Smyth, & Christian, 2009). The follow-up process can involve sending a reminder three weeks after the initial survey was launched. Three weeks after that reminder, another copy of the survey (or the link to the survey) can be sent to all non-respondents (if you know who the non-respondents are) with a request to complete the survey as soon as possible; if you do not know who the non-respondents are, you should send the link to the survey or a copy of the survey to everyone, asking those who have not yet responded to complete the survey.

Figure 3.8 summarizes the phases and steps for developing and implementing surveys. It also provides some additional hints.

1. Prepare.
   - Familiarize yourself with the background situation.
   - Speak with appropriate groups of employees to define and clarify jargon or technical terms.
   - Establish the purpose and expected outcomes for the survey.
2. Design.
   - Determine whether questions from previously developed surveys can be used in their entirety or in part.
   - Determine whether any commercial surveys can be customized.
   - Determine whether and how confidentiality will be maintained.
   - Consult with a technical specialist if an electronic or web-based survey will be used or if computerized analysis will be performed.
   - Determine how results will be analyzed and presented.
   - Determine whether outsourcing will be necessary.
   - Decide whether color schemes should be used.
3. Develop questions.
   - Ensure that each question has a purpose.
   - Determine which type of question (open- or closed-ended) will elicit the best response. (If the survey will be sent to a large number of people,

limit the number of open-ended questions to avoid needing an unreasonable amount of time for data analysis.)

- Ensure that each question asks for only one piece of information.
- Avoid leading or biased questions.
- Avoid negatively phrased questions.
- Avoid personal or identifying questions.
- Ask questions that the respondents are qualified to answer.
- Avoid jargon, abbreviations, and colloquialisms.
- Use gender-neutral terms.
- Write questions that are clear and concise.
- Arrange questions in a logical sequence from general to specific.
- Position difficult or sensitive questions at the end.
- Number items.
- Provide space for comments.
- Use boldface or italic type and underline where appropriate.
- Use plenty of white space.
- Number pages.

4. Write instructions.
   - Write instructions on how to answer questions.
   - Explain complicated or confusing terms.

5. Write a cover letter.
   - State the purpose of the survey.
   - Say who authorized the survey.
   - Provide a history of previous research or findings when appropriate.
   - Show the benefit to the user.
   - Explain why the respondent was selected.
   - State when and how the form should be returned.
   - Thank the respondent for completing the survey.

6. Pilot-test survey.
   - Select participants for the pilot test.
   - Conduct and observe the pilot test.
   - Analyze the data from the pilot test.
   - Make appropriate modifications based on results of the pilot test.
   - Conduct a second pilot test if necessary.
   - Make final modifications.

7. Conduct the survey and follow-up.
   - Distribute or post the survey.
   - Determine the response rate.
   - Send reminder memo, postcard, or email three weeks following the original survey.
   - Send a reminder and second survey three weeks following the first reminder.

FIGURE 3.8 *Hints for Preparing and Implementing Surveys*

Observation

Observation is another method used to collect data during needs assessments. When used systematically, observation can yield meaningful results. Like interview data, observational data can be collected in a structured or unstructured fashion. The time frame for the observation, whether structured or unstructured, is established. With structured observations, decisions as to exactly which factors will be monitored are made prior to the observation. For example, an analyst could use structured observation to monitor the number of employees in a kitchen who wash their hands prior to preparing food. With unstructured observations, the analyst collects information on all aspects of interest in a situation. For example, the analyst could observe the same kitchen to see and record all behaviors of interest.

Structured observations have some advantages:

- They reduce the potential for bias.
- They increase the reliability of observations.
- They provide an accurate way to report data.

As Rossett (1987) suggested, use the unstructured method to obtain an initial feel for a situation. Then follow up with a structured observation.

One problem that arises with observation, whether structured or unstructured, is that people often alter their behavior when being watched by others. To avoid this problem, use unobtrusive techniques. For example, observe people from an inconspicuous spot. You can reduce anxiety by dressing in attire similar to the attire of those you are observing.

The notes that document unstructured observations are usually recorded on notepaper or in a computer file that is labeled with the name of the observer, the location, and time of the observation. Forms are usually created to document structured observations. Here are a few hints for preparing structured observation forms:

- Include the name of the observer and the observation date and location.

- Include a checklist of items to be observed, including the individual tasks and subtasks performed during your observation and either the frequency of performance or the amount of time taken to perform a task. Also include the start and end times.

- Design the checklist with space for recording both qualitative and quantitative data.

- Provide space for comments and additional notes.

Documents and Artifacts

Another vital source of information in needs assessments is the data contained in current and historical documents and other artifacts, such as business plans, mission statements, job descriptions, performance reviews, websites, training evaluation forms, sales records, customer-service call records, personnel records, budgets, photographs, and newspaper articles. Such data can be qualitative or quantitative. The benefit of collecting such data is optimized when these data are collected in conjunction with another data-collection method.

Following are a few suggestions for using data from documents and artifacts:

- Be clear about the type of information you are seeking before undertaking an extensive search of records.

- Seek permission prior to using archival or company records.

- Look for trends and patterns in the data.

- Create a codebook for recording the data.

- Have two people use the codebook to record a small subset of the data. Determine the raters' level of agreement (the inter-rater reliability) on the coding.

- If the inter-rater reliability is low, rework the code book. Then redo the coding and check the inter-rater reliability.

Photos and Videos

Cell phones, laptops, and tablets are useful in collecting needs assessment data. For example, they can record conversations and capture pictures and videos that show the larger environment for the work or the ways in which the work is actually conducted. Such visual images can capture the emotions of clients and stakeholders that words and numbers cannot.

For example, Photovoice combines community grass roots needs assessment with photography and storytelling. Community residents take photographs that document their point of view and tell the stories of their photographs, then small and large groups discuss the photographs and stories and engage in critical dialogue that is designed to influence policy (Centers for Disease Control, 2010).

Needs assessments can also be informed by cell phone and email records. Be sure to consider the legal restrictions and the privacy issues before collecting such data. Figure 3.9 summarizes the primary collection methods discussed in this chapter. It also compares the time and cost for using them.

DATA ANALYSIS

In order to use the collected data to make decisions and prioritize needs, the data must be analyzed. *Quantitative* data can be gathered, scored, and analyzed more easily and quickly than qualitative data. They may be summarized and presented using various kinds of tables, charts, and graphs. In contrast, *qualitative* data are more difficult and time-consuming to collect and analyze, but they provide rich and detailed information.

The computer software for analyzing quantitative data (such as Excel, SPSS, and SAS) or qualitative data (such as NVivo and AtlasTI) improves the ease, accuracy, and speed of data analysis. The following paragraphs provide an overview of some of the basic analyses that can be used. More detailed and complex analyses are beyond the scope of

Method	When to Use	Time Required — Conduct or Implement	Time Required — Analyze Data	Cost	Resources Required — HRD	Resources Required — Management
One-on-One Interviews	Conduct complex, strategic, competency, job task analysis, or knowledge and skills assessment. Obtain sensitive information. Discuss complex issues that require explanations. Gain support.	High	High	Medium to high	Time Skilled interviewer	Budget Time
Phone Interviews	Conduct complex, strategic or knowledge and skills assessment. Gather small pieces of interviewer information. Ask follow-up questions. Obtain information when respondents are geographically disbursed. Obtain information from many sources quickly. Obtain non-sensitive information. Obtain more quantifiable and qualitative information. Save travel costs.	Low to medium	Medium	Low	Time Skilled interviewers	Budget Time
Focus Groups	Conduct complex, strategic, competency, job task analysis, or knowledge and skills assessment. Collect qualitative data. Gather information when group behavior determines job performance.	Low	High	Medium to high	Time Skilled facilitator Note-taker or recorder	Budget
Surveys	Conduct complex, strategic, competency, job task analysis, or knowledge and skills assessment. Use when individuals are geographically disbursed. Obtain quantifiable data. Responses to closed-ended questions can be categorized easily.	Low to medium	Low	Low	Time Knowledge of survey development Data-tracking skills Data-analysis skills	Budget Administrative support may be needed for complex or large surveys

FIGURE 3.9 *Comparison of Primary Data-Collection Methods*

Method	When to Use	Time Required		Cost	Resources Required	
		Conduct or Implement	Analyze Data		HRD	Management
Observations	Conduct complex, strategic, job and task analysis, or knowledge and skills assessment. Document performance. Observe frequency of performance. Document amount of time taken to perform a task.	Low	Low to medium	Low	Time Availability of individuals Knowledge of the performance to be observed Observation form	Permissions, if needed
Current and Historical Documents and Other Artifacts	Conduct complex, strategic competency, job task analysis, or knowledge and skills assessment. Provide background information. Collect qualitative or quantitative data.	Low	Low to medium	Low	Time The ability to interpret historical data. The expertise required to extract the relevant information contained in the documents and artifacts.	Permissions, if needed
Photographs and Videos	Capture visual images of the gaps between the current and ideal situations, how work is really performed, or what actually occurs.	Low	High	Depends on the cost of the photography and video equipment and if experts are hired to operate the equipment.	Time Must be available when the work is performed. Expertise to interpret the images that are captured.	Camera or video equipment, capability to develop photos or videos, photo release form from individuals in the photographs Permissions, if needed

FIGURE 3.9 *Comparison of Primary Data-Collection Methods* (Continued)

this book. However, many books and articles describe specific procedures for analyzing various kinds of quantitative and qualitative data, and Chapter Eleven contains references that will get you started.

Analyzing Quantitative Data

In most needs assessments, quantitative data analyses are limited to *descriptive statistics*. These analyses basically describe the survey data. Statistical software, such as SAS and SPSS, make it easy to do these calculations. However, you can also perform these calculations yourself by hand or by using Excel.

To begin analyzing quantitative data, create a spreadsheet that includes all the items for which such data were collected. Figure 3.10 shows an example of such a tally sheet for analyzing the quantitative data obtained from a survey question. Of course, you could create a similar tally sheet for qualitative data obtained through other methods (such as observations and interviews). The example shows the response choices for the item (such as extremely well, very well, and moderately well), the value of each response choice (for instance, 5 for extremely well), the frequency of each response (obtained by counting the actual responses), and the percentage of individuals who selected

Item	Response	Frequency	Percentage
How well did line	5 Extremely well	5	3
workers perform	4 Very well	14	8
the new process?	3 Moderately well	54	32
	2 Not well	51	31
	1 Not at all well	33	20
	No response	10	6
Total		167	100

FIGURE 3.10 *Example of Frequency and Percentage Calculation for a Quantitative Question Showing All Responses*

each response. Using this example, let us review how to calculate frequencies and percentages.

Frequency. This measure counts the number of times each response choice was selected. A quick glance at the frequency column in Figure 3.10 reveals that the greatest number of people (fifty-four) thought line workers performed the new process moderately well, but only five people thought line workers performed the new process extremely well.

Percentages. This measure is useful for comparing the categories of responses. To calculate the percentage for a response, divide its frequency by the total frequency. For example, in Figure 3.10 the percentage for the response extremely well was calculated by dividing its frequency (5) by the total (167) and then rounding the number (.02994 rounds to 3 percent).

It should be noted that, in the preceding example, the non-respondents are included in the calculation of the percentages. Another option would be to calculate the percentages based only on those who responded (with N = 157), but when doing so it would be important to include the frequency of non-respondents (that is, 10) and to indicate the total number of respondents plus non-respondents (that is, 167). Figure 3.11 displays these results. It should be noted that in this example the total percentage adds up to 99 because of rounding.

Item	Response	Frequency	Percentage
How well did line workers perform the new process?	5 Extremely well	5	3
	4 Very well	14	9
	3 Moderately well	54	34
	2 Not well	51	32
	1 Not at all well	33	21
	No response (10)		
Total		157	99

FIGURE 3.11 *Example of Frequency and Percentage Calculation for a Quantitative Question Showing Only Respondents*

Other Useful Measures

In addition to reporting the frequencies and percentages for each category, you can also report a single value that provides information about what is typical for a question. This value is called a "measure of central tendency." There are three different measures of central tendency: (1) the mode, (2) the median, and (3) the mean or average.

The *mode* is simply the most frequent response. Let us take the last example presented. In this case, the mode, or most frequent response, is "3 moderately well."

The *median* represents the middle-most point, or the point that would divide the distribution into the top 50 percent and the bottom 50 percent. If we again take the last example and add the percentages from the bottom of the scale (21 + 32), we see that 50 percent of the responses would fall into the category of "2 not well." This, then, is the median.

The *mean* is the average for the question. The steps for calculating the mean are as follows:

1. For each response, multiply the response value by the number of respondents. The calculations for the responses in Figure 3.11 are as follows:

Extremely well	5×5	$= 25$
Very well	14×4	$= 56$
Moderately well	54×3	$= 162$
Not well	51×2	$= 102$
Not at all well	33×1	$= 33$
		378

2. Add the products for all responses (in this case, $25 + 56 + 162 + 102 + 33 = 378$) and divide this total by the number of respondents (that is, $378/157 = 2.4076$). In the example in Figure 3.11, the mean or average is thus 2.41.

Finally, you can report on the values that indicate the degree of spread, or variation, in the data. These values are called *measures of variability*. Again, there are three options: (1) the range, (2) the interquartile range, and (3) the standard deviation.

The *range* simply measures the difference between the highest and the lowest response. So, in the preceding example, the range would consist of the difference between "5 extremely well" (the highest response) and "1 not at all well" (the lowest response), or 5 − 1 = 4. This measure communicates that in this case the highest and lowest response options were chosen by one or more of the respondents.

The *interquartile range* is the difference between the value at the 75th percentile and the value at the 25th percentile. In the case above, the value at the 75th percentile is "3 moderately well" and the value at the 25th percentile is "2 not well." So the interquartile range would be 3 − 2 = 1.

The *standard deviation* measures how much an individual value varies from the mean. A low standard deviation means that the responses vary little from the mean; a high standard deviation means that the responses vary greatly from the mean. One major advantage of the standard deviation is that it provides information needed for more advanced statistics. We use statistics software or math calculators to compute standard deviations. For the example in Figure 3.11, the standard deviation equals 1.02.

Although most needs assessments rely primarily on the descriptive statistics just discussed, there are occasions when it is necessary to undertake other types of analyses. These may involve making inferences from a sample group to the entire population (using inferential statistics), examining relationships (using correlational analyses), focusing on predicting relationships (using regression analyses), or testing for significant differences among variables or groups. To learn more about these types of statistics, refer to an introductory or advanced text on statistics and research methods.

Analyzing Qualitative Data

Analyzing qualitative data involves classifying the data into categories. These categories may come from other sources (such as previous data-collection efforts), or they may be derived from the current data. Categories derived from the current data can be developed by reviewing the entire data set and determining the major themes, or they can use specific words or phrases in the responses.

In most needs assessment projects, qualitative data include responses to open-ended questions. The software available to analyze such responses can report the various sentiments and themes that are contained in the comments; however, many analysts forgo using the software because of expense and because the software is less effective in interpreting sarcasm, sentiments, and organization-specific jargon. Instead, most analysis of open-ended responses involves reading and rereading the responses to determine the meaning of the statements.

Once the meaning of a statement has been determined, one can decide how to categorize the response. The following steps should be used when undertaking such analyses:

- Read and reread each statement.

- Make notes or underline important phrases.

- Develop codes, such as a name, acronym, or number, for each category.

- Assign codes to each statement and sort them into the categories.

- Review the statements within each category and revise the categorization.

- Have a colleague sort some of the data into the categories and compare the results with the earlier categorization of data to determine the level of agreement.

- Count the number of statements within each category.

- Decide how you will report the results.

Tip

The following chapter provides some helpful suggestions for using Excel to analyze qualitative data:

Ruona, W.E.A. (2005). Analyzing qualitative data. In R.A. Swanson & E.F. Holton III (Eds.), *Research in organizations: Foundations and methods of inquiry* (pp. 233–263). San Francisco, CA: Berrett-Koehler.

For more complex qualitative analyses, consult the resources listed in Chapter Eleven.

Reliability, Validity, and Trustworthiness Related to Data Collection and Analysis

Reliability, validity, and *trustworthiness* are terms that describe the level of confidence we have in the data collection and analysis. You would probably question data that were collected using a rubber ruler. The data would not be reliable, because the measurements would change depending on how taut the ruler was. Similarly, you should examine other data-collection instruments to determine whether they collect data consistently.

Reliability refers to the degree of consistency. For example, this consistency can be among raters (as with the agreement among different people categorizing qualitative data), among questions in a survey that measure the same concept, or among responses to similar surveys given at different times. Measures of reliability, such as Cronbach's alpha or test-retest reliability, can be calculated with most statistical software packages.

Validity refers to how well the data-collection method or instrument accurately reflects the concepts or phenomena being measured. For example, validity provides information about the extent to which a survey and the items it contains accurately measure employees' skills.

To obtain face validity, as well as some measure of content validity, have the data-collection methods reviewed by subject-matter experts. Other forms of validity require statistical analyses. More information on these analyses can be found in the resources listed in Chapter Eleven.

Trustworthiness is a concept closely related to reliability and validity, but it tends to be used for qualitative data and qualitative analyses. Guba and Lincoln (1981) proposed four criteria for trustworthiness:

- *Truth value:* the degree to which one can establish the "truth" of the findings, potentially by using multiple methods

- *Applicability:* the degree to which the findings may be applicable in other settings

- *Consistency:* the degree to which the results can be considered reliable and stable

- *Neutrality:* the degree to which the findings come from the study and not from the biases of the analyst

Being attentive to the data-collection methods and analyses and determining the levels of reliability, validity, and trustworthiness provides support for the needs assessment findings. We can place more confidence in rigorously collected and analyzed data than in shoddily collected and analyzed data. Further details on these procedures can be found in Russ-Eft and Preskill (2009) and in the resources provided in Chapter Eleven.

ORGANIZING DATA FOR DECISION MAKING

If your needs assessment relied on multiple methods of data collection and multiple sources of data, you may feel that you are drowning in data. To quickly organize the data for decision making, use the templates and worksheets in the Needs Assessment Toolkit in Section Four of this book. In addition to these forms, consider using a synthesis model to organize or communicate complex or large amounts of data

Synthesis Example: Priority of Organization Needs Based on Interviews and Survey Data

Data Source	Improve communication	Improve access to resources	Improve xyz skills	Improve IT
VP marketing interview	x			
VP manufacturing interview		x		
VP sales interview			x	x
VP HR interview			x	x
VP supply chain interview				x
VP IT interview				x
Focus groups with sixty-three top-performing employees			x	x

FIGURE 3.12 *Comparison of Priority Needs Identified from Different Sources*

so that they create meaningful information for decision making. For example, combine key data that were collected from surveys with key data from interviews by using a two-axis matrix or a graphic chart. The table in Figure 3.12 shows the priority needs for this needs assessment identified by each data source. The two-axis matrix clearly shows that improving IT has the greatest support among those interviewed and surveyed. Equally important, the synthesis shows who does not support this need as the top priority. For additional information on synthesis tools, see Swanson (2007), Watkins, Meiers, and Visser (2012), and Altschuld and White (2010).

CONCLUSION

Data collection and analysis are essential parts of needs assessment. This chapter has described the most commonly used methods of data collection. As seen, each method has its strengths and weaknesses. Needs assessments are optimized when a combination of data-collection methods is used. This chapter also has described methods for analyzing quantitative and qualitative data. Regardless of which methods are used to collect and analyze data, it is important to consider the reliability, validity, and trustworthiness of the data and to organize the data for decision making. Such data can provide the foundation for meaningful negotiations about which needs to address first and how to best address the needs.

The tools and concepts presented in this chapter will be used throughout the book. The next chapter describes how to collect and analyze data when conducting a knowledge and skills assessment.

II

Getting Down to Brass Tacks

FOUR Knowledge and Skills Assessment

PURPOSE

This chapter will enable you to accomplish the following:

- Determine what a knowledge and skills assessment is.
- Know when to use a knowledge and skills assessment.
- Recognize the benefits and drawbacks of the approach.
- Identify critical success factors for completing a knowledge and skills assessment.
- Examine the steps for undertaking a knowledge and skills assessment.
- Examine how knowledge and skills assessments were conducted in two organizations.

RELATED TOOLKIT JOB AIDS

The following job aids for use with the material in this chapter are available in the Needs Assessment Toolkit, which can be found in Section Four of this book:

- Knowledge and Skills Assessment Interview Guide
- Skills Assessment Survey

- Customer-Service Knowledge and Skills Assessment Survey
- Management Knowledge and Skills Assessment Survey
- Knowledge and Skills Assessment Curriculum Plan

OVERVIEW

As a human performance generalist for a medium-sized manufacturing company, you may need to implement a company-wide orientation program; as the training manager of a large health care facility, you may be asked to develop management training programs for supervisory staff; as the HRD manager within a financial organization, you may need to launch a sales training program; as the HPT specialist within a manufacturing company, you may be asked to introduce a system designed to improve productivity; as the learning specialist within an international agency, you may create a cultural awareness program; as the instructional designer for the online learning system for a university, you may need to develop an instructional program to introduce faculty to the new features of the system; or as the manager with an international development organization, you may be charged with redesigning a country's educational system. Before launching any training, learning, or development program, you usually must gather information about the learning needs of your target group or groups and determine whether training is, in fact, the appropriate solution.

By using a systematic approach, you can ensure that gaps in performance are identified correctly. Usually, only those gaps caused by lack of knowledge or skills can be improved through training. Performance deficiencies that occur because of lack of motivation, environmental problems, or systems issues require non-training interventions, such as changes in the selection process, the performance appraisal process, the reward system, or the production system.

When designing training programs, the roles of HRD, HPT, and ID professionals vary, but some of their more common responsibilities include the following:

- Creating a training agenda
- Developing a specific training program (course or module)
- Developing a training curriculum
- Implementing the agenda, program, or curriculum

A knowledge and skills assessment provides the information that is necessary for designing and implementing effective training programs. Its basic purpose is twofold:

1. To identify the knowledge and skills that people must possess in order to perform effectively on the job

2. To prescribe appropriate interventions that can close the knowledge and skills gaps

The amount of time spent conducting needs assessments varies. Although most knowledge and skills assessments are performed in less than a month, a few take a year or more to complete. The knowledge and skills assessment described in the case presented later in this chapter was completed in five weeks.

When to Use

A knowledge and skills assessment is most likely to be useful under the following circumstances:

- When new business opportunities arise
- When a new system or technology must be implemented
- When existing training or development programs must be revised or updated
- When people must assume new job responsibilities
- When jobs must be upgraded
- When organizations undergo downsizing
- When organizations experience rapid growth
- When communities need citizens who have specific knowledge and skills, such as emergency management skills

Benefits and Drawbacks

There are two main benefits from conducting a knowledge and skills assessment:

- It ensures that training programs are developed based on identified needs.

- It is relatively easy to implement.

The main drawback to the approach is that it lacks the detail of a job and task analysis, a competency assessment, a strategic needs assessment or a complex needs assessment. These assessment methods are described in Chapters Five, Six, Seven, and Eight.

Critical Success Factors

The following factors must be present for the successful completion of a knowledge and skills assessment:

- Support, both human and monetary, from senior officials or senior management as well as from the community members or line staff

- Buy-in from special interest groups, such as labor unions, especially if the assessment is perceived by some as a threat to their positions

- Access to the selected people for data-collection purposes

KEY PHASES

A knowledge and skills assessment is made up of five phases:

Phase 1: Gather preliminary data.

Phase 2: Plan.

Phase 3: Perform training requirements analysis.

1. Develop tools.

2. Collect data.

Phase 4: Analyze data.

Phase 5: Prepare and present a report.

Phase 1: Gather Preliminary Data

As mentioned earlier, deficiencies in human performance and changes in the environment often trigger the need for training. For instance, managers in Company A may be outstanding coaches but lack technical skills. Technical staff in Company B may not have problems operating machine X, because they are familiar with the procedures, but they may have problems operating machine Y, which was recently installed. Community members may understand the need for collaboration but lack the skills to successfully work together.

In any case, the analyst should begin by gathering some preliminary information about the training or performance needs of the target groups. As a first step, review available documents and records. These may include statements about the community's, organization's, or unit's goals; training records, and performance data (such as production records, error rates, safety violations, and performance appraisal records). (See Chapter Three for more details on reviewing records and documents.)

After the document review, some additional sources that can be tapped for this preliminary analysis include the following:

- Government officials
- Senior managers
- Members of the target group
- Functional heads or managers of the target group
- Subordinates of the target group

- Internal or external customers
- Suppliers
- Others (such as peers or technical support staff)

Because you are gathering preliminary information, it is usually best to conduct group interviews with three to five people. This will enable you to obtain different perspectives without devoting large amounts of time to the task. A key person however, may be unavailable for a face-to-face interview or group interview. In that case, the same information may be obtained through an individual phone interview.

For a manufacturing company, this preliminary group could consist of a senior manager, a mid-level manager, a subordinate, and a relatively new employee. For a health care facility, information could be obtained from a senior manager, a first-line supervisor, and a subordinate. For a global financial services organization, interviews could be undertaken with the senior vice president of sales, the senior vice president of marketing, a regional sales manager, and a sales associate. For an international development organization, information could be obtained from a government official, a funding partner, a senior manager, and regional associates. As indicated in these examples, it is critical to obtain the perspectives of one or two key decision-makers (such as senior managers) who are familiar with the issues that are the focus of the needs assessment.

The objectives of this phase are as follows:

1. *Establish the goals of the assessment.* As the following example illustrates, the goals expressed by various interviewees could be quite different from one another in purpose and scope.

- Goal 1: Determine the worldwide knowledge and skills of all Company Y technicians.
- Goal 2: Determine the knowledge and skills of all Company Y Level 1 and Level 2 technicians in the United States and Canada.

Therefore, clarify the purpose of the assessment with the client at the beginning of the project so that the appropriate data can be collected.

2. *Obtain a holistic perspective about the knowledge and skills.* In particular, it is important to determine whether the solution really should involve training or should focus on some other systemic issues. (See McLean, 2005, for some ideas about addressing non-training issues.) Use the general questions in Toolkit Form 4.1 to help elicit a broad understanding about whether and how a lack of knowledge and skills is affecting workplace productivity. The questions on the form also can be used to develop a better understanding with the client about what the needs assessment should accomplish. After all the necessary data have been obtained, summarize your findings in a brief report that contains the following elements:

- Statement of the problem
- Situation analysis
- Goals
- Preliminary findings
- Next steps

You can examine these elements in the report for an actual knowledge and skills assessment, which is on pages 96 and 97. The case describes an international humanitarian aid organization, identified by the pseudonym HumanitarianAid. Rebecca Roehm, a graduate student at Oregon State University, contributed the case.

Phase 2: Plan

This phase involves developing a work plan to ensure that you stay on target with your assessment. Sometimes this work plan is developed as part of a larger proposal, as discussed in Chapter Eight. When preparing a work plan, seek the input of your client or contact at the beginning of the project, because this person usually has the best knowledge of group operations, peak business periods to avoid, and so forth. The four steps for planning an assessment begin on page 98.

CASE

STATEMENT OF THE PROBLEM

HumanitarianAid provides members of the community as well as current volunteers with training that ranges from traditional classroom instruction to on-the-job trainings. In the majority of the trainings, volunteers are the instructors. They must complete required training and certifications in order to train new and existing volunteers.

SITUATION ANALYSIS

The organization recently updated their volunteer human resources software. The new software and website, VolunteerLink, streamlines the application process and instantly updates volunteer training information. When VolunteerLink was launched, a training session was held to introduce all volunteers (regardless of department or position) to the website and demonstrate how to use the new features. The training did not include how instructors would use specific features relevant to their job duties, such as looking up class rosters, adding or deleting attendees, researching who has previous disaster training, etc.

GOALS

The purpose of this needs assessment was primarily to determine the reasons why instructors were not using the new website.

APPROACH

A link to an online survey was posted for a subgroup of the volunteer instructors. One week prior to the survey launch, an email was sent to all of the volunteer instructors in the subgroup explaining the purpose of the survey. The email also stated that the only identifying information that would be collected would be the chapter that each participant was associated with and that completion of the survey would take less than ten minutes.

PRELIMINARY FINDINGS

At the end of two weeks, thirty-seven volunteers had responded, which represented 39 percent of the ninety-five volunteers in the subgroup. About 27 percent of the respondents reported that they had never used the website. Another 32 percent reported using the site once a week, and 19 percent reported using the website on a daily basis. (This last group of respondents could be disproportionately paid staff members who need to access the website as part of their job duties.) The majority of respondents (66 percent) used the site for viewing the events calendar and more than half (52 percent) used the site to view the rosters for upcoming classes. In addition, several people mentioned that they used the site for keeping up to date on disaster responses as well as applying for national disaster deployment. The question asking about comfort level with using the website showed about equal responses for the three options: "Not Comfortable Using," "Somewhat Comfortable Using," and "Very Comfortable Using." One respondent said, "Disappointed in all the prior computer interface HumanitarianAid programs. Tired of learning new useless ones and then also their replacements." The majority of the responses alluded to confusion about how the VolunteerLink website could benefit them as instructors or being told that specific features were not available. A few respondents had positive experiences and believed that the website was beneficial to their role as a volunteer instructor for the subgroup at HumanitarianAid.

NEXT STEPS

This assessment showed that not every volunteer was aware of the features and uses that could improve their experience as an instructor and volunteer. Furthermore, not every chapter permits access to some of the important features. A recommendation was made to provide a link on the homepage of the organization to a helpful video tutorial and to consider offering some additional training.

1. *Determine what types of data must be collected.* The goals established in the first needs assessment phase set the stage for data-collection efforts in this phase.

2. *Determine sources of data.* For groups with fewer than thirty members, include every person in your study. If your target audience includes different groups or hierarchical levels, select a representative sample from each group or level. For more information on sample sizes, consult *Performance Consulting* by Robinson and Robinson (1995) or *Evaluation in Organizations* by Russ-Eft and Preskill (2009). In addition, use the following guidelines when making decisions about whom to include in an assessment:

- When implementing a new system or technology, involve technical or subject-matter experts, the target audience, supervisors, and end-users.

- When assessing knowledge and skill needs for an existing process, involve subject-matter experts, job incumbents, supervisors, and other related internal or external customers.

- When revising or updating an existing training program or an HRD, HPT, or ID intervention, include the target audience and supervisors. Consider including subject-matter experts and other related internal or external customers if needed or required.

- When developing a new training program or an HRD, HPT, or ID intervention, include the target audience, subject-matter experts (if required), supervisors, and other related internal or external customers.

3. *Examine the purposes of the knowledge and skills assessment and determine the types of analyses that must be performed.* Figure 4.1 shows some of the common purposes of a knowledge and skills assessment and suggests the kinds of questions that will be addressed by the analyses. Usually, the specific business needs of an organization will determine whether any statistical analyses, such as correlations, must be computed. As mentioned in Chapter Three, if you lack expertise in

such areas as statistics or survey design, consider engaging someone with expertise in preparing data-collection instruments and in analyzing data.

4. *Identify the types of methods that will be used to collect data.* Typically, using two or three different data-collection methods increases the validity, trustworthiness, and reliability of data. For instance, you could supplement surveys with follow-up interviews or observations, or you could use focus groups as your primary data-collection method and collect additional information through observation. An overview of the primary data-collection methods, including their benefits and drawbacks, is given in Chapter Three.

After you have completed the four steps of Phase 2, inform the people involved about your plan through letters, phone calls, or email, and obtain approval from the client and advisory group to proceed with the assessment.

---

1. Learner analysis (What do learners know or need to know, and what do they not know?)
2. Subject-matter analysis (What do subject-matter experts say is important?)
3. Comparison of knowledge levels: current versus desired (How does the current level of knowledge differ from what is needed or desired?)
4. Comparison of skill levels: current versus desired (What are the current skills, and how do they differ from what is needed or desired?)
5. Attitude toward learning (What is the attitude toward learning within the target group?)
6. Attitude toward change (What is the attitude toward change within the target group?)
7. Attitude toward existing training programs (What is the attitude about the current training programs?)
8. Attitude toward a new system or technology (What is the attitude toward the new system or technology?)
9. Quality of existing training programs (What is the quality level of the existing training programs?)

FIGURE 4.1 *Common Purposes of a Knowledge and Skills Assessment*

Phase 3: Perform Training Requirements Analysis

A performance gap is the difference between the current condition (or what is) and the desired condition (or what should be). A knowledge and skills assessment helps to define such a gap by identifying where performance deficiencies exist. The first two phases helped to lay the groundwork for developing the assessment instruments or tools. The third phase consists of two steps: develop the assessment tools and collect the assessment data.

Step 1: Develop Assessment Tools

Because every organization's assessment requirements are unique, the best strategy is to follow the basic guidelines for preparing interview and observation forms, surveys, and focus group questions discussed in Chapter Three. As a guideline, allow about two days to prepare each instrument, but be prepared to allow additional time if special features must be included.

Figures 4.2 and 4.3 are examples of instruments for measuring gaps in skill proficiencies. Figure 4.2 is a simple self-assessment instrument that was used to monitor job activity levels at a major hospital. Figure 4.3 shows a portion of a performance skills profile for assessing the knowledge and skills of employees at an insurance company. The Needs Assessment Toolkit in Section Four contains templates that you can customize to collect these types of data. (See Toolkit Form 4.2: Skills Assessment Survey, Toolkit Form 4.3: Customer Service Knowledge and Skills Assessment Survey, and Toolkit Form 4.4: Management Knowledge and Skills Assessment Survey.)

In addition, Toolkit Form 4.3, a customer-service training survey, and Toolkit Form 4.4, a management development survey, are included to help you start to develop these types of assessments. Note that Toolkit Form 4.4, the management development survey, can be administered to the managers' managers, their subordinates, or both to obtain many perspectives about managerial effectiveness in the organization. Following are some additional suggestions to consider when developing tools:

- Refer to the goals and objectives of your assessment.

- Include an opening paragraph (a statement of purpose and instructions for completing a survey, or an overview and

Importance
1 – Unimportant
2 – Minor
3 – Important
4 – Very Important
5 – Critical

Amount of Time Spent
0 – Never do this task
1 – Very little compared to other tasks
2 – Somewhat less compared to other tasks
3 – Same amount as other tasks
4 – More compared to other tasks
5 – A great deal more compared to other tasks

Performance
1 – Have low or no skill
2 – Perform well enough to get by
3 – Perform in this area without any problem
4 – Have a definite strength or high skill
5 – Have maximum skill

Instructions: For each task activity, circle the number corresponding to its importance for your job, the amount of time you spend on it, and how well you feel you perform it.

Medicare Tape Run	Importance	Amount of Time Spent	Performance
Edit Lists	1 2 3 4 5	0 1 2 3 4 5	1 2 3 4 5
Tape List Claims	1 2 3 4 5	0 1 2 3 4 5	1 2 3 4 5
Paper Claims	1 2 3 4 5	0 1 2 3 4 5	1 2 3 4 5
Sort Error Claims for Reviewers	1 2 3 4 5	0 1 2 3 4 5	1 2 3 4 5
Call on Medicare Tape Runs	1 2 3 4 5	0 1 2 3 4 5	1 2 3 4 5
Work All Railroad EOB's	1 2 3 4 5	0 1 2 3 4 5	1 2 3 4 5
Check All Payments	1 2 3 4 5	0 1 2 3 4 5	1 2 3 4 5
Review All Rejects	1 2 3 4 5	0 1 2 3 4 5	1 2 3 4 5
Resubmit with Correct Information	1 2 3 4 5	0 1 2 3 4 5	1 2 3 4 5
Meet with Supervisor for Major Problems	1 2 3 4 5	0 1 2 3 4 5	1 2 3 4 5
Work on Groups	1 2 3 4 5	0 1 2 3 4 5	1 2 3 4 5
Call Patients to Correct Primary Insurance	1 2 3 4 5	0 1 2 3 4 5	1 2 3 4 5
Call Medicare to Update Insurance	1 2 3 4 5	0 1 2 3 4 5	1 2 3 4 5

FIGURE 4.2 *Example of a Job Activity Self-Assessment*

1. About You

Name: _____ Date: _____

a. Department: _____ Date of Employment: _____

Title of Current Job: _____

Objective of Current Job *(Describe in ten words or less.):* _____

_____

b. What equipment do you routinely use in your current work? *(Check all that apply.)*

____ Telephone   ____ Computer (terminal)   ____ PC

____ Typewriter   ____ Calculator   ____ Fax

____ Microphone   ____ Other

c. List other equipment here:

_____

_____

2. About Your Formal Education *(optional)*

Circle the highest scholastic level achieved: 11 or below, 12, 13,
                                                  14, 15, 16, 17, 18, 19 or more

3. About Your Work Experience

a. What *other* positions have you held? *(List most current first.)*

Title	Brief Description of Job Objective

b. Equipment used in these jobs *(other than those listed above)*

_____

_____

4. About Your Computer Experience

Listed below are some of the most common computer applications used at our company.

In column A, rate your skill level in the application used in your current job.

In column B, rate your skill level in the application not used in your current job but in which you possess prior experience.

If an item is not applicable, place a check mark in the NA column.

FIGURE 4.3 *Example of a Performance Skills Profile*

Use the following scale:

None	Poor	Average	Good	Excellent
1	2	3	4	5

A   B   NA

A	B	NA		
____	____	_____	Active Directory	User interface
____	____	____	CMW	Medical billing system
____	____	____	Dragon Naturally Speaking	Voice-activated system
____	____	____	EMR	Electronic medical records
____	____	____	End Notes	Notes and citation system
____	____	____	HTML	Hypertext markup language
____	____	____	Lotus Notes	Email and forms
____	____	____	WordPerfect	Word processor
____	____	____	XML	Markup language
____	____	____	Access	Database
____	____	____	Excel	Spreadsheet
____	____	____	Outlook	Calendar and email
____	____	____	PowerPoint	Presentation
____	____	____	Project	Project management
____	____	____	Publisher	Publication
____	____	____	Visio	Flow charts, process, and so on
____	____	____	Word	Word processor
____	____	____	Visual Studio	Programming
____	____	____	Netware Utilities	Novell application
____	____	____	Windows	User interface

Please add any additional computer applications that you use on the job or know and rate them.

____ ____   _____

____ ____   _____

____ ____   _____

5. About Training Related to Your Occupation

List below any formal training received *during the last five years* relating to any job you held at *any company.* List in sequence beginning with the most current.

Date	Name of Training Course	Date	Name of Training Course
1. _____		5. _____	
2. _____		6. _____	
3. _____		7. _____	
4. _____		8. _____	

(If you need more space, use a separate sheet and print your name on it.)

FIGURE 4.3 *Example of a Performance Skills Profile* (continued)

6. About Assessing Your Training Needs

Given your current duties, accountabilities, and position objectives, assign two ratings to each of the items listed below.

In column A, rate *your need* for training.

In column B, rate *its importance* to your job.

If an item is *not applicable,* place a check mark in the NA column.

Provide a rating, as above, for any entry you make on the "other" line.

Use the following scale:

Very low	Low	Average	High	Very high
1	2	3	4	5

A   B   NA   *Communication Skills*

___ ___ _____   **a.** Oral communication skills

___ ___ _____   **b.** Written communication skills (letters/e-mails/reports)

___ ___ _____   **c.** Formal presentation skills

___ ___ _____   **d.** Leading effective meetings

___ ___ _____   **e.** Other. Please specify: _____

Customer-Service Skills

___ ___ _____   **a.** Telephone skills

___ ___ _____   **b.** Listening/questioning skills

___ ___ _____   **c.** Handling difficult customers and complaints

___ ___ _____   **d.** Other. Please specify: _____

Performance Management Skills

___ ___ _____   **a.** Monitoring performance/correcting problems

___ ___ _____   **b.** Providing feedback/motivation

___ ___ _____   **c.** Coaching, counseling

___ ___ _____   **d.** Conflict management

___ ___ _____   **e.** Other. Please specify: _____

FIGURE 4.3 *Example of a Performance Skills Profile* (continued)

introduction for interviews and focus groups), an indication of the confidentiality of the responses, the main section (the questions), and a closing (possibly demographic questions in the case of surveys, or closing remarks for conducting interviews or focus groups).

- Separate and label sections clearly.

- Include appropriate labels when using a rating scale.

- Decide whether to use an even-numbered rating scale, such as a four-point or six-point scale, or an odd-numbered scale, such as a five-point or seven-point scale. An odd-numbered scale allows respondents to choose the middle rating rather than be forced to choose one end of the scale or the other. Scales that have more points give respondents more choices, but if the group is too small, make it difficult to see patterns in the data.

- If you use two sets of rating scales per question (shown below) and want to combine them, seek the expertise of someone who can interpret the results accurately. For example:

	Proficiency				
	Very Low	Low	Average	High	Very High
Operate DVD	1	2	3	4	5
	Importance to Job				
	Very Low	Low	Average	High	Very High
Operate DVD	1	2	3	4	5

- Limit the number of questions so that interviews and focus groups can be concluded in two and a half hours and surveys can be completed in ten minutes.

- Limit the number of items to be assessed in a survey. For instance, if you listed more than fifty items and the majority received a rating of 3 or below (indicating that training is needed), you would need to develop a training plan that could accommodate all these programs. Because most people attend an average of seven training programs per year, it could take several years to train everyone. A more effective strategy is to prioritize the items to be included in a survey on the basis of the most critical requirements for the job.

- Pilot-test the data-collection instruments and revise them based on feedback.

Step 2: Collect Data

After you have prepared your instruments, you will be ready to begin the data-collection process. Here are a few suggestions to remember when collecting data:

- When working in a team, ensure that everyone follows the same procedure.
- Limit the time allowed for returning surveys, usually to ten days.
- Have supervisors or managers follow up if instruments have not been received after the ten-day limit.

Phase 4: Analyze Data

After completing Phase 3, you will have collected data from surveys, interviews, or focus groups. To analyze the data, use the process for compiling results that you selected for your plan in Phase 2. Following are a few strategies for ensuring success:

- Limit responsibility for this task: assume it yourself or delegate it to one or two individuals whose judgment and skills you trust.
- Review the data for discrepancies, deviations, and irregularities.
- Present irregularities in the data in a separate section.
- Always keep your client apprised of discrepancies in the data.
- Omit extraneous or irrelevant data; for example, eliminate facts or details that do not pertain specifically to the assessment and its objective. (This includes extraneous information that you may have gathered while interviewing or conducting focus groups.)

- List responses that do not fall into a previously defined category in a separate section titled "other."

- Establish codes for qualitative data (that is, data that are not numerical) so that you can group responses into categories. For example, review the responses to the open-ended survey questions to determine whether there are major themes or categories. If the majority of responses to a question fall into three main categories, assign codes A, B, or C (or relevant descriptive words) to the data according to the three predetermined categories. This coding scheme can then be used as you review the notes or recordings from the interviews or focus groups. As you review the data, you may need to add additional categories that emerge.

- Next to each category, list the frequency of responses. For example:

  Q. Why do you think team training is needed?

TYPE OF RESPONSE	NUMBER OF RESPONSES
A. People don't know how to work in teams.	15
B. There is lack of cooperation among units.	10
C. There is lack of clarity about team roles.	11

- When faced with conflicting data, seek the opinion of an expert or individual qualified to make a judgment.

Phase 5: Prepare and Present a Report

The final phase of a knowledge and skills assessment is preparing and presenting a formal report. Reports generally contain the following elements:

- Executive summary

- Goals or objectives

- Overview of data-collection methods

- Findings or conclusions

- Recommendations

- Appendix

Chapter Nine provides additional information on report writing. Other examples of formal reports can be found in Phillips and Holton (1995). In addition, Torres, Preskill, and Piontek (2005) provide a variety of reporting formats.

Here are a few guidelines for presenting your conclusions and recommendations to your client and interested stakeholders:

- Tailor the presentation style to the culture of your organization.

- Verify budgetary constraints so that recommendations are on target.

- If appropriate, present your recommendations in a table with the following headings: cost, urgency, availability of resources (monetary and nonmonetary), and feasibility.

- Research the feasibility of each recommendation thoroughly and offer alternatives where needed.

- Use benchmarking data when available.

- Provide cost/benefit information, if appropriate.

- Support your recommendations with citations and "best practices" from authorities in the field or industry.

If you are preparing and presenting a curriculum plan, following is a suggested list of content areas to include:

- Overview

- Statement of the problem

- Learner analysis

- Detailed course objectives

- Course outlines

- Training schedule (quarterly, bi-annual, or annual)

- Training delivery strategy

- Evaluation strategy

Toolkit Form 4.5 can be used to develop high-level and detailed curriculum plans. The plan can include a core or advanced curriculum or both. Usually, core curriculums are more appropriate for beginning or intermediate learners.

This chapter has presented the methods and tools for performing a knowledge and skills assessment. Here is a case study of an assessment completed for Packaged Delivery, Inc. The information for this case was contributed by Jeanne Strayer, a training and performance improvement consultant based in Oceanside, California. Although all events are real, the company has been given a fictitious name at the request of the contributor. The case shows the approach used to conduct a needs assessment in preparation for a new company-wide training program. The key tool shown here is a set of interview questions used for lead drivers, first-line supervisors, and senior managers.

CASE

Packaged Delivery, Inc., is one of the largest packaged product delivery companies in the United States. It manufactures and distributes products through home and commercial delivery, as well as through retail outlets, such as supermarkets. The company has six regions in ten states. Each region has between four and six branches. Each branch is responsible for delivering its product to customers on designated routes. Depending on the size of the branch, lead drivers may report to two or more sales supervisors.

THE NEED

Packaged Delivery, Inc., recognized that lead drivers were being asked to expand their job duties. Because of their seniority, leads were expected to coach and train their peers—those responsible for driving routes and delivering products. The leads benefited because coaching offered a balance to their driving, delivery, and bookkeeping duties. The company benefited because the leads often noticed and corrected performance problems with new trainees. Yet the leads did not necessarily have the skills to be effective trainers and coaches. Although they had sound technical skills, developing people required a different type of skill. The company saw the need for a program to help drivers learn to train and coach others.

THE APPROACH

A five-phase approach to conducting the needs assessment was used. The major steps and findings in each phase are summarized here.

Phase 1: Gather Preliminary Data

Preliminary data were gathered when the designated course developer met with the HR director and two regional vice presidents. The group confirmed the situation but also pointed out some unique characteristics of the leads' situation that had to be addressed:

- Leads were placed in a position of responsibility but had little or no authority.
- It was difficult for leads to find time to train and coach, because their regular duties consumed so much time.
- Leads needed to strike the right balance between resolving problems behind the scenes and going to the supervisor when management intervention was required, which was especially true because of union regulations.
- Leads were often promoted within the same group, a situation that sometimes led to new dynamics and tensions with their former peers.

Phase 2: Develop a Plan

1. The HR director and two regional vice presidents agreed to the scope of the training and the plan for the needs assessment. All operational leads in the company (approximately

110 people) would be trained. The needs assessment would involve interviews with members of the target audience (the leads), their supervisors, and selected HR personnel who were seen as experts in coaching skills and union practices.

2. The following goals were identified for the interviews:

- Determine the gap between current and desired levels of training and coaching skills.
- Assess the leads' attitudes toward training.
- Obtain stories about real-life situations that could later serve as examples, case studies, or role plays during the training.

Phase 3: Conduct a Needs Assessment

1. Interview instruments were created for the leads (see Figure 4.4), their supervisors (see Figure 4.5), and the company's vice presidents (see Figure 4.6).
2. Instruments were reviewed and approved by the HR director.
3. Interviews were conducted with fourteen leads, six supervisors, and two regional vice presidents. Interviews with the supervisors and vice presidents confirmed the data collected from the leads.
4. Interviews with HR personnel were particularly helpful in determining the types of coaching and training skills needed for nonsupervisory positions. These interviews also provided valuable insights into the constraints faced by the leads when working as union members.

Phase 4: Analyze the Data

1. Recurring themes in the qualitative interview data were noted, organized into categories, and coded. For example, responses to a question about obstacles to coaching others while working on the job were grouped into three categories:

- Lack of time to coach
- Physical environment (open spaces with no privacy)
- Personal reluctance to coach former peers

2. The interviews also yielded quantitative, or numerical, data that helped to determine and rate the deficiencies in the leads' skills. The items and their ratings included the following (on a 5-point scale with 1 as low and 5 as high):

- Listening empathetically   3.2
- Giving directions clearly   3.2
- Giving feedback constructively   3.0
- Involving people rather than telling them what to do   2.5

Phase 5: Write a Report

1. The report prepared for the HR director summarized the results of the needs assessment and provided specific recommendations for the content, skills, examples, and issues to be covered during training. The report included a proposed outline of the training program, which incorporated all the recommendations and also showed the sequence of topics (see Figure 4.7).
2. The report was submitted, and the proposed outline approved. Some modifications were made prior to course development.

THE RESULTS

The program was well received by management and the leads, because it met their identified needs. In addition, the examples used in the training came from real-life stories. The course served as a stepping stone for those leads who aspired to becoming supervisors. The company, the leads, and the drivers benefited from the program.

All items that received a rating of 3.5 or under were earmarked for training.

1. According to the job description, a lead driver spends time training new hires and coaching experienced drivers as well as covering open routes. What percentage of your time do you estimate is spent on training and coaching?
2. What common performance problems do new hires have? Experienced drivers?
3. What sorts of situations call for coaching on your part?
4. What are the biggest challenges of a lead driver's job?
5. What were the biggest pitfalls you encountered as a new coach and trainer?
   Follow-up question 1: What mistakes did you make at first?
   Follow-up question 2: What lessons have you learned over time?
6. What do you do when someone is having trouble or not meeting standards?
7. Can you tell me about a successful experience you have had coaching someone?
   Follow-up question 1: What made it successful?
8. Tell me about a not-so-successful experience you have had coaching someone.
   Follow-up question 1: Why was it not successful?
9. How do you encourage and motivate other lead drivers?
   Follow-up question 1: Do you use incentives or rewards?
   Follow-up question 2: Do you try other things (for example, pay compliments, recognize people, give personal attention)?
10. What keeps you from being a good coach on the job?
11. Have you received training in coaching people?
12. Please rate yourself on the following skills on a scale of 1 (low) to 5 (high). These ratings are confidential and will not be attributed to any one person.
    a. Listening empathetically
    b. Giving directions clearly
    c. Giving feedback constructively
    d. Involving people rather than telling them what to do
    e. Demonstrating a new skill in such a way that another person understands the critical aspects, that is, does it correctly
    f. Guiding a team member to a solution for a problem
    g. Knowing how to recognize someone for a job well done
    h. Pointing out how someone's behavior is negatively affecting indicators and key measures
13. What topics would you like to see covered in training?

FIGURE 4.4 *Interview Questions for Lead Drivers*

1. According to the job description, a lead driver spends time training new hires and coaching experienced drivers, as well as covering open routes. What percentage of a driver's time do you estimate is spent doing training and coaching?

2. What are some of the skills you expect a lead driver to demonstrate as a coach or trainer?
   Follow-up question 1: Do the lead drivers currently perform these skills?
   Follow-up question 2: Why or why not?

3. What would the impact be on your branch if lead drivers were used effectively as coaches and trainers?

4. What kinds of situations call for coaching by drivers?
   Follow-up question 1: What measures should be taken?

5. What is a common performance problem for a new hire?
   Follow-up question 1: For an experienced driver?

6. What are the biggest challenges lead drivers face as coaches?

7. What are the biggest pitfalls you have seen new coaches fall into?
   Follow-up question 1: What mistakes do they commonly make?

8. To what extent do lead drivers have to help solve a problem? Or do they just bring it to the person's attention?
   Follow-up question 1: For example, can a lead driver come up with strategies to help someone increase sales, improve customer satisfaction ratings, and so on?

9. Think about the lead drivers who report to you now. How would you rate them on the items below using a scale of 1 (low) to 5 (high). These ratings are confidential and will not be attributed to any one person.
   a. Listening empathetically
   b. Giving directions clearly
   c. Giving feedback constructively
   d. Involving people rather than telling them what to do
   e. Demonstrating a new skill in such a way that another person understands the critical aspects, that is, does it correctly
   f. Guiding a team member to a solution for a problem
   g. Knowing how to recognize someone for a job well done
   h. Pointing out how someone's behavior is negatively affecting indicators and key measures

10. Does anything keep lead drivers from being good coaches on the job?
    Follow-up question 1: Are there physical constraints, time constraints, or other factors?

11. Have lead drivers received any training in coaching people?

12. What topics would you like to see covered in training?

FIGURE 4.5 *Interview Questions for Supervisors*

1. How would you like to see lead drivers used as coaches and trainers for new hires?
2. What impact would the lead drivers have if used effectively as coaches or trainers?

   Follow-up question 1: What key measures or indicators would be affected?
3. What are the biggest challenges lead drivers face on the job as coaches or trainers?
4. What would you like to see emphasized in a coaching skills program for lead drivers?

FIGURE 4.6 *Interview Questions for Vice Presidents*

   I. Welcome to Coaching
     A. Welcome
     B. Factors affecting how much you are able to coach
     C. Course objectives
     D. Exercise: Think about a coach you had in the past
     E. Are you coaching now?
  II. The Coach as Trainer
     A. Giving directions
     B. Exercise: Benefits and drawbacks of showing and telling versus not showing and telling
     C. Exercise: Lessons learned
 III. The Coach as Counselor
     A. Introduction
     B. The ABCs of understanding behavior
     C. Listening empathetically
     D. Giving feedback
     E. Performance coaching: A seven-step model
 IV. The Coach as Motivator
     A. Leading by example
     B. Getting to know each person
     C. Incentives and rewards
  V. Achieving Success
     A. Challenges faced by lead drivers in their roles as coaches
     B. Lessons learned from others
     C. When and where to coach
     D. Handling problem situations
     E. Working with your supervisor

FIGURE 4.7 *Course Outline*

CONCLUSION

A knowledge and skills assessment is one of the most basic and common forms of needs assessment conducted by HRD and HPT professionals in the workplace. This chapter has described a five-phase approach for doing such an assessment. The key to performing a successful knowledge and skills assessment is to follow a few simple guidelines.

1. Adapt and modify your strategy based on the situation. Although it is recommended that more than one data-collection method be used for a needs assessment, the case in this chapter shows that a program can be successful with interviews alone.

2. To facilitate the data-collection process, consider using existing or "found" data.

3. Limit the size of the group from which information must be obtained. This simplifies the data-analysis phase considerably. If large groups must be used, be sure you have established a sound data-collection and analysis methods.

The next chapter describes how to conduct a job and task analysis.

FIVE Job and Task Analysis

PURPOSE

This chapter will enable you to accomplish the following:

- Define a job and task analysis.

- Recognize when to use a job and task analysis.

- Recognize benefits and drawbacks of the approach.

- Identify critical success factors for doing a job and task analysis.

- Identify key elements, including job responsibilities and job tasks.

- Examine three phases for conducting a job and task analysis.

- Identify shortcuts to the process.

- Examine how a job and task analysis was conducted at Boehringer Mannheim Corporation.

RELATED TOOLKIT JOB AIDS

The following job aids for use with the material in this chapter are available in the Needs Assessment Toolkit, which can be found in Section Four of this book:

- Job Analysis Questionnaire
- Job Training and Non-Training Recommendations I (Professional/Supervisory/Management)
- Job Training and Non-Training Recommendations II (Administrative)
- Job Task Analysis Checklist

OVERVIEW

Jobs and tasks are common in for-profit and not-for-profit organizations, government agencies, and communities. A *job* is defined as anything a person is expected to do, while a *task* is a piece of work that is expected of a person. Some jobs and tasks are paid; some are not. Examples of community jobs include first responder, volunteer firefighter, and community worker.

Job analysis is a method for gathering, organizing, evaluating, and reporting work-related information (Brannick & Levine, 2002; Butruille, 1989; Fine & Cronshaw, 1999). Task analysis is a method for determining the knowledge, skills, tools, conditions, and requirements needed to perform a job (Callahan, 1985; Shepherd, 2001). Although some people consider these separate types of analyses, we combine them because of their similarities. The primary objective of a job and task analysis is to gather information about the scope, responsibilities, and tasks for a particular job function or functions.

Information from a job and task analysis is useful in preparing job profiles or position descriptions. Job and task analysis also provides the foundation for training and development programs that are based on the work that is actually done.

Doing a job and task analysis helps people gain a clearer picture of what specific jobs entail and what is expected. It also helps supervisors and managers establish criteria for job performance and thus lay a foundation for performance management and career planning systems.

Undertaking a job and task analysis is not as difficult as it appears. After you understand what it is and how it is done, the analysis can usually be accomplished without problems. The amount of time required to complete a job and task analysis can vary from a few days to several months. The amount of time that such a project takes depends on the number of job analyses that must be developed, recognizing that each position can encompass many different jobs and tasks.

When to Use

A job and task analysis is most valuable under the following circumstances:

- When new or existing job descriptions or position profiles for managerial and non-managerial jobs must be developed as part of a performance management system

- When jobs must be redesigned and tasks (including the requisite knowledge, skills, attitudes, and behaviors) for each job identified

- When a consistent set of training requirements must be created, especially those involving highly technical or specialized job functions

- When specific knowledge, skills, and behaviors must be identified for testing and certification purposes

Benefits and Drawbacks

Conducting a job and task analysis has several benefits for an organization:

- It stimulates buy-in and interest, because people are directly involved in defining their jobs and tasks.

- It provides supervisors with a profile of the skill sets that are necessary for people to perform competently in a given job function.

- It serves as a basis for distinguishing the skill requirements of various job classifications or levels within a position (such as entry-level versus senior positions).

- It serves as a benchmark for determining what additional knowledge, skills, attitudes, and behaviors people must acquire to move across categories or upward within a job category.

- It supports the growth and professional development of people within an organization.

- It can provide the foundation for community development and international development efforts.

The approach has drawbacks:

- It does not take into account external factors that may affect performance.

- It may not take into account different cultures and cultural issues.

- It takes extensive time and commitment.

- It is costly.

- When this approach is conducted as a foundation for community or international development, remember that jobs and tasks with the same names are often performed in differing ways. For example, the job of a community organizer differs across communities encompassing different tasks. In order for the needs assessment to reflect how the work is actually done, these differences must be reconciled before the needs assessment is conducted

Critical Success Factors

A few prerequisites are crucial to the successful completion of a job and task analysis project or initiative:

- Support from senior management or senior officials

- Availability of both human and monetary resources

- A stable environment (It is difficult to question people about their jobs during downsizing, mergers, or takeovers; furthermore, the jobs and tasks may be changing.)

- Open communication about why the analysis is being prepared and how it will impact the job incumbents

- A willingness to collaborate by both those who perform and those who have stakes in the jobs and tasks.

Both the organization and its employees have much to gain from a job and task analysis, given the right approach and the right environment. We begin by defining a few key terms. Then we present guidelines for writing effective job task statements and standards. Finally we discuss the steps for conducting a job and task analysis.

Definition of Terms

Before we provide guidelines for writing job task statements and standards, we define a couple of terms:

- *Job responsibility.* The scope of activities for a job function or job position. For example, a job responsibility of an operations manager is to *ensure that staff members participate in the annual corporate professional education program.*

- *Job task.* What must be done to fulfill a responsibility. Usually four to six tasks are associated with each responsibility. Continuing the example of the operations manager, one job task associated with the above job responsibility is to *develop an annual professional education program for each staff member.*

WRITING JOB TASK STATEMENTS

Most people are familiar with the term "responsibilities." A person has control over his or her responsibilities and is accountable for them. For the supervisor position, one responsibility may be to manage work performance. Another may be to conduct performance reviews. Each responsibility comprises several job tasks. A job task statement essentially describes the what, why, and how of a job, as shown in the following example:

What?   Type a report
Why?   To document the minutes of a meeting
How?   By using a word-processing program

In general, it is useful to follow a few basic rules when writing job task statements:

- Restrict each sentence to one idea.

- Avoid using jargon.

- Avoid using negatives, such as "will not participate in the fund-raising campaign."

In addition, job task statements should always begin with a specific verb. Following are a few verb substitutions for increasing specificity:

INSTEAD OF	CONSIDER USING
Communicate	Write, speak
Gauge	Evaluate, identify, measure, assess, determine
Strive	Accomplish, meet, conduct

The following statements have been rewritten to begin with a specific action verb:

1. Work under direction of supervisor to develop an employee pension plan.

   Write an employee pension plan under direction of supervisor.

2. Interface monthly with business unit heads.

   Meet monthly with business unit heads.

3. Interact with treasury department to support implementation of new credit policy.

   Conduct weekly meetings with treasury department staff to support implementation of new credit policy.

4. Serve as lead for presentation of updated tariff policy plan.

   Lead presentation on the updated tariff policy plan.

WRITING STANDARDS

Occasionally, job task statements add another component—a standard—at the end of the statement. A standard specifies how a task should be performed. For instance:

- Calculate correctly the number of home closings per quarter.
- Monitor implementation of the corrective action policy by reporting employee deviations to management each month.
- Process new claims courteously in ten to fifteen minutes.

For example:

ASSEMBLY OF HELP DESK MANUALS

Task statement   Assemble help desk manuals.

Standards   Make twenty copies of each one-hundred-page binder using a copier, without assistance, within five business days. Insert five tab dividers into each binder in the proper places.

It is relatively easy to specify standards for administrative and technical jobs, because the degree of accuracy required for job performance is both specific and high. However, because of the time required to obtain and spell out such standards, completing a job and task analysis for a skilled worker takes longer.

KEY PHASES

There are three phases in conducting a job and task analysis:
Phase 1: Prepare.

1. Identify high performers.

2. Prepare job analysis questionnaire.

3. Prepare materials.

Phase 2: Conduct job task analysis work session.

1. Prepare for the work session.

2. Refine job responsibilities.

3. Identify job tasks.

4. Identify training and non-training requirements.

Phase 3: Develop and present job training and non-training recommendations.

Phase 1: Prepare

This phase consists of several tasks. Start by assembling a project team. Depending on the scope of your project, a team may be limited to you and a facilitator who leads the job and task analysis work session (see detail in Phase 2), or it can include field personnel and subject-matter experts. For high-profile projects, an advisory committee or expert panel may be necessary.

Identify High Performers

Select four to six key people in a range from above average to high performers in the job category being analyzed. The criteria for selecting high performers is explained in Chapter Six (see pages 152 and 153). Occasionally, a job function expert—that is, someone within or outside the organization who is considered an expert in a particular job task—can be used as a resource person. Job function experts are especially helpful when the job being analyzed is very technical or specialized.

During this preparatory stage, inform participants that they have been selected to provide input for a job and task analysis. Also inform their supervisors. If employees are located elsewhere, make travel and other arrangements. Brief participants about the process.

Prepare Job Analysis Questionnaire

Figure 5.1, Sample Toolkit Form 5.1, shows a sample job analysis survey that can be used to obtain job-related information prior to holding a work session. A week before the scheduled date of the session, distribute the survey to participants via email, the web, or mail. In addition to starting participants' thinking about the critical tasks involved in

---

TOOLKIT FORM 5.1 *Job Analysis Questionnaire*

Purpose: The purpose of this questionnaire is to gather information about your job.

Directions: Answer all the questions. Return the survey to [name/ department] by [date].

Name:_____

Sample Questions:

1. List all of your major responsibilities. Then prioritize each item by assigning a number to it. For example, assign the number "1" to the responsibility you consider the most important.

Develop data record layouts, input forms, record formats, testing schemes, and test data.	*1*
Write computer programs using logic flow charts, record layouts, and record formats.	*2*
Ensure program accuracy by creating test programs, conducting spot checks, and reviewing output.	*3*
Document programs, operations, and projects in accordance with company standards.	*4*
Assist computer operations personnel with implementation of programs.	*5*

FIGURE 5.1 *Sample Toolkit Form 5.1: Job Analysis Questionnaire*

TOOLKIT FORM 5.1 *Job Analysis Questionnaire* (continued)

2. Why are these responsibilities important to your job?

I need the specifications from the project lead to ensure that the logic

programs and operating techniques I produce are efficient. I use the

software programs and manufacturer routines in areas of sort, utility, and

bulk media conversion. I require a PC for documentation and program

development, and the disk storage device for creating permanent files.

3. What equipment and tools do you use in your job?

PC computer, disk storage device, software programs, computer

manufacturer routines, and job flow specifications from the

project leader.

4. Describe some specific duties or tasks that you perform in your job, as related to your major responsibilities. List the responsibilities that you previously mentioned. After you indicate the specific duty or task, please state how often you perform this duty or task.

Develop data record layouts: I review and evaluate job flow specifications

to make sure they are clear and that the project can be completed in the

specified time. I do this about every three months.

Write computer programs: I write or modify computer programs including

testing them almost daily.

Assist computer operations: I assist operations with the implementation of

programs about once a week.

5. What knowledge do you require to perform your job successfully?

I need to know about accounting and manufacturing systems and data

management techniques, and to have some understanding of

communication concepts.

FIGURE 5.1 *Sample Toolkit Form 5.1: Job Analysis Questionnaire*

TOOLKIT FORM 5.1 *Job Analysis Questionnaire* (continued)

6. What qualities are necessary to make you successful in your job?

I need to be able to work in a fast-paced environment and meet

deadlines.

I need to have good interpersonal skills to work with project leaders and

operations personnel. I also need to be detail-oriented and to care about

quality control.

7. What prior knowledge, skills, attitudes, and behaviors did you bring to your position that helped to make you successful in your job?

To be successful in this job takes either a college degree or one or

more years of programming experience. You need to be aware of

the latest techniques in data processing, especially if it affects

programming.

8. List any courses, workshops, or training programs you attended in the past that you feel have helped you succeed in your job.

I took a communications course last year that helped me understand

myself and others better. It made it easier for me to work with and

understand the project leaders. I also completed a course in data

management techniques, which was helpful because the field

changes so frequently.

9. Describe any other contributing factors that you feel have made you successful in your job.

The systems project leader is very supportive. He helps me whenever

I have a question or a problem with computer operations or data

conversion personnel. He also lets me know where I stand and gives me

feedback on my work.

FIGURE 5.1 *Sample Toolkit Form 5.1: Job Analysis Questionnaire* (continued)

performing a job, the survey stimulates their interest in the process of job and task analysis.

Prepare Materials

Spend time reviewing the returned surveys and transcribing key job responsibilities from the surveys into one document, such as a flip chart, handout, or computer-based presentation, so they can be shared with the project team. For example:

EMPLOYEE	PRIMARY JOB RESPONSIBILITIES
Sue	**1.** Execute marketing and strategic initiatives for asset management group.
	2. Develop advertising, direct mail, customer communication, and public relations program for asset management group products.
John	**1.** Manage product development, competitive pricing analysis, and reporting for asset management group products.
	2. Implement strategic and marketing programs worldwide for asset management group.

Phase 2: Conduct Job Task Analysis Work Session

The work session to elicit information from participants requires a skilled group facilitator. The primary objective of the work session is to identify key responsibilities and job tasks required for effective on-the-job performance. Once these requirements have been obtained, the group can further define the training and non-training requirements for a job.

Prepare for the Work Session

Prepare an agenda for the work session. The following sample agenda can be used as a guide. Immediately before the session, gather materials, including the completed surveys, copies of the agenda, blank flip charts, markers, the needed computer equipment, handouts, or prepared flip charts. Also reserve a meeting room. When setting up the meeting room, post the prepared flip charts in a prominent place.

TIME	ACTIVITY
8:00 A.M.–8:30 A.M.	Orientation • Introduce everyone. • Review purpose and significance of the session. • Review agenda. • Discuss "housekeeping" issues: ground rules, breaks, restrooms, lunch, phone, interruptions, use of cell phones, protocol.
8:30 A.M.–10:00 A.M.	Refine list of responsibilities. • Review prepared flip chart of responsibilities. • Brainstorm additional responsibilities. • Combine similar responsibilities.
10:00 A.M.–10:20 A.M.	Break
10:20 A.M.–1:00 P.M.	Identify tasks for each job responsibility. • Use data from questionnaires to brainstorm tasks. • Review list and omit non-essential tasks.
1:00 P.M.–2:00 P.M.	Lunch break
2:00 P.M.–3:15 P.M.	Identify the knowledge, skills, attitudes and behaviors required to perform each task.

3:15 P.M.–3:30 P.M.	Break
3:30 P.M.–4:15 P.M.	Identify training and non-training requirements necessary to acquire the knowledge, skills, attitudes, and behaviors for each task.
4:15 P.M.–4:45 P.M.	Prioritize the training needs based on consensus about the tasks most critical to job performance.
4:45 P.M.–5:00 P.M.	Close • Review next steps in the process. • Ask for subject-matter expert's availability for reviews. • Thank participants.

Note: The time required to complete the analysis may vary. An additional half day or day may be needed, depending on the complexity of the job responsibilities, the number of participants, and the facilitator's skills.

Refine Job Responsibilities

The first order of business during a work session is to obtain consensus from participants about the key responsibilities involved in performing their jobs. The group then works to refine the list of prepared job responsibilities by combining similar statements under one statement. For example, Sue's first statement and John's second statement from the earlier example can be rewritten as follows: Conduct marketing and strategic initiatives worldwide for the asset management group.

Identify Job Tasks

Next, ask participants to use the information from their completed surveys to brainstorm a list of tasks for each job responsibility. Post these on a flip chart or key them into a computer presentation. Ask participants to review the list of tasks and delete all nonessential tasks.

Finally, ask participants to identify the knowledge, skills, attitudes, and behaviors required to perform each task.

Identify Training and Non-Training Requirements

Ask participants to identify the training needed to acquire the knowledge, skills, attitudes, and behaviors for each task. For example:

Position:	**Project Leader**
Job responsibility 1:	Manage multiple systems projects.
Job tasks:	Manage project schedules.
	Manage internal technical experts, project team, and vendors.
	Prepare interim and final reports.
Knowledge:	Project management, software architecture.
Skills and abilities:	Team leadership, resource management, oral and written communication skills.
Attitudes:	Highly motivated, future-oriented.
Behaviors:	Listen carefully to requests, record conversations in detail, monitor schedules, communicate status of projects, and collaborate with team members to troubleshoot projects.
Prerequisite	Computer operating systems, client-server knowledge and skills systems, work flow, and imaging implementation.
Training required:	Advanced project management, team management, writing business reports, presentation skills.

Finally, ask participants to prioritize training and non-training needs on the basis of tasks they consider most critical to job performance.

Phase 3: Develop and Present Job Training and Non-Training Recommendations

The purpose of this phase is to review and organize the information obtained from the work session. Prepare a preliminary draft of the job responsibilities, the tasks, and the training and non-training recommendations. Present this draft to supervisors for review. Ask supervisors to refine the list by adding or deleting tasks. After the draft has been approved, prepare a final copy of the job training and non-training recommendations. You can use Toolkit Form 5.2 to prepare the job training and non-training recommendations for professionals and supervisory and management personnel, and Toolkit Form 5.3 to prepare the job training and non-training recommendations for administrative jobs. Figures 5.2 and 5.3 give sample job training and non-training recommendations for a marketing manager and an administrative assistant.

TOOLKIT FORM 5.2 *Job Training and Non-Training Recommendations (Professional/Supervisory/Management)*

Job Title: Marketing Manager

Department: Marketing

Location: New York

Job Responsibility 1: Develop advertisements

1. Job Task: Define client needs
2. Job Task: Write ad copy
3. Job Task: Establish rapport with newspaper representatives
4. Job Task: Track ad response
5. Job Task: Manage advertising budget

Competencies: Grammar, understand the process of placing ads, math, organizational skills, ability to meet deadlines, interpersonal skills, word processing

Training Requirements: Features and process of writing advertisements, time management

Non-Training Requirements: Computer system for tracking

FIGURE 5.2 *Sample Toolkit Form 5.2: Job Training and Non-Training Recommendations (Professional/Supervisory/Management)*

TOOLKIT FORM 5.2 *Job Training and Non-Training Recommendations (Professional/Supervisory/Management)* (continued)

Job Responsibility 2: Develop direct mail

1. Job Task: Write promotional materials, newsletters, pamphlets
2. Job Task: Identify potential audience
3. Job Task: Maintain database
4. Job Task: Evaluate vendor services and pricing structures
5. Job Task: Track response rates

Competencies: Grammar, math, market research, database management, analytical skills, computer skills

Training Requirements: Writing, database management, marketing, desktop publishing

Non-Training Requirements: Computer tools for database management and desktop publishing

Job Responsibility 3: Maintain and develop customer communications

1. Job Task: Call customers once a quarter
2. Job Task: Respond to phone inquiries
3. Job Task: Mail appropriate materials to customers
4. Job Task: Request referrals

Competencies: Interpersonal skills, ability to handle multiple tasks, follow-through skills, product knowledge

Training Requirements: Time management, communication, product information, stress management

Non-Training Requirements: Availability of needed materials

Job Responsibility 4: Develop public relations

1. Job Task: Attend Chamber of Commerce meetings
2. Job Task: Identify community charities
3. Job Task: Identify and participate in community activities
4. Job Task: Write articles for local newspapers
5. Job Task: Conduct presentations at schools, colleges, and professional meetings

Competencies: Grammar, community awareness, interpersonal skills, writing skills, assertiveness, presentation skills,

Training Requirements: Assertiveness, writing, interpersonal skills, public speaking, graphic design

Non-Training Requirements: Notification of Chamber of Commerce meetings, notice of deadlines for newspapers and meetings

FIGURE 5.2 *Sample Toolkit Form 5.2: Job Training and Non-Training Recommendations (Professional/Supervisory/Management)* (continued)

TOOLKIT FORM 5.2 *Job Training and Non-Training Recommendations (Professional/Supervisory/Management)* (continued)

Job Responsibility 5: Benchmark company performance

1. Job Task: Review competitors' materials
2. Job Task: Review industry literature
3. Job Task: Attend professional association meetings

Competencies: Knowledge of competition, awareness of industry publications, research techniques, analytical skills, interpersonal skills

Training Requirements: Communication, market research, interpersonal skills

Non-Training Requirements: Vendor to obtain competitors' materials, access to industry literature

FIGURE 5.2 *Sample Toolkit Form 5.2: Job Training and Non-Training Recommendations (Professional/Supervisory/Management)* (continued)

TOOLKIT FORM 5.3 *Job Training and Non-Training Recommendations (Administrative)*

Job Title: Administrative Assistant
Department: Accounting
Location: New York

Job Responsibility 1: Track accounts receivable

1. Job Task: Use spreadsheet to record accounts receivable
2. Job Task: Supply chief financial officer (CFO) with weekly summary report
3. Job Task: Contact delinquent accounts
4. Job Task: Reconcile ledger discrepancies

Knowledge: Accounting, math, knowledge of customer base

Skills/Abilities: Spreadsheet, word processing, interpersonal skills, organizational skills, attention to detail

Attitudes: Team player

Behaviors: Completes work and double-checking in a timely fashion

Standards: Balanced accounts, timely and accurate reports, no accounts receivable balances more than forty-five days old

FIGURE 5.3 *Sample Toolkit Form 5.3: Job Training and Non-Training Recommendations (Administrative)*

TOOLKIT FORM 5.3 *Job Training and Non-Training Recommendations (Administrative)* (continued)

Training Requirements: Accounting, math, spreadsheets, word processing, time management, procedure for contacting delinquent accounts, phone skills

Non-Training Requirements: Up-to-date accounting software

Job Responsibility 2: Pay accounts payable

1. Job Task: Review invoices for accuracy
2. Job Task: Rectify invoice discrepancies
3. Job Task: Balance payable accounts
4. Job Task: Prepare and mail payments

Knowledge: Accounting, math

Skills/Abilities: Attention to detail, spreadsheet word processing, interpersonal skills, organizational skills

Attitudes: Team player

Behaviors: Completes work and double-checking in a timely fashion

Standards: Accounts balanced, all discrepancies rectified, payments made within forty-five days of the due date

Training Requirements: Accounting, math, spreadsheets, interpersonal skills, organizational skills

Non-Training Requirements: Up-to-date accounting software

Job Responsibility 3: Prepare financial reports

1. Job Task: Review monthly records for accuracy
2. Job Task: Collect financial information for use in statistical analysis and business plans
3. Job Task: Prepare statistical summaries for management reports
4. Job Task: Duplicate and supply copies of the summary to senior management

Knowledge: Accounting

Skills/Abilities: Attention to detail, analytical skills, math, word processing, writing skills, time management, operation of the copy machine

Attitudes: Team player

Behaviors: Completes work in a timely fashion

Standards: Accurate, complete, and timely reports provided to all senior managers

Training Requirements: Accounting, company standards and practices, word processing, writing skills, time management, copy machine operations

Non-Training Requirements: Access to company standards, computer and word processing software, access to copy machine

---

FIGURE 5.3 *Sample Toolkit Form 5.3: Job Training and Non-Training Recommendations (Administrative)* (continued)

TOOLKIT FORM 5.3 *Job Training and Non-Training Recommendations (Administrative)* (continued)

Job Responsibility 4: Assist CFO with communications

1. Job Task: Prepare memos
2. Job Task: Prepare meeting summaries
3. Job Task: Monitor email, internal mail, and direct inquiries
4. Job Task: Handle phone calls

Knowledge: Phone and email systems, names and positions of company personnel

Skills/Abilities: Writing skills, word processing skills, organizational skills, interpersonal skills

Attitudes: Outgoing, team player

Behaviors: Completes work in timely fashion, notifies CFO of problems or delays

Standards: Memos and reports are concise, understandable, and timely; email, internal mail, direct inquires, and phone calls are handled professionally

Training Requirements: Writing skills, word processing skills, phone system, email, internal mail systems, organizational skills, interpersonal skills

Non-Training Requirements: Access to computer, email, phone, and internal mail systems

Job Responsibility 5: Track sales force activity

1. Job Task: Review sales reports, compare actual sales with forecast sales
2. Job Task: Review sales expenses and compare with budget
3. Job Task: Charge expenses to appropriate customer or product accounts
4. Job Task: Prepare monthly sales expense report
5. Job Task: Calculate sales bonus and commission compensation

Knowledge: Actual sales, forecast sales, budget allowances, knowledge of customer and product accounts, compensation rates

Skills/Abilities: Analytical skills, math, word processing

Attitudes: Team player

Behaviors: Completes work in a timely fashion

Standards: Monthly sales expenses are charged to appropriate accounts; sales reports are accurate and prepared monthly; bonuses and commissions are accurately calculated by last Friday of each month

Training Requirements: Company financial reports, internal and external accounts, math, word processing

Non-Training Requirements: Timely access to company financial records, internal and external accounts

FIGURE 5.3 *Sample Toolkit Form 5.3: Job Training and Non-Training Recommendations (Administrative)* (continued)

You may need to obtain additional approval from the human resources department. After you have received approvals from all appropriate sources, present and distribute the final statement to senior management and the target audience.

To facilitate the process of conducting a job and task analysis, use the checklist provided in the Toolkit section, Toolkit Form 5.4, which lists the steps that should be followed when conducting a job and task analysis.

Tip

A job and task analysis can be a time-consuming process. Following are a few ways to save time during the process:

- Ask for existing position descriptions or documents that describe the jobs or tasks, but be aware that such descriptions may or may not be current. If they are current, you can use this information to refine your survey. Asking more focused survey questions can reduce the amount of time spent in a work session.
- Eliminate one step in the process by asking participants' supervisors to attend the latter portion of a work session for the purpose of reviewing the preliminary draft of the job training and non-training recommendations statement as it is developed by the group. Doing this reduces the amount of time spent sending out the statement and waiting for approvals.

Your situation may require detailed documentation on how high-performing employees actually accomplish tasks. Such additional work analysis is often required for developing technical, systems, or managerial training. Examples include training operators on the exact steps of a procedure (such as how to operate a complicated machine), training employees how to troubleshoot a process that involves many people performing interrelated tasks (such as shipping an order with many parts), or training new managers how the firm's experts perform unobservable knowledge work (such as targeting potential clients). You could document such information-intensive work by following a job and task analysis with more specific analysis procedures, such as those described by Swanson (2007).

- Stay aware of the goal for the job and task analysis and avoid collecting and analyzing data that do not relate to your goal. Notice, for example, that the case study presented shortly, which focuses only on training needs, does not analyze non-training needs.

This chapter has presented the methods and tools required to perform a job and task analysis. Take a look at how the process was actually done at Boehringer Mannheim Corporation. The information for the following case was contributed by Mary Keller, HR consultant for Boehringer Mannheim Corporation. This case shows how a job and task analysis was carried out to go beyond a set of recommendations in order to develop a training plan for a quality control inspector. The end product is a position training plan.

CASE

Boehringer Mannheim Corporation (BMC) is a privately held worldwide health care device manufacturer. This bio-technology company has a diverse portfolio of "in vitro" diagnostic test systems, automated clinical chemistry systems, heterogeneous and homogenous testing, therapeutics, and biochemical products.

BMC products are used by physicians and life science research laboratories in many ways, including for diabetes monitoring, patient sample analysis, and coagulation. BMC-West, located in Pleasanton, California, researches, develops, and manufactures medical diagnostic kits. This West Coast company employs about 270 employees.

THE NEED

As a part of the requirements for obtaining ISO 9001 certification, the company had to meet the standard set by Element 4.19: Training. This element, one of twenty in the standard, required employees to be qualified to perform their jobs. Documentation of their qualification was also needed.

At BMC, this requirement was satisfied by putting in place a training record system, position training plans, updated resumes, and company-wide training programs. All training systems, plans, and programs were strategically linked with the business goals of the company.

THE APPROACH

Before examining the job and task analysis approach used by BMC to develop its position training plans, it is useful to review a couple of terms that were specific to BMC's situation.

- A position training plan (PTP) is a table that lists the knowledge, skills, attitudes, and behaviors needed for an individual to perform a job. It also contains the training and development activities that are necessary for acquiring minimal competencies.
- A learning channel is a method for acquiring knowledge, skills, attitudes, and behaviors. Learning channels are broad categories of employee and manager activities that facilitate learning and development. They include the following:

OJT	On-the-job training
A	Assignment or project
M	Mentoring or coaching
W	Workshop, class, or seminar
C	Continuing education
S	Self-directed study

To meet the requirements spelled out by a position training plan, an employee must complete the training and development activities, show evidence of previous comparable training, or demonstrate proficiency on the job. The PTPs are used as a guide by managers to identify the competencies an employee must have to perform on the job and the suggested learning channels for acquiring those competencies.

You can review some of the steps below that BMC took in using the job and task analysis process to develop position training plans.

Phase 1: Prepare

1. The human resource and quality assurance departments identified the jobs for which PTPs needed to be written. Production jobs were given priority, because these jobs were more likely to be audited by the ISO review team.
2. The job analysis questionnaire was prepared.
3. Descriptions for the targeted jobs were completed. They included the responsibilities, the scope of decision making, and the knowledge, skills, attitudes, and behaviors for each job function.

Phase 2: Conduct Job and Task Analysis Work Session

1. Human resource consultants met with managers and supervisors in small groups to explain the function of the PTPs and the process that would be used to develop them.
2. The following process was used to develop the PTPs:
   - Managers worked primarily on the PTPs for the jobs of persons reporting to them.
   - Each knowledge, skill, and ability (KSA) from the job description was listed on the PTP.
   - Managers then added to and refined the KSAs.

- One or more learning channels was listed next to each KSA, which permitted flexibility in planning for acquiring the new skill or knowledge and at the same time acknowledged that formal workshops or classes were not always the best way to acquire a skill.
- Comments were added (for example, a firm deadline for meeting a certain training requirement was stated).
- The human resources department reviewed the draft PTPs and issued final approvals.

Phase 3: Develop and Present Recommendations and a Job Training Plan

1. Managers and the human resources department signed the final PTP.
2. PTPs were made available to all employees.

   A sample PTP for a quality control inspector is shown in Figure 5.4.

THE RESULTS

PTPs were issued for fifty-nine non-exempt jobs in the company. The requirements for Element 4:19 of ISO 9001 were met. Job descriptions, PTPs, managers' requirements for job performance, and the training needed to develop the requisite skills for a job were firmly and logically linked.

CONCLUSION

Job and task analysis is a powerful tool that HRD, HPT, and ID practitioners can use to develop workforce potential. The information obtained from this process can serve as an important link in the evolution of many other related human development endeavors.

Department: Operations, QA/QC

Knowledge

Training/Education	Learning Channel	Comments
High school or equivalent	C	
Basic understanding of GMPs and their application to the job	OJT, W, C, M	
Advanced working knowledge of critical and non-critical chemical inspections	OJT, A, M	Demonstrates independent judgment. Resolves problems and makes decisions and recommendations within the advanced scope of inspection.
Advanced working knowledge of packaging materials inspection	OJT, A, M	
Advanced working knowledge of packaging line, filling line, and labeling line clearance	OJT, A, M	

List what is required in each of these areas for minimal competence in performing the job:

Knowledge

- Business
- Areas of Expertise

Approved by: _____ Date: _____

HR Approval: _____ Date: _____

FIGURE 5.4 *Quality Control Inspector Position Training Plan*

142

A job and task analysis is particularly useful in industries where jobs are highly technical or specialized. Many state and federal agencies, such as the U.S. Departments of Defense and Labor, have used the method to develop standardized training requirements for their employees.

This chapter has described a job and task analysis approach to needs assessment. It has established a context for the process by defining key terms and concepts, describing the writing of job task statements and standards, and reviewing the steps in the process. The case described a biotechnology company's experience with the analysis process and its outcomes. The next chapter presents details on undertaking a competency-based assessment.

SIX Competency-Based Needs Assessment

PURPOSE

This chapter will enable you to accomplish the following tasks:

- Determine the purpose of a competency-based needs assessment.
- Decide when to use the approach.
- Identify the benefits and drawbacks of the approach.
- Recognize critical success factors for performing a competency-based needs assessment.
- Explain key terms, such as competency dictionary, core cluster, competency model, and individual learning and development plan.
- Identify five phases for conducting a competency-based needs assessment.
- Examine online competency assessment tools.

RELATED TOOLKIT JOB AIDS

The following job aids for use with the material in this chapter are available in the Needs Assessment Toolkit, which can be found in Section Four of this book:

- Competency Project Plan Worksheet
- Competency Interview Worksheet
- Competency Dictionary Worksheet
- Competency Model Worksheet
- Individual Learning and Development Plan

OVERVIEW

As a professional, you must be able to communicate and interact effectively with peers, supervisors, and internal and external customers. As a manager, you must be able to lead, solve problems, and act decisively. As a front-line supervisor, you must be able to assume ownership of customer-service problems. A *competency* is a knowledge, skill, attitude, or behavior that enables a person to perform effectively the activities of a given occupation or to function to the standards expected in employment (International Board of Standards for Training, Performance, and Instruction®, 2005). For example, a competency statement for a leadership position at XYZ firm is "coaches direct reports."

Competencies and competency assessment were introduced by psychologists Robert White (1959), David McClelland (1973), and Spencer and Spencer (1993). McLagan (1980) observed, "Without clear competency criteria, recruiters select, managers manage, trainers train, and career planners plan to different (and sometimes even conflicting) images of the capabilities required to do a job" (p. 23). Competencies have been developed by many organizations. Just a few examples include the U.S. Army, Microsoft, the Chartered Accountants of Canada, and Engineers Australia.

The purposes of a competency-based needs assessment are as follows:

- Identify the competencies necessary for superior job performance.
- Create a composite picture or best-practice model of the competencies necessary for a particular job function or functions.

- Define incompetence and determine the knowledge, skills, attitudes, and behaviors that should be avoided for optimum performance.

In a competency-based approach, the focal point is the person, or performer. A competency-based needs assessment seeks to identify the knowledge, skills, attitudes, and behaviors the performer needs in order to excel in a job.

The time needed to complete a competency study varies. Although some studies take a few months to complete, others take several years. The amount of time needed depends on the project's scope and level of complexity.

When to Use

A competency-based approach is most effective under the following circumstances:

- *When competencies for management, supervisory, or professional jobs must be identified.* In some cases, upper management may demand that competencies be identified. In other cases, you, as the analyst, may feel that a competency approach is warranted.

- *When a credible system or "template" must be created for recruiting, hiring, developing, and promoting individuals within specific jobs* (Boyatzis, 1982). The competency approach can aid in creating needed job specifications.

- *When the competencies for a particular professional group must be examined across many different organizations and even many different cultures and nations.* Often, organizations that develop training programs for specific professional groups will use a competency approach.

- *When the competencies need to be identified for a specific group as part of a community or international development effort, the competency approach will help with this identification.*

Benefits and Drawbacks

The benefits of a competency-based needs assessment are as follows:

- It establishes the qualities or characteristics that distinguish average from exemplary performance.
- It provides in-depth information about current and future predictors of job performance.
- It helps to increase job satisfaction, because people have a clear vision of what is expected of them.
- It can be used to create standardized training and development programs.
- It can be used to develop standards and assessments for certification.
- It can be used to show career progression paths for a job or a job family.

The approach has several limitations:

- It is time-consuming, because it requires the involvement of many people, including managers and senior managers and, occasionally, such external agencies as regulators and customers.
- It can be costly to implement.
- It requires good project management skills.

Critical Success Factors

Several factors are essential to the success of a project (Griffiths, 1997):

- Competencies must produce outcomes that are consistent with the needs and goals of an organization or community.
- There must be a sponsor or driver who can leverage a project.
- Users must have ownership; that is, people must recognize what is in it for them.

- The model must be simple enough that people can easily access and use it.

- The model must be flexible so it can complement existing performance management systems within an organization.

Before outlining the steps for doing a competency-based needs assessment, let us review a few terms that are used in this chapter.

As mentioned on the previous page, *competency* refers to knowledge, skills, attitudes, or behaviors that enable one to perform the activities of a given occupation or to function to the standards expected in employment (International Board of Standards for Training, Performance, and Instruction, 2005). This knowledge or these skills, attitudes, or behaviors should be observable and measurable. That is, you and others should be able, for example, to test the person's knowledge, observe the person performing the skills, or determine the person's attitude through an assessment.

A *performance statement* is a detailed explanation of the activities that are summarized in a competency statement (Richey, Fields, & Foxon, 2001), but it is not simply a list of tasks. For example, one of the program evaluator competencies is: "Communicate effectively in written, oral, and visual form," and an associated performance statement is: "Use verbal and nonverbal language appropriate to the audience, context, and culture" (Russ-Eft, Bober, de la Teja, Foxon, & Koszalka, 2008, p. 49). The performance statement can provide greater clarity about the specifics of the competency.

Domain is a cluster of related competencies grouped together under a broad dimension. For example, leadership as a domain might consist of such competencies as delegation, coaching, and team building.

A *competency model* organizes "identified competencies into a conceptual framework that enables the people in an organization to understand, talk about, and apply the competencies" (Marrelli, 1998, p. 10). A competency model can focus on one job function (for example, sales manager), a job family (such as sales associate, sales manager, or sales executive), or multiple job families (for instance, sales, production, or research and development). The competency assessments in a community could result in competency models for community organizers, members of certain committees, and volunteers.

A *competency dictionary* is an organized list of definitions for individual competencies. For example, the definition of the competency that focuses on prospecting for salespeople might read: "Evaluates current and future market conditions and uses this information to develop sales projections and goals."

An *individual learning development plan* shows the learning activities, support, resources, success indicators, and measures for improving a person's performance.

PHASES OF A COMPETENCY NEEDS ASSESSMENT

Various scholars have offered approaches for conducting a competency needs assessment. There are two main approaches:

1. Critical incident and behavioral event interviewing (Bergmann, Hurson, & Russ-Eft, 1999; Flanagan, 1954; McClelland, 1973; Russ-Eft, 2004; Spencer & Spencer, 1993)

2. Expert development and validation (Klein, Spector, Grabowski, & de la Teja, 2004; Richey, Fields, & Foxon, 2001; Rothwell, 1996; Russ-Eft, Bober, de la Teja, Foxon, & Koszalka, 2008; Koszalka, Russ-Eft, & Reiser, 2013)

Although both approaches focus on the knowledge, skills, attitudes, and behaviors that people must have to perform a given occupation or job function, they differ in some aspects. Readers who are interested in comparing the approaches are invited to check out the references listed above.

The following are the phases for the critical incident and behavioral event interviewing approach.

Phase 1: Develop a project plan.

1. Establish parameters.

2. Identify key players.

3. Develop work plan.

Phase 2: Conduct behavioral interviews.

1. Design the behavioral interview guide.

2. Obtain behavioral information.

3. Analyze behavioral information.

Phase 3: Construct competency model.

1. Create competency dictionary.

2. Create competency model.

Phase 4: Assess gaps.

1. Identify gaps.

2. Analyze results.

Phase 5: Implement model.

Phase 1: Develop a Project Plan

This phase involves refining the scope and objectives for a project, creating a project team, and establishing a project management structure. Sometimes, a needs assessment committee is formed to guide a competency-based needs assessment, including the development of a project plan.

Step 1: Establish Parameters

First, it is essential to determine the focus of the competency model and define how it will be used. This is usually done by conducting one-on-one interviews with senior leaders. The following questions can be asked during these interviews:

- What is the purpose of the competency study?
- How will the competency study meet the needs of the organization or community?
- How many competency models must be created? For example, will a model be needed for a job function, such as sales manager; a job

family, such as sales associate, sales manager, or sales executive; or multiple job families, such as sales, production, and research and development?

- For what purposes will the competency models be used? For example, will they be used for recruiting, hiring, training, performance management, or career planning?

- What resources of time, personnel, and budget are available for this effort?

- What additional constraints are anticipated, such as deadlines or input from external customers?

- How will the competency materials be maintained and updated? If talent management software will be used, learn the requirements of the software.

Step 2: Identify Key Players

After project parameters are established, identify the people who will participate in the project. Most small to medium-sized projects require a sponsor, a group of high performers, the target audience, a human resource manager, field personnel, and one or more training professionals. Large-scale projects may also require a steering committee and project liaison person to coordinate and administer a project. Subject-matter experts are required when the job content for developing a competency model is highly technical and complex terms must be translated.

High performers are the main source of information about the behaviors and actions that are necessary to do a job successfully. High performers are people who

- Consistently meet or exceed organization or unit objectives

- Achieve "very good" to "excellent" ratings on their performance reviews

- Are informally labeled "masters" or experts by their peers and managers

- Are sought for their knowledge of or expertise in a particular subject

- Are respected by others, which is particularly important in situations in which close teamwork is necessary

Usually human resource personnel and managers can identify high performers within an organization. In addition to the high performers, consider interviewing others who are considered average performers. This will allow you to compare the responses of the high performers and the average performers to determine the specific behaviors that distinguish the two groups. (See Spencer & Spencer, 1993, for more detail on this approach.)

Step 3: Develop Work Plan

After key players have been identified and their availability has been determined, the next step is to develop a work plan. Figure 6.1 shows a sample high-level work plan for two hundred people. A form to scope out tasks in more detail can be found in Toolkit Form 6.1.

After the project plan is developed and approved, it is time to begin the data-collection process.

Phase 2: Conduct Behavioral Interviews

This phase involves gathering and analyzing data to build a competency model. Several of the data-collection methods described in Chapter Three, such as surveys, individual interviews, focus groups, and observations, can be used.

The main advantage of surveys is that, once they are designed, they can be used to collect data from many different people in many different locations. However, such problems as low response rate or the lack of detailed behavioral information could diminish their effectiveness.

The main advantage of individual interviews is that detailed information can be gathered, particularly when the interviewer has the opportunity to probe and further clarify responses. However, conducting individual interviews requires a great deal of time and effort.

Schedule of Events - Overview (Sample)

Task Name	January	February	March	April	May	June	July
1 Establish Parameters							
2 Assemble and Orient Project Team							
3 Prepare Interview Form							
4 Conduct Interviews							
5 Analyze Interview Data							
6 Develop Competency Dictionary							
7 Develop Competency Model							
8 Hold Steering Committee Meeting							
9 Design Assessment Instrument							
10 Administer Assessment Instrument							
11 Analyze Results							
12 Prepare Summary							
13 Hold Steering Committee Meeting							
14 Return Survey to Managers/Employees							
15 Prepare Manager Briefing							
16 Hold Manager/Employee Meeting							
17 Send Copy of Plan to Human Resources							

FIGURE 6.1 *Competency-Based Needs Assessment Project Plan*

154

The main advantage of focus-group interviews is that information from many different people can be gathered at one time. However, negative group dynamics could interfere with the data-collection effort. Furthermore, focus groups may not produce a variety of views. Excellent facilitation skills and the ability to develop and ask effective questions are important prerequisites for conducting focus group interviews.

The technique described in this chapter for using behavioral interviews—with individuals or groups—to gather the very specific behavioral information for building a competency model is adapted from Flanagan's (1954, 1974) Critical Incident Method. The basic purpose of behavioral interviews is to obtain two types of information from interviewees:

- Background and job-related information

- Information about what high performers do (or do not do) that makes them successful and what low performers do (or do not do) that makes them fail

Consider these purposes as you design the data-collection instruments and as you collect and analyze data.

Step 1: Design the Behavioral Interview Guide

Chapter Three provides information on how to design data-collection instruments. In addition, Figure 6.2 shows a sample script you can use to start developing a behavioral interview. Note that the sample script is appropriate for one-on-one interviews. However, you could modify it and use it for group interviews and surveys.

After you complete this preliminary introduction, you can give participants the opportunity to talk about themselves and their job responsibilities, then you can ask the questions that target specific job and performance information.

SAMPLE SCRIPT FOR A BEHAVIORAL INTERVIEW

Thank you for meeting with me to discuss [name of job] and to identify the knowledge and skills and the competencies that help people succeed in the [name of job] position at [name of organization].

Your supervisor identified a group of experts who are highly skilled and/or knowledgeable about this job. You are one such expert. I am interviewing people in this group, including you, to better understand what it takes to be successful in the job. Our interview will take about an hour.

I will combine the information from many interviews to create a model—a picture—of the competencies for [name of job] at [name of organization]. The model will be used to enhance recruiting, hiring, and training at [name of organization]. For example, HR will use the model to hire people who most likely will succeed on the job. This will benefit the person and the company. Also, trainers and managers will use the model to help those who perform the job to enhance their knowledge, skills, and competencies so they can perform the job at a high level. This, too, will benefit the person and the company.

During our interview, I will be inviting you to think about your experience with this job during the past year and asking you to talk about how the [name of job] is performed, including the responsibilities and the knowledge and skills required. Also, I will ask you to describe specific situations that led to either valued successes or noted problems and unsuccessful results.

Before we begin, I will start the recorder so that nothing you say during the interview will be overlooked. Do you have any questions or concerns?

FIGURE 6.2 *Sample Script for a Behavioral Interview*

Step 2: Obtain Behavioral Information

The following sample questions can be used to obtain both job-related and behavioral information. For a sample interview worksheet, see Toolkit Form 6.2 in the Toolkit section of the book and online at www.wiley.com/go/needs3e.

1. What are the five main responsibilities of your job? (Probe for quantifiable results, such as, "Meet sales quota every quarter.")

2. What skills and abilities do you need to accomplish each of these responsibilities? (Probe for quantifiable behaviors and actions, such as, "Make five new cold calls per month.")

3. What other skills and abilities do you require to make you successful in your job? (Probe for behaviors and actions, such as, "Be courteous to customers.")

4. Now, think about a specific time [in the past week, month, or year] when you or someone else experienced success as a [name of job].

What was the context? When did it happen? Who was involved? (Probe for behaviors and actions, such as, "Took the initiative, made quick decisions, listened carefully.")

What did you feel or think? (Probe for behaviors and actions, such as, "I felt empowered and handled the problem myself.")

What did you say? Why were these actions and words effective? (Probe for behaviors and actions, such as, "I took the initiative and called to authorize the overdue shipment of several cartons of tape. This pleased the customer.")

What were the results? What significance does this event have? (Probe for behaviors and actions, such as, "I learned that by acting quickly and decisively, I saved the company from losing a customer.")

5. Now, think about a specific time [in the past week, month, or year] when you or someone else experienced failure as a [name of job].

What was the context? When did it happen? Who was involved? (Probe for behaviors and actions, such as "Failed to take the initiative, could not decide, did not listen carefully.")

What did you feel or think? (Probe for behaviors and actions, such as, "I felt guilty, disappointed, or angry.")

What did you say? Why were these actions and words ineffective? (Probe for behaviors and actions, such as, "I failed to solve the customer's problem. He became angry and upset.")

What are some other actions you did not take at the time that could have helped you succeed? (Probe for specifics.)

What were the results? What significance does this event have? (Probe for behaviors and actions, such as, "I lost a good customer.")

Questions 4 and 5 can be repeated to obtain additional critical incidents.

Most behavioral interviews take between two and two-and-a-half hours to complete. In the beginning of an interview, it is essential to establish the right tone. Techniques for doing this include building rapport and maintaining a neutral attitude.

Learning to develop effective follow-up questions during an interview takes time and experience. There is no comprehensive list that is appropriate for all interviews. However, here are a few suggested prompts:

- Describe for me . . .
- Tell me about a time when . . .
- Tell me about a situation that . . .
- Can you be more specific about . . . ?
- Can you give me an example of . . . ?
- What specifically happened next?
- What was your response?
- What did you think when . . . happened?
- When you said . . ., what did you mean?
- I'd like to hear more about . . .

Pitfalls to Avoid

A key to successful outcomes is avoiding the following pitfalls:

- *Using the wrong questions.* For example, asking "why" questions that require interviewees to justify, explain, or rationalize their behavior or asking leading questions

- *Encouraging guesses.* For example, asking interviewees to guess or anticipate their future actions or reactions or asking them to guess or anticipate how others might act or react

- *Using ineffective prompts.* For example, encouraging responses through your body language, intonations, or comments, or inaccurately paraphrasing an interviewee's responses or interrupting the interviewee with questions

- *Making assumptions.* For example, jumping to conclusions without knowing the facts or anticipating an interviewee's next words (such as completing sentences for the interviewee)

- *Interrupting*

Step 3: Analyze Behavioral Information

To analyze the incidents, you can follow the guidelines set forth by Flanagan (1954, 1974). These include the following:

1. Select a frame of reference. For example, later in the chapter we provide sample forms for a competency assessment on the job category "sales performance." The title serves as a frame of reference for distinguishing this competency model from one created for the job category "customer service." We recognize that in some organizations sales and customer service are aspects of the same job category. For these organizations, the frame of reference could be expanded to "sales and customer service."

2. Sort a sample of incidents into a few categories according to the selected frame of reference.

3. Develop tentative headings for major categories, for example, leadership and knowledge of the industry.

4. Sort additional incidents into these major categories and develop subcategories as needed. For example, under the leadership category you might identify coaching and vision.

5. Prepare tentative definitions for major categories, including general statements about each category. For example, the definition for leadership could read, "Uses the company vision to help others achieve personal and organizational goals."

6. Decide on the level of specificity or generality to be used. For example, you could decide whether to group *listening skills* with *interpersonal* to reduce the number of major categories.

7. Redefine major categories and subcategories as needed while continuing to classify incidents.

8. After all incidents have been classified, review definitions and revise where needed.

9. Arrange to have experts in the field or a select group of inter-viewees complete an independent check of the classification system.

Phase 3: Construct Competency Model

The analyzed data from the previous step results in a preliminary draft of a competency model. You may want to obtain an independent check of it and enlist the client and the stakeholders in considering its applicability to the organization or community before you complete the two steps of this phase: create a competency dictionary and create a competency model.

Step 1: Create Competency Dictionary

Review and edit definitions that were created in the previous phase until you are satisfied with them. Finally, write an overall statement that describes each dimension. Figure 6.3 shows Toolkit Form 6.3, the Competency Dictionary Worksheet, filled out with information for a sales position. Two dimensions, leadership and interpersonal, are shown in the example. The description for the dimension leadership is: "Uses the company vision to help others achieve personal and organizational goals." The description for the dimension interpersonal is: "Projects an attitude that is positive, perceptive, and sensitive to audience needs."

Step 2: Create Competency Model

The model is essentially a high-level depiction of the dimensions and competencies contained in the dictionary. Figure 6.4 shows a sample competency model for the job family sales using Toolkit Form 6.4. Note that certain positions require certain competencies, while others require different competencies. After creating the first draft of the competency model, obtain approval of it from senior management and the human resources department. If necessary, make additional changes to the dictionary and the model based on their feedback. Prepare a final copy.

TOOLKIT FORM 6.3 *Competency Dictionary—Sales*

1. Leadership: Uses the company vision to help others achieve personal and organizational goals.

Competencies/Core Clusters	Definitions
Coaching	Assists others to advance to their knowledge and skills by providing advice, encouragement, and feedback.
Influencing	Uses authority and personal charisma to gain support and commitment for goals.
Vision	Recognizes future opportunities for the organization and establishes long-term goals to maximize their potential.

2. Interpersonal: Projects an attitude that is positive, perceptive, and sensitive to audience needs.

Competencies/Core Clusters	Definitions
Articulation	Expresses facts and emotions with clarity; generates an interest in the audience.
Listening	Uses active listening skills to understand the audience's point of view and to improve communication.
Self-Awareness	Is aware of how his or her personal actions and attitudes affect others; is perceptive and understands own strengths and weaknesses.

FIGURE 6.3 *Sample Toolkit Form 6.3: Competency Dictionary Showing Two Domains for a Sales Position, Three Competencies in Each Domain, and Their Definitions*

Phase 4: Assess Gaps

When the competency model is complete, you can use it to identify the gaps in the proficiencies of individuals who perform the job functions. It is only after these gaps have been identified that appropriate interventions can be developed to close them. This phase consists of two steps: identify gaps and analyze results.

TOOLKIT FORM 6.4 *Competency Model—Sales Positions*

Dimensions	Competencies/Core Clusters		
	Sales Associate	**Sales Manager**	**Sales Executive**
1. Leadership Uses the company vision to help others achieve personal and organizational goals.	Influencing	Coaching Influencing	Coaching Influencing Vision
2. Interpersonal Projects an attitude that is positive, perceptive, and sensitive to audience needs.	Articulation Listening Self-awareness	Articulation Listening Self-awareness	Articulation Listening Self-awareness
3. Knowledge of the Industry Maintains an up-to-date understanding of the industry by reading industry journals, attending meetings and conventions, and networking.	Product and service knowledge Market knowledge	Product and service knowledge Market knowledge	Product and service knowledge Market knowledge
4. Management Uses company resources and personnel to meet or exceed company goals.	Decision making	Decision making Budget control Staffing Team building	Decision making Budget control Staffing Team building
5. Sales Skills Meets or exceeds sales goals by anticipating and responding to clients' needs for services and products.	Prospecting Presentation Persuasion Customer service	Presentation Persuasion Customer service	Presentation Persuasion Customer service
6. Personal Attributes Possesses values, attitudes, qualities, and behaviors that are consistent with the industry and the organization's standards.	Initiative Integrity Flexibility	Initiative Integrity Flexibility	Initiative Integrity Flexibility

FIGURE 6.4 *Sample Toolkit Form 6.4: Competency Model for Sales Positions*

Step 1: Identify Gaps

As explained in Chapter One, a gap is the difference between an actual condition and an ideal condition, or the difference between what performance is and what performance should be. Surveys are an effective tool for gathering this type of data. You will need to decide who should receive the survey. You can involve all of the key players mentioned earlier or you involve the target group only. You also must consider whether the survey is confidential. If an individual's manager will see his or her survey responses, then the survey is *not* confidential.

Figure 6.5 shows a simple rating scale that can be used to obtain information. Note that in an actual survey the competencies that were identified in the competency assessment would be listed in the left column.

SAMPLE SURVEY QUESTIONS

Instructions: On the following rating scale, fill in the bubble that corresponds most closely to the degree with which you agree or disagree that the statement represents a critical part of the job.

	Strongly Disagree	Disagree	Neutral	Agree	Strongly Agree	Not Applicable
Coaching: Assists others in advancing their knowledge and skills by providing advice, encouragement, and feedback.	⬭	⬭	⬭	⬭	⬭	⬭
Influencing: Uses authority and personal charisma to gain support and commitment to goals.	⬭	⬭	⬭	⬭	⬭	⬭

FIGURE 6.5 *Sample Rating Scale for Competency-Based Survey Questions*

Note also that the survey could use other types of scales, such as "How important is this competency for success on the job?" or "How frequently do you do this competency?" or both.

Step 2: Analyze Results

After the surveys have been distributed and returned, data can be analyzed by using one of the software packages that are available for this purpose, or they can be tabulated by hand. As discussed in Chapter Three, you may want to examine the frequency of responses, a measure of central tendency (such as the average, median, or mode), and a measure of variability (such as the standard deviation, the inter-quartile range, or the range). If you surveyed people from different groups (such as the top performers and the average performers in the job), you may want to examine the differences among the groups.

Tip Reviewing an actual competency assessment could provide useful insights for your project. Russ-Eft (2004) described a competency assessment that involved 460 customer service providers from companies in North America, Europe, and Asia.

Phase 5: Implement Model

Competency models have many applications. They can be used to create individual learning development plans and to develop selection, hiring, and other performance-management systems. Here we discuss one application: individualized learning development plans.

The first step in developing individualized learning development plans is to share the employees' completed surveys with managers. After managers receive a copy of the survey results, a brief meeting can be held with them to explain how to develop and use learning development plans. During this meeting, copies of Toolkit Form 6.5, Individual Learning Development Plan, can also be distributed. Managers can adapt the following agenda to conduct a meeting with employees:

1. Review the team's strengths and identify opportunities for development.

2. Identify the support and resources required to facilitate performance.

3. Develop an action plan that best meets the needs of the learners.

4. Create a schedule for implementing learning and development activities.

5. Discuss a follow-up plan.

After a competency model has been implemented, results can be monitored at both the organizational and the individual levels. At the individual level, managers can conduct quarterly or annual progress checks with their employees. At the organizational level, the impact of the assessment can be measured using other data, such as client satisfaction surveys or reorders or other performance data results that are relevant to the employees and management.

The preceding sections presented the methods and tools for conducting a competency-based assessment. The next section focuses on how to jump start your process by using competencies models that are already available.

Using Already Available Competency Models

A competency needs assessment requires the investment of both time and resources. You can jump start your competency needs assessment with competency models that are already available. For example, competency assessment instruments for specific professions can be found on the Internet. In addition, vendors offer competency models that may be very useful. For example, Lominger's Success Profile Architect (which can be found at www.Lominger.com) is a web-based tool that helps organizations create competency profiles. A few keystrokes produces pre-loaded research and expert-based profiles that target specific employee groups and contexts.

When researching available competency models, confirm that they contain competencies that are current and consistent with the needs, goals, and context of your organization or community. Also check the costs as some competency models are quite expensive.

Now it is time to see a competency needs assessment that was conducted by a group of graduate students for a government agency. The pseudonym for the government agency is Agency Q. This case was submitted by Brenda Nickel, United States Coast Guard; Shari Stein, Team-4-Community L3C; and Dave Torres, United States Coast Guard.

CASE

THE TARGET FOR THE NEEDS ASSESSMENT

Government Agency Q ensures the readiness of Division One through tactics, techniques, procedures, training, assessment, standardization, and exercise support. The ten training managers (TMs) assigned to Division One are responsible for ensuring that Government Agency Q personnel are ready to perform their required duties and responsibilities by providing effective training and the certifications required to perform their functions. Each TM is responsible for a different demographic within the organization. TMs, especially in their first year, wasted a large amount of time contacting various entities within the organization in an attempt to determine what they had to do in order to execute their job. TMs would be more productive if time was spent performing their job duties instead of trying to figure out what is required of them.

WHY THE NEEDS ASSESSMENT WAS CONDUCTED

The purpose of conducting a needs assessment was to determine the root causes of low TM performance at Government Agency Q's Division One during their first year. This case study used an evidence-based approach to determine the root causes of

TM struggles and provide recommendations to improve TM performance.

WHO CONDUCTED THE NEEDS ASSESSMENT

Boise State University (BSU) graduate students

WHO SPONSORED THE NEEDS ASSESSMENT

Government Agency Q—(pseudonym)

THE NEEDS ASSESSMENT PROCESS

The BSU graduate team conducted a competency-based needs assessment using on the approach outlined in Gupta, Sleezer, and Russ-Eft (2007), the course's needs assessment textbook. The team collected the data using open-ended interviews for general familiarization with Government Agency Q and the TMs' role. A subsequent round of semi-structured interviews and survey questions were developed using The Competency Interview Worksheet (Toolkit Form 6.2 from the textbook) and Gilbert's Behavior Engineering Model (BEM). The interviews and survey questions were used to collect data from TMs, TM supervisors, and personnel who receive support from TMs.

The resulting data were used for three project outputs:

- Development of the TM competency model/dictionary
- Identification of TM core and collateral processes
- Findings and recommendation to improve TM performance

The TM competency model/dictionary below was developed using the critical incident and behavioral event interviewing approach, a systematic framework outlined in Gupta, Sleezer, and Russ-Eft (2007).

OUR DATA-COLLECTION PROCESS

Phase 1: Develop Project Plan

1. The BSU team conducted exploratory interviews to determine the focus of the competency model and define how it will be used.
2. During the interviews the team gathered information on key players by asking with whom the TMs support and interact during the conduct of their job.
3. The team developed a work plan that included all future steps of the project including which personnel to interview and to survey.

Phase 2: Conduct Behavioral Interviews

1. The team created surveys and interview questions to gather behavioral information.
2. After data collection, the team analyzed TM behavioral information by sorting all data into five major dimensions (Project Management, Communication, Technical Knowledge, Interpersonal, and Advocacy/Liaison).

Phase 3: Construct Competency Model

1. The competency dictionary was created by developing definitions for all major headings and all behavioral data within each heading.
2. Definitions for each behavioral data point under each category were removed to create the competency model.

Phase 4 (assess gaps) of the competency-based needs assessment approach was not executed for this project because the purpose of this project was to assist newly assigned TMs. Newly assigned TMs have to learn TM roles and responsibilities in their entirety due to their lack of experience, so, by default, the gap was already defined.

Asking all TMs the following question during interviews identified the core and collateral TM process: "What are the five main responsibilities of your job?"

Functions shared by all TMs were categorized as core; all others were categorized as collateral. TM process data was validated through triangulation with the TM supervisors and the personnel who receive support from TMs.

Findings and recommendations were identified through further analysis of the data collected through surveys and interviews. To efficiently manage the data, protect the identity of the respondents, and link the findings and recommendations to the data, the team developed codes for respondents and data results.

RESULTS

TM Core and Collateral Processes

The project team was able to confirm that TMs do not have a formal set of roles and responsibilities to guide their efforts. The project team identified four core and six collateral TM processes. During a project presentation, Government Agency Q staff indicated that they would use the TM process information to formalize the TM role with policy. New incoming TMs will benefit from the use of the materials that resulted from the competency-based needs assessment by knowing what they are supposed to do instead of realizing their job functions over time.

Examples identified by the project team:

TM Core Process

- Curriculum Management: Involves approving curriculum per Government Agency Q's standard operating procedures

(SOPs) and striving for accreditation (curriculum content management and curriculum review)

Collateral Process

- Rating Management: Occupational analysis every three or four years

TM Competency Model

The competency model produced by the project team captures the knowledge, skills, attitudes, and behaviors that enable TMs to perform their job effectively. The competency model is currently being used to guide the development of a TM job definition document by Government Agency Q staff. This information is also being used by Government Agency Q to formalize the TM role with policy.

THE OUTCOMES OF THE NEEDS ASSESSMENT

The needs assessment produced a competency dictionary and a list of competencies that a TM should possess in order to perform the job effectively. Government Agency Q now has an actionable recommendation list to improve the overall efficiencies of training managers. Additionally, Government Agency Q also provided the data to two instructional design courses at BSU to develop two separate onboard courses for TMs. Government Agency Q is confident that these efforts will improve the performance of newly assigned TMs and increase their productivity.

INTERESTING CHALLENGES OR ISSUES

The BSU team had to learn the overall managerial structure and culture of Government Agency Q. Collecting these data was essential in order to gain an understanding of the multifaceted and complex role of a training manager. TMs provide a myriad of services to multiple entities within Government Agency Q. Interview data uncovered numerous competencies, and it was challenging to identify core competencies shared by all TMs, since the team found that TMs specialize in different services.

LESSONS LEARNED

It was critical for the BSU team to understand the organizational structure as well as the terminology of Government Agency Q. Most organizations speak their own "language," so it is important to become familiar with the culture of the organization being analyzed. Familiarity with an organizational structure and culture allows for more effective open-ended interviews, which can lead to an improved data collection.

CONCLUSION

Organizations must have ways to maximize human capital by identifying and closing gaps in performance. Performance gaps can be measured more easily when an ideal model exists.

The competency-based needs assessment approach helps an organization define the knowledge, skills, attitudes, and behaviors necessary for people to perform efficiently in their jobs. The results can be applied in many ways to achieve higher levels of performance. This chapter has shown how individual learning development plans can be created after a competency model has been built. The case study described how a competency-based needs assessment was used to improve on-boarding and training for new training managers for a government agency.

The chapter described a process for identifying the competencies necessary for people to perform successfully in their jobs. The focus was on the ways an individual performed in his or job. The next chapter on strategic needs assessment focuses on using needs assessment to identify and achieve long-term aims and interests for a community or organization.

SEVEN Strategic Needs Assessment

PURPOSE

This chapter will enable you to do the following:

- Describe the purpose of a strategic needs assessment.
- Recognize when to use the approach.
- Identify the benefits and drawbacks of the approach.
- Recognize critical success factors for performing a strategic needs assessment.
- Identify five phases for conducting a strategic needs assessment.
- Examine how a strategic needs assessment was performed at the fictitious Company XYZ.

RELATED TOOLKIT JOB AIDS

The following job aids for use with the material in this chapter are available in the Needs Assessment Toolkit, which can be found in Section Four of this book:

- Strategic Issues Worksheet
- Fisher's Models of Organizational Performance Worksheet
- Process Map Worksheet
- Gap Analysis Worksheet
- Change Readiness Checklist
- Performance Improvement Planner

OVERVIEW

Organizational leaders use strategic thinking and planning to anticipate issues and situations so they can shape them to gain the competitive advantages that are required for the organization's long-term
health. Many people view strategic needs assessment as a systematic
approach for determining the needs of a business firm; however, the
strategic needs assessment approach also can be used in other types of
organizations, such as an organizational unit, a nonprofit organization,
a community, an inter-organizational entity, or an entire country. For
example, a strategic needs assessment for a community could examine
the internal and external factors that will affect its long-term strategy
for economic, social, and environmental well-being. For your ease of
reading, we use the term "organization" in this chapter to refer to all
such possibilities.

All organizations face a variety of performance problems during the
course of their annual cycle. The scope and magnitude of these performance problems differ, but when the problems affect core business
processes, using quick-fix solutions to close performance gaps can be sur-
prisingly harmful. In such situations, strategic interventions are necessary.

Before implementing a strategic intervention to improve organizational performance, it is essential to examine the performance gaps
within the context of the organization's environment and operations.
Only then can appropriate solutions be prescribed and a road map for
closing the gaps be followed.

A strategic needs assessment examines the internal and external factors that affect performance within the context of an organization's strategy for its long-term health and identifies the gaps between the current and desired conditions that must be closed to achieve the organization's long-term success.

Implementing a strategic needs assessment requires a partnership between the analyst who implements the needs assessment and the client who is responsible for organizational results. What does the analyst bring to the partnership? Credibility, trust, a willingness to gain a deep knowledge about the organization, and knowledge and skills in such areas as HRD, HPT, community development, and international development.

When to Use

A strategic needs assessment is most effective in the following situations:

- When performance improvement needs are linked to the strategy of an organization

- When the organization is undertaking long-term performance improvement or strategic change initiatives

- When organizational processes that do not add value must be identified

- When changes in the external or internal environment could affect the organization's future

Benefits and Drawbacks

A strategic needs assessment offers many benefits. For example, it allows an organization to do the following:

- Develop long-term solutions to existing performance problems.

- Solve problems that affect core business processes, such as product development, order processing, or service delivery.

- Deal with future performance issues, such as a community's expected loss of tax revenues or a predicted increase in crime.

The main drawbacks to the approach are as follows:

- It can be time-intensive.
- It often requires participation by many people.
- It can be costly.
- It requires the analyst to use advanced organization development skills.

Critical Success Factors

The success of a strategic needs assessment project depends on several factors:

- Sponsorship from organization leaders
- Proactive participation by senior, middle, and line managers
- Access to customers, suppliers, business managers, and the public
- Organizational readiness to change

Following are a few terms that will be used in the chapter:

- *Mission*: A broad statement describing an organization's future plans and directions
- *Goal*: A statement describing a measure or target that will be achieved during a certain period, for example: "$100 billion in revenue by the year 2020" or "20 percent reduction in the crime rate by 2021"
- *Business unit*: A department or function within an organization, such as production or operations or the police department

- *Business process*: A series of activities that provide products, deliver services, or manage resources. In communities, programs and departments often rely on business processes to assure that their structured activities and tasks produce the desired product or service. Examples of such business processes include handling accounts receivable within the finance business unit or monitoring alarms by the fire department

- *Process map*: A graphic illustration of the steps or activities that are performed in a process (see the example in Figure 7.6 later in this chapter)

- *Process boundary*: An arbitrary "line" that shows where a process begins or where it ends, such as the process boundaries for an order management process that begins when the customer-service unit sends a mail order and ends when a product is received by a customer

- *Performance improvement planner*: A blueprint that documents all the performance projects that must be undertaken to improve an organization

KEY PHASES OF A NEEDS ASSESSMENT PROJECT

A strategic needs assessment has five phases:

Phase 1: Gather preliminary information about the situation.

Phase 2: Examine the external environment and identify relevant opportunities and threats.

Phase 3: Examine the internal environment and identify relevant strengths and weaknesses.

1. Validate the strategy.

2. Document current performance.

3. Identify causes of performance gaps.

Phase 4: Chart the future environment.

Phase 5: Develop a performance improvement plan.

1. Assess the organization's readiness for change.

2. Select specific interventions.

You probably noticed that a strategic needs assessment encompasses a SWOT analysis, which identifies the organization's *strengths (S), weaknesses (W), opportunities (O),* and *threats (T)* relative to the larger environment.

Strengths and weaknesses are internal to the organization.

- Examples of strengths include patents, strong brand recognition, trust among the decision-makers, and a highly educated workforce.

- Examples of weaknesses include high labor costs, lack of critical knowledge and skills, and an inadequate information technology infrastructure.

Opportunities and threats are external to the organization.

- Examples of opportunities include unfilled customer needs and technological advances that provide easier and faster communications.

- Examples of threats include lack of access to target groups, security problems, or new regulations that create disadvantages.

Scanning the internal and external environment with a SWOT analysis assures that the needs identified in the strategic needs assessment will align the organization's resources and capabilities with its larger environment.

In the workplace, some organizations have comprehensive and useful strategic plans, and others have not completed their plans. Because a strategic needs assessment relies on a thorough understanding of the organization's strategy, the following discussion includes background information on strategic planning.

Phase 1: Gather Preliminary Information About the Situation

The purpose of this phase is to develop a better understanding of a current or future performance need. For example, a 30 percent increase in security issues would indicate that a current problem exists. A mandate from leaders stating that all organizational units must be prepared for the demographic changes that will occur by 2020 would indicate a future performance need.

During this phase, discussions with a few key people will provide enough information to establish preliminary process boundaries and a definition of the performance problem or opportunity. A good first action is to conduct interviews with a few senior leaders from the organization. Later, the span of inquiry can be widened to include middle managers and first-line supervisors or various stakeholder groups. Secondary sources, such as transcripts of conversations with customers or newspaper articles, also can provide useful information.

Tip

Usually a strategic needs assessment for a community involves encouraging *as many* community members as possible to provide input and feedback on the most critical community needs.

Toolkit Form 7.1 contains a Strategic Issues Worksheet that can be used to examine an existing performance problem or to address a future performance need. Figure 7.1 shows some sample questions from that worksheet. After completing a preliminary analysis, it is important to document the findings in a report that includes the following elements:

- The background of the problem or need
- The scope of the problem or need

- The performance improvement goals
- The evidence examined

Use the information in the report to plan the remaining phases of the needs assessment.

TOOLKIT FORM 7.1 *Strategic Issues Worksheet—Sample Questions*

- What are the key organizational issues that must be addressed?
- What are the consequences of not addressing these issues?
- What are the performance improvement goals?
- What is preventing these goals from being achieved?
- What individuals and groups have a stake in addressing these issues and should participate in the needs assessment?

FIGURE 7.1 *Sample Questions from Toolkit Form 7.1: Strategic Issues Worksheet*

Phase 2: Examine the External Environment

Many external factors can affect organizational performance. During Phase 2, this information is collected and the data analyzed. The purposes of this phase are to

- Identify and isolate external factors, especially the opportunities and threats, affecting the performance need.

- Determine the implications of these external factors.

Porter's classic model (1980, 2008) identified the following forces that determine the long-term profitability for an industry:

- **Direct competitors**: The struggle among established rivals for profits and market share can be fierce.

- **Suppliers' bargaining power**: Suppliers can haggle for higher prices for their goods and services, reducing the profit for others.

- **Buyers' bargaining power**: Buyers, or customers, can pressure the organization to lower prices.

- **The threat of new entrants**: The potential of new market competitors is dangerous because of the innovative capacities they can bring to the competitive market and because of their ambitions for market share).

- **The threat of substitute products or services**: Substitutes rely on a different means to provide a similar function. For example, iTunes became a substitute product for many people who had purchased music CDs.

The extended competition among the forces listed above, called the intra-industry rivalry, shapes an industry's structure and also the nature of its competition.

As an example, consider a few illustrations of how recent Internet advances created new opportunities and risks for retail organizations:

- Competition is no longer limited by geographic area. For example, retail organizations that now can compete directly with each other through online shopping include Walmart, M&S, Carrefour, and Costco.

- Suppliers to these retail organizations can increase their own profits by using electronic commerce in ways that benefit them (such as facilitating the profitable financing and payment aspects of business transactions). Suppliers also can use the Internet to market and sell their products and services directly to buyers.

- Buyers can hold prices down by using the Internet to comparison shop.

- The threat of new market competitors became a reality when online businesses, such as Amazon, successfully competed with established brick-and-mortar retail businesses.

- Many buyers substituted online shopping for in-store shopping.

- The intense and extended rivalries from all the forces in the retail industry produced price discounts, service improvements, enhanced marketing, and so forth.

By analyzing all these forces, organizational leaders can gain a clearer picture of how an industry is changing and strategies that could be more profitable for the organization. The leadership team should completely analyze each force, including the positives and negatives, the current situation, and potential future changes.

All types of organizations, including communities, organizational units, and not-for-profit entities, can benefit from considering this model. A full-fledged analysis is beyond the scope of this book; however, Figure 7.2 shows some questions about the forces that a city leadership team could use to start analyzing its external environment.

Usually, information about the external forces can be obtained from discussions with the organization's senior leaders. Also, the following secondary sources can be helpful:

- Industry reports
- Industry conferences and proceedings
- Business newspapers, such as the *Wall Street Journal*
- Dow Jones Industrial Index
- Specialized trade journals
- Market research data
- Customer-satisfaction surveys
- Notes from meetings with customers or suppliers
- In-house sales or purchasing databases
- Secret shoppers
- Dun & Bradstreet reports
- SEC reports
- Regional or local newspapers
- Police and fire reports

Phase 3: Examine Internal Environment

Phase 3 provides answers to the questions: What are the organization's performance goals given its external environment, and what is the strategy

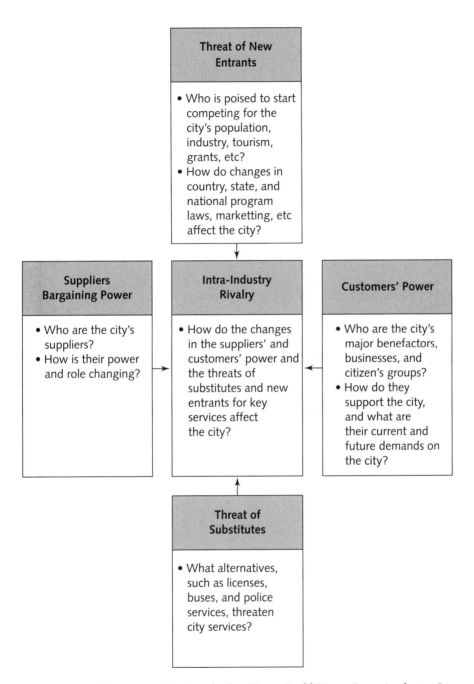

FIGURE 7.2. *Questions a City Leadership Team Could Use to Start Analyzing Its External Environment*

for reaching the goals? What are the organization's strengths and weaknesses? Which processes are affected by the performance problems or opportunities? and What are the performance gaps? Depending on the scope of the performance need, this phase can take a few days or several months to complete. The three steps of this phase are validate the strategy, document current performance, and identify causes of performance gaps.

Step 1: Validate the Strategy

This is a good time to identify the organization's strengths and weaknesses relative to the strategies that pertain to your particular project. A strategy is the set of policies, plans, and directions that an organization uses to achieve its goals and fulfill its mission. One or more strategies

---

Mission

　Become the community's vendor of choice in our product lines

Goal

　Capture 50 percent of the market in our product lines

Strategies

- Introduce fifteen new product offerings per year
- Focus advertising to expand the market to include middle-aged males
- Provide associates with training on how to sell the new products

Other components of a business plan:

- Critical success factors
- Market analysis
- Competitive analysis
- Tactical analysis
- Financial analysis including cash flow (actual and projected)
- Head count plan
- Profit and loss statement (actual and projected)
- Balance sheet (actual and projected)

FIGURE 7.3 *Components of a Simple Business Plan*

support each organizational goal. Each strategy describes how the organization's long-term goal will be achieved. Validating that the strategies are accurate and current at the start of the needs assessment saves both time and frustration. Strategies can be found in the business plan or the community comprehensive plan. Figure 7.3 shows some sample mission, goal, and strategy statements and also some components of a simple business plan. If the plan is not available or if the information is dated, you could conduct individual or group interviews with senior leaders to obtain the needed data.

An organization's strategy sets the direction for learning and performance improvement initiatives. Problems often arise when organizational goals are misaligned across levels, units, and processes (Gephart & Van Buren, 1996; Rummler & Brache, 1995).

Strategic business plans and comprehensive community plans can be very detailed. For instance, see example business plans at the U.S. Small Business Administration website, http://sba.gov. When reviewing a business plan, focus on the strategies and tactics that pertain to your particular needs assessment project. For example, if you are seeking to discover reasons for declining production, examine the section of the business

CASE

A community that was struggling with recession and loss of manufacturing jobs used community asset mapping as part of their needs assessment. Asset mapping is an approach to community development that focuses on depicting and understanding a community's individual and organizational resources (such as community institutions, citizen networks, and the gifts, skills, and capacities of community members). The resulting "map" showed connections between individuals, between individuals and organizations, and among organizations. It also led community members to realize that the community had many resources that could be harnessed to address their needs.

plan that contains production goals. If you are seeking to discover reasons for declining health services in a community, examine the section of the community comprehensive plan that pertains to health services.

Step 2: Document Current Performance

This step in a strategic needs assessment focuses on documenting, or mapping, exactly how current performance occurs. The process of documenting the elements and relationships that affect the organization's particular need can highlight the deficiencies and discrepancies in the performance system.

Figure 7.4 shows sample performance measures that can be used to document business process activities during this stage of the analysis. As the figure illustrates, the quality of services provided by an accounting unit can be measured by the number of errors per bill. In the same way, customer satisfaction can be measured by the number of invoices that were incorrect. Any deviation from a stated objective is an indication that a problem exists.

An organization can contain hundreds of processes; therefore, mapping performance is no simple undertaking. However, as Mankins and Steele (2005) point out, performance bottlenecks are often invisible to top management. Moreover, without good information about how and why poor

Process	Cost	Quality	Customer Time	Satisfaction
Accounting/ Billing	Bills processed per person	Number of errors processed per bill	Amount of time taken to process a bill	Number of bills generated incorrectly
Treasury/ Accounts Receivable	Bank reconciliation per person	Percentage of receivables outstanding past ninety days	Average number of days sales outstanding	Number of posting errors
Production	Average cost per unit below ten cents	Number of defects produced per billion	Number of orders shipped on time	Number of returns per thousand units sold

FIGURE 7.4 *Sample Performance Measures*

performance is occurring, top management finds it virtually impossible to implement appropriate corrective action (Rummler & Brache, 1995).

In a hierarchical organization, some processes cross individual, group, and organizational levels. Examples include those that contribute to high-level organization goals (for example, product launches typically involve marketing, product development, and sales). Such examples also include groups that contribute to the overall organization (for example, human resources, IT, and accounting). Some processes may not cross hierarchical levels, but they involve different aspects of performance goals, such as a team accomplishment that also increases its learning and its capacity for future accomplishment.

Many tools are available for documenting current performance. Three that provide especially powerful insights are (1) organizational performance models, (2) the SIPOC diagram, and (3) process mapping. Brief descriptions of these tools are provided below.

Organizational Performance Models. Fisher's (2000) theory of organizational performance in for-profit organizations contains models that are useful for mapping current performance at the individual, group, and organizational levels. These models show the aspects of performance at each level, and they reflect our current understanding of systems theory (that is, the interactions among capacity, production process, learning process, and accomplishments). Fisher's models also show cross-level performance relationships.

Toolkit Form 7.2 contains the Fisher models (Fisher, 2000; Fisher & Sleezer, 2003) and provides a brief description of each. Use these models to map the processes for your particular situation, to show how your performance need is linked to organizational performance, and to point out where potential deficiencies and discrepancies in a performance system might be occurring. In addition to providing visual images, the models contain useful language for discussing the processes that contribute to a particular performance need.

When using these models, pay attention to how learning and performance changes are transferred. For example, a needs assessment that recommends improving an organization's performance by training individuals should specify the processes by which such learning improves organizational performance. It should detail exactly how increased individual knowledge and skills will produce increased individual performance and also how the increased individual performance will eventually increase organizational performance.

Measurement is important when specifying how learning and performance improvements transfer to performance. For example, are individual behaviors pooled to achieve organizational performance? Or are they averaged? Or does performance emerge from a complex combination of diverse individual contributions toward team performance that is subsequently identified as an organizational performance? The answers depend on the situation.

Mapping precisely how the transfer of learning and improved performance actually occur in a complex organization requires heavy-duty analysis work. However, this important work is valuable because breakdowns in the transfer-of-learning and the transfer-of-performance processes often result in wasted resources.

Tip

When mapping organizational performance, save time by starting with the accomplishments that are delivered to the product market.

SIPOC Diagram. SIPOC stands for suppliers, inputs, process, outputs, and customers. This tool reflects the systems view of organizations that was described in Chapter One. A SIPOC diagram is useful for finding out and documenting at a high level the inputs, outputs, and work flows of a specific process. Start by asking about the outputs:

- What results or outputs does the process deliver?
- What inputs are required to make the process successful?
- Who provides the inputs to the process?
- Who are the customers of the process?

- What do the customers of this process require?
- What steps are involved in completing the process?

  A SIPOC diagram for car repair is shown in Figure 7.5.
  The steps for completing a SIPOC diagram are as follows:

1. Use the information gathered during Phases 1 and 2 of the strategic needs assessment to define the scope of the project and the specific process you will examine.

2. Use the outputs to define the end point of the process and the inputs to define the starting point for the process. The SIPOC does not identify processes that occur before the starting point or after the end point.

3. Record the process outputs, or results, and the customers who receive them.

4. Record the process inputs and the suppliers for each input.

5. Record the supports, or enablers, for the process.

6. Label the SIPOC diagram with a title identifying the process it illustrates.

7. Review the completed SIPOC diagram with the project sponsor and other involved stakeholders for verification.

Process Mapping. One major reason for performance gaps is activities that do not contribute to the performance needs of the organization. Non-value-added activities result in waste and increased costs. These activities must be understood and documented so that gaps in performance can be minimized. Common real-life examples of non-value-added activities include unnecessary duplication of tasks; idle or waiting time when no task is being performed; and checking, logging, or approving tasks that were performed correctly.

A process map uses graphic symbols, such as ovals and arrows, to show the steps of a process and the flow of information. Process boundaries show where a process begins and ends. For example, the process

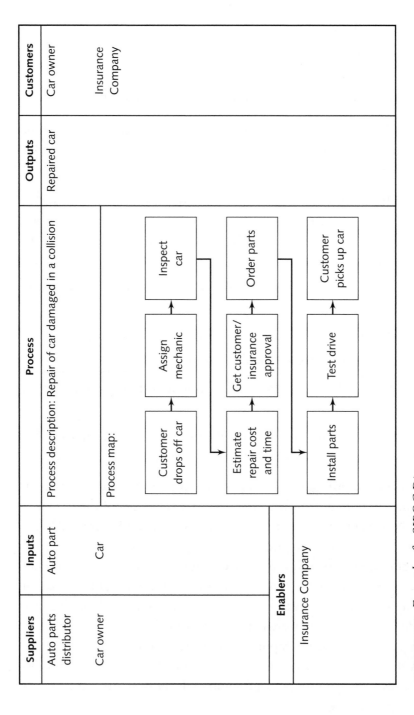

FIGURE 7.5 *Example of a SIPOC Diagram*

Source: Used with permission from www.shmula.com/suppliers-inputs-process-output-customers-sipoc/3289/

boundaries for order management in an organization begin when a customer-service unit sends a mail order and ends when the product is received by a customer. You can use Toolkit Form 7.3 as an aid in mapping a process. As an example, the process for filling a customer's order in one organization is shown in Figure 7.6. Many software packages are available that quickly and easily produce process maps (for example, Visio, Corel Flow, and Lucidchart).

When completing a process map, it is important to maintain perspective about how much detail is needed. You need to capture all the details that matter but avoid wasting time in documenting extra details that do not provide relevant information for your problem or need.

Once a process map is completed, it should be examined to identify such opportunities for performance improvement as bottlenecks, weak links, poorly defined activities, and activities that do not add value. Also, the map can be used to document responsibilities, standards, and measures for each step of the process.

Tip

If you plan to institute a new process or improve a process in an organization, consider benchmarking industry leaders. Benchmarking involves measuring the products and processes of industry leaders and using the information to improve your product or process. When benchmarking, be sure to consider the larger systems, because a product or process that works well for one organization may not do well in other organizational systems.

Step 3: Identify Causes of Performance Gaps

Comparing the current documented performance to the desired performance reveals the existence, location, and nature of gaps in such areas as quality of equipment, completeness of available information, and worker knowledge, skills, attitudes, and behaviors. Techniques—such as root cause analysis, brainstorming, fishbone diagrams, and procedure analysis—can be useful in uncovering the real cause of problems and thus produce significant long-term performance improvement.

TOOLKIT FORM 7.3 *Process Map Worksheet*

A process map uses graphic symbols to show the steps of a process. It also shows where a process begins and ends. Following are the graphic symbols to use:

1. To show information received from a source OUTSIDE a process boundary, such as a customer, customer request, or another business unit, use a RECTANGLE. ▭
2. To show any activity that is being carried out WITHIN a process, such as completing a form, use an OVAL. ⬭
3. To show the FLOW between activities (INPUTS and OUTPUTS), use an ARROW. ⟶

TIPS FOR PROCESS MAPPING

1. Before mapping a process, define the starting and ending points and the level of detail that is needed.
2. Document steps in sequence. Try to restrict your diagram to major steps at first. Do not become bogged down in too much detail.
3. Begin by identifying the output and the input. Then identify the first major process activity, such as processing quotes, as shown in Figure 7.6. Determine the flow of information to and from this process. Use single-pointed arrows for information that flows in one direction. For information that flows back and forth between two units or processes, use two-pointed arrows.
4. Identify the next major process. Document the inputs and outputs to this process.
5. Link all major processes as well as the inputs and outputs.
6. If you cannot define intermediate steps, make notes. Come back to these steps later.
7. When you have finished creating your process map, retrace steps to verify accuracy of the information collected.
8. Review the process map with the project sponsor and other involved stakeholders for verification.

FIGURE 7.6 *Sample Toolkit Form 7.3: Process Map Worksheet for an Order Management Process*

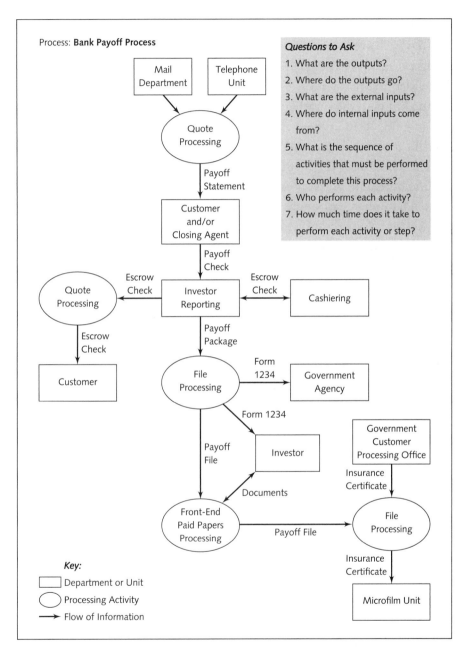

Process: **Bank Payoff Process**

Questions to Ask

1. What are the outputs?
2. Where do the outputs go?
3. What are the external inputs?
4. Where do internal inputs come from?
5. What is the sequence of activities that must be performed to complete this process?
6. Who performs each activity?
7. How much time does it take to perform each activity or step?

Key:

- ☐ Department or Unit
- ○ Processing Activity
- → Flow of Information

FIGURE 7.6 *Sample Toolkit Form 7.3: Process Map Worksheet for an Order Management Process* (continued)

Root Cause Analyis. This was developed from the insight that most often symptoms of performance problems rather than their underlying causes were being addressed. Root cause analysis is a procedure for identifying the most probable causes of problems, so organizations can eliminate them rather than continue to deal with their symptoms. Using this technique involves continuing to ask "Why?" until the pattern becomes evident and the causes of the problem become obvious.

Brainstorming is a method of problem solving in which group members contribute ideas spontaneously. To encourage creativity, the ideas are not evaluated or discussed until everyone has contributed. Often an idea that originally seemed far-fetched leads to the solution.

A fishbone, or Ishikawa, diagram is used to show all the causes (or inputs) for a single problem. Figure 7.7 shows a sample fishbone diagram. To create such a diagram, first fill in the problem statement, which in this example is that workers are dissatisfied. Then identify all the categories of problems, which in the example are management, labor, materials, and machines. Then show causes of the problem. Finally, arrange them by category and by their level of importance. The result is a picture that shows relationships among the potential causes of a problem.

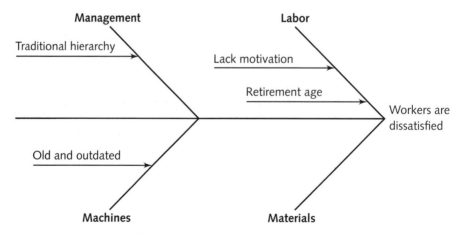

FIGURE 7.7 *Sample Fishbone Diagram Showing Causes for Workers Dissatisfaction*

Procedure Analysis. Procedure analysis is a systematic technique for documenting, step-by-step, the process for completing a complex or important task. Often the subject expert demonstrates the task, and the analyst records the steps that are performed to complete the task. Swanson (2007) provides information on how to conduct such an analysis.

CASE

When a pump manufacturing firm found a high number of defects in its popular small pump, the division vice president told the chief learning officer (CLO) to "Fix it, now!" As a first step, the CLO conducted a speedy strategic needs assessment. He examined the external environment by talking with the vice president of marketing and reviewing some industry reports. He learned that the demand for the pumps had increased and would likely remain strong. Product defects were the major barrier to retaining customers. Looking internally, the CLO found that:

- Many new workers had been hired, and more new hires were expected.
- Training new hires was done on the job using knowledgeable workers who had previously been trained by the product engineer or the director of quality.
- The parts-acquisition process had not changed.

To document current performance, the CLO asked the director of quality and the product engineer to demonstrate the procedure for assembling the pump. At first they did not see the need for the demonstration, but they eventually agreed to do it and gathered the parts for assembling two pumps.

Interestingly, just before beginning the demonstration, the director of quality joked with the product engineer that performance would really improve when all employees could assemble pumps as well as they did. You can almost guess what happened next. While demonstrating the correct assembly steps, these subject experts saw that they each used different procedures. They first hotly argued about whose procedure caused more defects. They then decided to work together to improve the assembly process, which the CLO documented using procedure analysis. The resulting document was used to train employees, which resulted in fewer defective pumps.

To document the performance gaps that were identified in Phases 1, 2, and 3, use the Gap Analysis Worksheet (Toolkit Form 7.4). An example using the form to document performance gaps is shown in Figure 7.8.

Phase 4: Chart Future Environment

After deficiencies and causes of performance gaps have been identified, start documenting the desired processes and performance. The map created in this phase is a reconfigured process map at the same level of detail as the one created in the previous phase. Usually, new organizational charts, job classifications, performance measures, or team structures are needed to support the new process. Minimizing unnecessary specialization and rigidity in job content can improve performance at the organizational, process, and job levels. To access guidelines for performing an analysis at the job and task levels, see Chapter Five.

Phase 5: Develop Performance Improvement Plan

In this phase, the analyst essentially transforms the information that was mapped in the earlier phase into a performance improvement plan, which is a blueprint that documents all the performance improvement projects to be undertaken to improve the overall effectiveness of an organization. This phase involves two steps: assess readiness for change and select interventions.

Step 1: Assess Readiness for Change

It is essential to assess whether an organization and its people are ready to implement a performance improvement plan. A formal plan

TOOLKIT FORM 7.4 *Gap Analysis Worksheet*

Process	Current Performance Indicators	Performance Gap	Effect
Quote processing	5 business days	Customers expect quote within 2 days	Lost business; dissatisfied customer
Escrow check processing	7 business days	Tax data not received on time	Processing delay
File processing	10 business days	Payoff package incomplete	Processing delay

FIGURE 7.8 *Sample Toolkit Form 7.4: Gap Analysis Worksheet*

to determine change readiness is particularly necessary when the performance improvement plan will require significant changes in processes, systems, or jobs. For example, the implementation of a new call-management system may involve establishing standards and instituting a training program, a communications program, and a performance-management system. The Change Readiness Checklist (Toolkit Form 7.5) contains questions that can help you assess the organization's readiness for change. The answers to these questions can help prioritize the performance improvement gaps, and they also provide insight into actions that can improve the organization's readiness for change.

Creating or maintaining an open work climate can help to minimize people's resistance to change. When launching a change initiative, it is usually best to assign the initiative to a project leader or facilitator who is well respected and can manage the whole effort. See Toolkit Form 7.5 for a checklist that can be used to guide this effort.

Step 2: Select Interventions

Next, select the interventions that will most effectively support the implementation of a performance improvement plan. The Performance Improvement Planner (Toolkit Form 7.6) shows the factors that must be considered, such as critical success factors, prerequisites for starting a project, and other related project requirements. Using the Performance Improvement Planner (Toolkit Form 7.6) in conjunction with the Change Readiness Checklist (Toolkit Form 7.5) allows the value and cost of each performance improvement project to be assessed quickly and easily.

This chapter has presented the methods and tools for doing a strategic needs assessment. Here is how it was done at XYZ Corporation. This fictitious case was contributed by Bob Carroll, an organizational consultant. Carroll has been involved in several performance improvement initiatives for a major computer company. The key tools shown here are a Business Issues Worksheet and a Performance Improvement Planner.

CASE

Andre Adams, a training director at XYZ Corporation, used the strategic needs assessment approach to develop a long-term performance improvement plan for the company. XYZ Corporation is a large wholesale distributor of electronic goods. With over $3 billion in assets, the company markets computers, television and video equipment, and cameras to Far Eastern countries.

The Need

The electronics division of XYZ had not been keeping pace with its other store divisions or with its competition. Sales targets had not been met for two years. The division had been, and could again be, a very lucrative operation for the company. Management wanted to know what was causing a drop in sales and what actions, if any, were needed to turn things around.

The Approach

The training director used a five-phase approach to conduct the strategic needs assessment.

Phase 1: Assess Current Situation

1. The training director conducted a series of interviews with the president, two senior vice presidents, and a representative sample of middle managers and first-line supervisors from the electronics division.

2. The training director reviewed one hundred customer-satisfaction surveys taken during the period just before sales began to drop off, then reviewed another one hundred surveys taken during the period when sales went into decline.

3. The training director established preliminary performance improvement goals based on system capabilities and prepared a report that summarized the key findings from the first two steps.

Phase 2: Examine External Environment

1. The training director researched the business environment in which XYZ and its competitors operated. This was background for a more detailed examination of the consumer electronics market. He consulted industry and trade journals and reviewed customer-satisfaction surveys.

2. He also conducted focus groups with a sample of the division's customers. As a result of these inquiries, the training director learned that much of the customer dissatisfaction resulted from a new Asian competitor who was offering lower prices and longer credit periods to his organization's current and potential customers. The competitor also delivered products faster.

Phase 3: Examine Internal Environment

1. The business plan was reviewed for its applicability to the changing environment. It revealed that the division had planned to emphasize quality and speed of delivery rather

than lower prices. This plan was being executed despite the fact that the new competitor's low price policy was hurting sales. Figure 7.9 shows the business issues for XYZ Corporation.

2. Process maps for shipping and purchasing were created, and performance gaps between ideal and actual were identified.

Phase 4: Chart Future Environment

1. The senior leaders of the company and the training director identified the performance needed to regain lost market share. They decided that the division would emphasize quality and speed by reducing product defects and the time required to ship orders. They also decided to cut costs and extend credit and to work with the division to place greater emphasis on customer relationships.

2. A reorganization of the shipping and purchasing departments was included in the new plan, which called for improved relationships with wholesalers and distributors.

Phase 5: Develop Performance Improvement Plan

1. To ensure that the plan would be implemented smoothly, the training director assessed the organization's readiness for change.

2. Based on that analysis, the following major performance-improvement projects were identified:

- Implement a new order-management system.
- Train to support the implementation of the new order-management system, including team building, relationship management, and customer-service training.

Figure 7.10 shows the performance improvement planner that was used for this project.

Key business issues	Order delivery takes too long
	Order-management system is inefficient
	Linkage between shipping, receiving, and product delivery is ineffective
	Poor quality service to customers
	Poor supplier relationships
	Lack of ownership in order delivery process
	Prices are too high
	Credit period is too short
Length problems existed	2 years
Consequences of not solving problems	Lose even more customers
Business processes affected	Shipping, sales, purchasing, credit, finance, marketing
Performance improvement goals	Reduce order delivery time by 50 percent
	Reduce product costs by 10 percent
	Extend credit by 30 days
Obstacles to success	Inability of suppliers to ship goods from overseas on time
	Union rules
	Limit on number of hours shipping and receiving personnel will work on the job

FIGURE 7.9 *Business Issues: XYZ Corporation*

The Results

The new order-management system was fully implemented one year later and led to increased sales. XYZ Corporation regained the market share it had lost. A follow-up survey showed that customer-satisfaction levels were as high as they had been before the new competitor captured some of XYZ's market share.

Project Identification Number: 123

Project Description: Order delivery performance improvement

Project Sponsor (Name/Business Unit): Chuck Brady/Sales

Performance Improvement Goal: Reduce order delivery time from twenty days to ten days.

Critical Success Factors
1. Participation of purchasing, shipping, and sales units
2. Communication of program benefits to customers and employees
3. Pilot program in two regions before nationwide rollout

Obstacles to Success
1. Current shipping vendor's performance
2. Union rules
3. Aging inventory computer software
4. Lack of performance measures for purchasing and shipping supervisors

Prerequisites for Starting the Project
1. Improved understanding of customer needs
2. Shipping vendor participation in sales planning

Project Structure: Steering committee composed of unit heads from purchasing, shipping, and sales; project manager; and one analyst from each business unit who understands the processes.

Team Requirements: Knowledge of unit policies; two years' experience in purchasing, shipping, and sales process; operating knowledge of computer software

Resources: Budget, staff

Expected Cost: $1.2M

FIGURE 7.10 *Performance Improvement Planner: XYZ Corporation*

Benefits
1. Improved sales: $2.0M
2. Reduced returns: $1.0M
3. Reduced inventory: $2.0M

Timeline

Milestone	Expected Start Date	Expected Completion Date
1. Analysis	1/1	2/28
2. Cost/benefit analysis	3/1	3/5
3. Plan pilot	3/6	3/15
4. Perform pilot	3/16	3/31
5. Launch program	4/1	4/15
6. Rollout program	4/16	4/30

Completed by: _____   Approved by: _____

Date: _____   Date: _____

FIGURE 7.10 *Performance Improvement Planner: XYZ Corporation* (continued)

CONCLUSION

A strategic needs assessment addresses the performance processes that are linked to an organization's core strategies for long-term performance. It should be used whenever performance problems or opportunities affect strategic processes.

The success of a performance improvement initiative depends on several factors, including an assessment of the readiness to change and a carefully crafted performance improvement plan. In this chapter we described how to examine factors in the organization's external and internal environments that can affect performance. The focus was on the organization and its processes. The next chapter describes the process for conducting a complex needs assessment.

EIGHT Complex Needs Assessment

PURPOSE

This chapter will enable you to

- Describe the purpose of a complex needs assessment.
- Recognize when to use a complex needs assessment.
- Identify the benefits and drawbacks of the approach.
- Describe the three phases of a complex needs assessment.
- Recognize critical success factors for performing a complex needs assessment.
- Describe examples of complex needs assessments.

RELATED TOOLKIT JOB AID

The following job aid for use with the material in this chapter is available in the Needs Assessment Toolkit, which can be found in Section Four of this book:

- Complex Needs Assessment Planning Template

OVERVIEW

The complex needs assessment approach is the appropriate choice when an organization's or a community's needs appear to include both training and non-training, or systemic, issues. For example, consider the required data collection and analysis to assess the needs for a community that is implementing a new inventory software system that will enable all departments to share surplus materials and equipment. To be successful, the analyst must assess the training needs to operate the software. In addition, the analyst will likely work with those who have a stake in the project to assess such non-training needs as the following:

- The ideal schedule and process for uploading inventory information into the software

- The current surplus cataloguing and reporting process as compared to the proposed process

- The way in which departments catalogue inventory that is not available to be shared (such as sand that is inventoried for road crews to use on icy roads)

- Change management (people often have strong feelings that their department's approach to managing inventory is the best and that all the other departments should use their approach)

As the example highlights, some situations cannot be assessed using only the knowledge and skills assessment, job and task analysis, competency-based assessment, or strategic needs assessment approaches. The complex needs assessment approach is the appropriate choice in such situations.

Some scholars use the term generic needs assessment (Altschuld & Kumar, 2010; Witkin, 1984). We prefer the term *complex needs assessment*, because the needs are multifaceted and may require the analyst to adapt aspects from the other needs assessment approaches and/or apply expertise from other subject areas (such as inventory management, change management, and so forth). Most importantly, implementing a complex needs assessment compels the analyst to innovate.

Below are some examples of situations that call for a complex needs assessment:

- Assessing the training and non-training needs of a dysfunctional team

- Responding to an increase in tuberculosis by assessing a community's tuberculosis prevention programs

- Determining the information technology security that a city will need to meet its strategic plan for growth in the upcoming decade

- Assessing learning needs for employees in an organization that was recently acquired by another company

When to Use

While reading the examples above, did you realize that the needs could not be determined with only a job-related competency assessment or a knowledge and skills assessment? Did you also realize that neither a job and task analysis nor a strategic needs assessment would be sufficient? The complex needs assessment approach is used when the other needs assessment approaches alone are insufficient. A complex needs assessment also is used when flexibility is required to determine what the important needs are and how to close the gaps in learning and performance.

Benefits and Drawbacks

The greatest benefit of a complex needs assessment is that it can easily be tailored to match the situation. This is also the greatest drawback of the approach. Such flexibility requires the analyst to have strong expertise in needs assessments and deep knowledge of the various alternative approaches, along with a background in both quantitative and qualitative data collection and analysis processes. In addition, implementing a complex needs assessment usually requires the analyst to apply organization development and/or other kinds of expertise and to innovate.

KEY PHASES

A complex needs assessment has three phases:
Phase 1: Conduct the pre-assessment.
Phase 2: Conduct the needs assessment.
Phase 3: Conduct the post-assessment.

Phase 1: Conduct the Pre-Assessment

Activities in this phase include getting organized, forming a needs assessment committee, specifying the boundaries for the needs assessment, and planning the data collection, analysis and reporting processes.

Phase 2: Conduct the Needs Assessment

Activities in this phase include collecting and analyzing data on the current condition and the desired condition, prioritizing the needs based on the data, identifying the solution criteria and potential solutions, and reporting the needs assessment results.

Phase 3: Conduct the Post-Assessment

The post-assessment may be limited to a follow-up meeting with the client to assure that all the appropriate actions for the complex needs assessment have been completed. However, in some cases, this phase involves more extensive activities.

The process of implementing the first two phases of a complex needs assessment provides the analyst with expertise in the needs and the context, and also builds relationships with the client, the decision-makers, and other stakeholders. After the needs have been determined, the client may ask the analyst to continue supporting the project as the client and stakeholders address the needs. For example, the analyst might collaborate with stakeholders to develop action plans that address the needs, provide feedback on the implementation of the action plan, or evaluate results. Thus, it is important in this phase to monitor the contract so that project creep is avoided.

The Complex Needs Assessment Planning Template (Toolkit Form 8.1) can be used to guide the planning for each phase of a complex needs assessment.

In the following real-life case study, the analyst worked at a manufacturing firm as an organization development practitioner.

CASE

The vice president of manufacturing (VP) requested that the analyst work with a twelve-person work team that reported to him. The VP indicated that the team members' interactions with each other had caused the team to miss a major performance goal. The team members had sufficient expertise to accomplish their individual goals, but they were not working well together. Missing the performance goal was a critical event, because the firm had begun marketing the team's products to new clients in another region of the world and counted on this venture to open up new markets for the entire firm.

The analyst realized that the gaps in this situation could not be determined by implementing only a knowledge and skills assessment, a job and task analysis, a competency assessment, or a strategic needs assessment, and she implemented a complex needs assessment. As you read the case, notice how the process of assessing the gaps between the ideal and actual team performance influenced the team's behaviors.

Phase 1: Conduct the Pre-Assessment

The pre-assessment, which was called "planning" in this case, included:

- Establish a needs assessment committee (NAC).
- Define the needs assessment participants.
- Select the needs assessment instrument.
- Plan the implementation of the instrument.
- Plan the reporting of the individual feedback and the team feedback.

The NAC was comprised of the VP, the work group's supervisor, and the analyst. During the first NAC meeting, the VP and supervisor described multiple instances when team members' conflicts interfered with individual and team performance and some instances that affected the larger organization. They expressed particular concern that the team's conflicts could derail current efforts to acquire new Latin American customers.

The NAC expected the needs assessment to provide a learning opportunity for team members and also to offer opportunities for the VP, the supervisor, and the analyst to observe and evaluate the behaviors of individual team members. The NAC determined that data would be collected about the first-shift team members' work styles and shared with the team.

The NAC reviewed several assessment instruments. Many team assessment instruments can be found on the Internet, including The Five Dysfunctions of a Team: Team Assessment (www.tablegroup.com/dysfunctions/), the Myers-Briggs Type Indicator™ (www.myersbriggs.org), and DiSC® (www.everythingdisc.com). The NAC elected to use DiSC for this project.

The NAC developed the following needs assessment plan:

- The supervisor will communicate to the team members the expectations about their participation in the needs assessment and the training.
- Team members will individually complete the online DiSC survey.
- The analyst will use the DiSC reports to give individual team members feedback on their styles.
- All the team members will participate in training to learn the DiSC profile for the team. This training will include strategies for working together more effectively.

The VP asked the analyst and supervisor to observe the behaviors of the team members during the individual feedback sessions and also during the training session to identify the person or persons who could be the source of the problems, and to provide a recommendation about who should be reassigned to a different work group.

Phase 2: Conduct the Needs Assessment

The plan that was created in Phase 1 guided the activities of this phase. Each team member completed the online DiSC survey and within the next two weeks had a private feedback session with the analyst. Many team members commented during their feedback sessions that they viewed the assessment and training as an opportunity for personal development.

Less than a week later, the training session for the team was held. The VP welcomed everyone to the training and described how important the team was to the organization. The analyst then introduced the team results for DiSC and provided each person with a copy of the DiSC team profile. The team members openly discussed how well the profile reflected the team. This discussion revealed that most team members were strong-willed, and they dealt with problems actively and aggressively. However, several members relied on different styles. For example, the logistic manager's style was to adhere strictly to the rules and regulations. His favorite saying was "Do it right the first time." The account manager's style emphasized being deliberate, consistent, and unemotional. The team members quickly recognized that their conflicts were a function of their differing styles.

During the training, all team members actively participated in identifying ways they could use the feedback. For example, several team members grinned in agreement with one member's comment that it was a good thing the logistics manager adhered to "every blasted rule," because the customs agents for some countries held up product delivery to customers for the smallest infractions. The active discussion during training gave the members a new language for talking openly about conflicts and helped team members see situations differently. One member commented that many of the team's conflicts, in retrospect, seemed pretty childish.

The tone of the meeting changed when a team member wondered aloud about the styles of their customers. The team grew quiet as realization dawned that the intense and aggressive style of most team members could be off-putting to the potential Latin American customers. Then the training room grew abuzz with conversation as the team members brainstormed how to better use the styles of the entire team to market to new customers. Someone asked the VP and the supervisor if the team responsible for marketing to new customers in Latin America could be reconfigured to include the low-key team member who adhered to rules and regulations. The other team members showed their support for this request with such comments as "good idea" and "yeah" and nodding. The VP asked if the idea had support from the entire team. It did. He asked the team to put the suggestion in writing by the next week.

When someone asked to have additional training sessions, the VP indicated that he wanted to see the "stickiness" of this training first and be assured that it made a difference to the team's performance. Several participants argued that because they now understood the team differently they could not return to the old ways of behaving, but the VP stood firm.

After the training, the VP, supervisor, and analyst briefly met in the hallway. The VP and supervisor stated that the training had gone well. They decided to observe how the team got along during the next week and to hold off on identifying team members who would be reassigned.

Phase 3: Conduct the Post-Assessment

The VP approved the proposal to reconfigure the customer support group. He also coached the supervisor in ways to monitor and mentor the team to assure that the old ways of interacting did not reappear. The VP and supervisor decided that, based on the team's positive response to the needs assessment, there was no need to remove anyone from the team.

The only evaluation for this needs assessment was the congratulations of the VP and supervisor, who commented to the analyst at the final NAC meeting that they were pleased that the project resulted in the immediate decrease of conflict among the team members. They expected the change to improve the team's interactions with the customers. Both the VP and the supervisor said they would continue to remind team members of the benefits of their different styles.

Tip

If you use an instrument developed by a vendor, check the assumptions, models, and research that support the instrument. Often the vendor can provide such information. Useful information may be found in professional journals, such as the *Journal of Applied Psychology* or *Human Resource Development Quarterly*.

COMMUNITY AND ORGANIZATION SURVEYS

Community surveys are a popular tool for driving improvements to public services. For example, community workforce surveys can identify the characteristics of people who are interested in becoming potential employees within a community. The survey results can be used to recruit new employers and develop community-sponsored training programs. In some cases, community members may undertake surveys within a certain area of the community to identify the major issues of concern. As part of the community organizing effort, the survey results can be presented to community leaders in a large group forum that encourages some actions on the identified issue or issues.

Organizational surveys are a popular tool for creating environments that attract, focus, and retain talent. Examples of organizational surveys include employee satisfaction, attitude, and engagement surveys. These surveys allow comparisons of high- and low-rated items across organizational units and also comparisons of high- and low-rated items within organizational units. The complex needs assessment is the best approach for implementing such surveys.

Employee engagement surveys are currently popular, because they measure employees' discretionary effort and also their intent to continue working for the organization. Research has shown that a relationship exists between employee engagement and organizational outcomes (Gallup, 2013) and that engaged employees are more productive (Buckingham & Coffman, 1999). Today, many vendors offer such surveys.

Figure 8.1 shows some vendors who posted employee engagement survey items and information on their web pages.

Figure 8.2 lists the activities in each phase of a complex needs assessment for an employee engagement survey. Notice that the heaviest workload occurs during the pre-assessment phase. Before using this list to guide an engagement survey in your organization, be sure to consider whether there are any unique aspects of your organization that should be taken into account.

Gallup	www.gallup.com/strategicconsulting/121535/Employee-Engagement-Overview-Brochure.aspx
Sirota	www.sirota.com/employee-engagement-model
Towers Watson	http://towerswatson.com/assets/pdf/2012-Towers-Watson-Global-Workforce-Study.pdf

FIGURE 8.1 *Some Vendor Sites with Employee Engagement Survey Information*

Using a Complex Needs Assessment to Conduct an Employee Engagement Survey

Phase 1: Conduct the Pre-Assessment

- Decide whether the survey will be administered in-house or by a vendor. (Using a vendor is expensive, but can assure confidentiality for individual employee responses.)
- Identify who will participate in the survey. (All employees? A department? A specific subset of employees?)
- Establish the needs assessment committee, which often is called the employee engagement team. (Consider including representatives from the organization's communications, information technology, HR and human resource information system (HRIS) teams, along with the vendor's team.)
- Brand the survey. (Create a logo and marketing campaign.)
- Create a survey timeline. (Determine such details as: (a) when the survey will be administered, (b) how long the survey will be available, (c) when survey reminders will be sent to employees, (d) when survey results will be shared with managers and employees, (e) when action planning on issues identified by the survey will be completed, and (f) when and how the outcomes of action planning will be shared with managers and employees).
- Decide whether the survey will be administered online, via paper, or a combination of both. (If respondents have access to computers, online surveys are less expensive and produce results faster.)
- If multiple languages are needed, decide the languages for the questionnaire and the communications. (Have one person translate and have a second person back-translate the questionnaire. Then have a third person who is conversant in both languages and also familiar with the jargon used in the organization review and confirm that the translated version conveys the content and the meaning of the original version. Also, determine how responses to the open-ended items in the various languages will be analyzed.)
- If the survey is confidential, determine the number of individuals in a unit who must respond to the survey in order for the unit's data to be reported.
- Decide how the survey results will be analyzed and reported. (For survey items that respondents rate, determine whether the reports will include means and standard deviations or agreement scores, which are the percentages of respondents who agreed with each item.)
- Determine who will review the responses to open-end items, what criteria will be used to categorize and analyze responses, and whether there will be any review or double-checking of that categorization. Also decide on how any red flag comments, which describe harming employees or property, will be handled.

FIGURE 8.2 *Activities in Each Phase of an Employee Engagement Survey*

- Create report templates that show the survey results and ask leaders to approve the report templates before the survey is administered. (This assures that the survey reports will provide exactly the information that the leaders expect. Note that two templates are needed if senior leaders will receive an enterprise report and managers will receive survey reports for their units.)
- Plan how the survey will be administered. (Will each employee receive a unique survey? Many surveys vendors rely on information from the organization's human resource information system [HRIS] to distribute the survey and organize the data. If so, plan how the names of employees, their managers, the organizational units, and other demographics will be entered into the survey database.)
- Decide how the data will be stored and the results rolled out. (Will leaders learn the results first and share them with managers and then with employees? Will managers share the reports with employees? Will the HR team have access to the results so they can support the leaders and managers? How long will the organization have access to the data?)
- Determine how the communication of survey results to employees will be managed. (What mediums will be used for the communications? How can the survey be tied to the organization's vision and strategy? Will employees receive a summary of survey results at the enterprise level and at their unit level?)
- Determine the action planning process. (Will the development and implementation of action plans will be monitored? Will action planning be conducted at the organization level? At the unit level? At all levels?)
- Create the survey questionnaire, communications, and action planning resources.

Phase 2: Conduct the Needs Assessment
- Disseminate the communication materials.
- Distribute the employee engagement survey questionnaire.
- Distribute reminders to complete the survey.
- Monitor the survey response rates, answer questions, and troubleshoot problems. (Share the response rates with senior leaders and generate friendly competition to improve the response rates.)
- Analyze the survey data and create the reports.
- Distribute the survey results.
- Compare the survey responses at the enterprise level and at the unit levels to identify the high- and the low-rated survey items. Also compare the ratings within organizational units to identify what is working and what needs improvement. Also compare the survey results for the parent organization and the subsidiaries. (For example, in one organization Global Marketing is the parent organization, and it has two subsidiaries, Eastern Hemisphere Marketing and Western Hemisphere Marketing.)
- Share the results of the employee engagement survey, as planned in Phase 1.

FIGURE 8.2 *Activities in Each Phase of an Employee Engagement Survey* (continued)

> **Phase 3: Conduct the Post-Assessment**
> - Create action plans that address the issues identified in the survey results.
> - Monitor the implementation of action plans to assure ongoing actions that improve the workplace. Also monitor and encourage communications to employees of improvements in the workplace.
> - If the engagement survey will be implemented repeatedly, conduct an after-action review to collect data and opinions on what worked and what could be improved.

FIGURE 8.2 *Activities in Each Phase of an Employee Engagement Survey* (continued)

The case study below, which was submitted by Cathy McCullough, McCullough Group, LLC, describes a complex needs assessment that relied on an organizational survey.

CASE

Phase 1: Conduct the Pre-Assessment

Transitioning from one CEO to the next can be a daunting task for the whole organization. Employees must adjust to a new leadership style and expectations, while the new CEO must understand the organization's culture. In this case, the new CEO took a careful approach to implementing his plan by first understanding the organization, then molding it in the direction he felt was best, and measuring the results to determine the degree to which the stated new strategy was understood and acted upon by the employees. The aim of the needs assessment was to link stated metrics to desired outcomes. The first survey, the Denison Organizational Culture Survey (DOCS), was administered in 2002. (You can find more information about this survey at www.denisonconsulting.com/model-surveys/denison-surveys/organizational-culture).

The DOCS Model aligns leadership behaviors with a high-performing culture to allow organization leaders to pinpoint, with laser-like accuracy, the key aspects of the culture that are working well for the organization as well as those that are not. The survey measures an organization's culture using groups of items about Mission, Involvement, Adaptability, and Consistency.

Phase 2: Conduct the Needs Assessment

The leadership team was first introduced to the DOCS via a two-hour session with a facilitator. For purposes of creating a unified leadership response to any questions that might be asked by employees, it was important that everyone understand the reason for the assessment and the research that supported the assessment. Employees were asked to sign up for small-group sessions in which they heard an overview of the culture survey process. Confidentiality was assured during this session, and questions were answered. The survey was administered to 218 employees. After the survey process was complete, the facilitator analyzed the results and met with the CEO, followed by a two-hour debriefing with the entire leadership team. After the leaders were informed, the CEO shared an overview of the results at an all-employee meeting.

The 2002 results identified key strengths, especially in the area of too close Team Orientation and Capability Development (Involvement) as well as Vision and Strategic Direction and Intent (Mission). There were notable cultural gaps, however, in internal operations, such as living the stated Core Values, reaching Agreement, and Coordination and Integration. Also noted was a minor gap in understanding the actual Goals and Objectives. The overall Strategic Intent was understood, as was the Vision; however, the specific "steps" identified by leadership to create forward movement were not as clear as they could be. There were also significant gaps in the organization's ability to Create Change, Customer Focus, and Organizational Learning.

When the results of the survey were analyzed by division, the leader of each functional area learned how his or her area was performing. In the end, the results in most functional areas looked much like those of the organization. However, the data in certain functional areas contributed significantly to the gaps noted in the organization's results.

Phase 3: Conduct the Post-Assessment Activities

Members of the leadership team were asked to prepare a plan of action, or roadmap, for addressing the strengths and the gaps in their functional areas. The leaders subsequently presented the roadmaps to the leadership team and to their own divisional leaders.

In 2008, the CEO wanted to formally measure the organization against the 2002 results. Over the years, the CEO had used the 2002 results to guide the development of annual strategic plans. Division leaders and function directors had used the results as a guide for leading more effectively. In addition, the CEO had provided coaching to the leaders who needed more support.

The 2008 survey was administered to 226 employees. The results of the second culture survey provided data that identified organizational improvements. It also supported the CEO's efforts to pinpoint areas of weakness in leadership and coach specific leaders toward higher levels of skill and greater successes.

An increase in people seeking to work for this organization was also seen as validation of the survey and follow-up actions. The CEO recognized that the new and potentially skilled employees provided additional bench strength to the organization.

This example shows how a complex needs assessment was used to conduct an organizational culture survey. Next, we examine how the complex needs assessment approach was used to determine an organization's environmental and occupational safety and health needs.

EOSH Training

Environmental and occupational safety and health (EOSH) regulations and requirements play an important role in assuring workplace health and safety. So it is not surprising that federal, state, and local governments and industries and organizations have them. In some cases, these regulations and requirements overlap and/or give conflicting guidance. Thus, assessing an organization's EOSH training needs requires:

- An in-depth understanding of the organization

- Knowledge of the applicable EOSH regulations and requirements

- Expertise in assessing knowledge and skill needs

Below is a case study, shared by Thomas Wood, MS, CSP, that assesses an organization's strategic training needs for EOSH. Notice that this case shows how a knowledge and skills assessment was supplemented to include the identification of applicable EOSH regulations and requirements for the organization and for various organizational departments.

CASE

PHASE 1: CONDUCT THE PRE-ASSESSMENT

Gather Preliminary Data

The objective of this needs assessment was to identify the required EOSH knowledge and skills for the Flight Inspection Services Aircraft Maintenance and Engineering Group (AMEG). Among other responsibilities, this group maintains and operates a fleet of aircraft. Although extensive EOSH training had been conducted, operational changes and the results of surveys and audits by internal and external parties pointed to the need for improved regulatory compliance and improvements to the organization's EOSH training process.

This needs assessment had the simple goal of identifying the existing and desired states of the EOSH training program and also determining the means to close the gap between the two. The

intended outcome of the project was an EOSH strategic training plan that would include the training profiles that showed the
required training for each job, information about the training gaps,
and the training schedule necessary to achieve compliance at the
earliest feasible date.

Plan for Data Collection, Analysis, and Reporting

The needs assessment plan was to

1. Identify the applicable EOSH regulations and requirements,
2. Collect information from supervisors on the EOSH requirements for each job,
3. Collect data from employee training records on the EOSH
   training that had been acquired,
4. Analyze the information from the first two steps to
   identify patterns and then use a training profile to document the required EOSH training for the jobs in the
   organization,
5. Identify training gaps by comparing the training profiles with
   employees' training records,
6. Create an EOSH training schedule that established compliance with mandatory training as soon as possible, and
7. Prepare and present the results to the organization's management team.

Wood was charged with spearheading the project, assisted
by three other members of the EOSH technical team and an
employee who represented a standing employee work group. These
individuals comprised the needs assessment committee. They were
responsible for implementing the needs assessment and developing
the EOSH strategic training plan. The EOSH strategic training
plan was to be reported to the director of maintenance and all
second-level managers within AMEG.

Phase 2: Conduct the Needs Assessment

During this phase, the needs assessment plan was implemented. The steps of the needs assessment built on each other.

The EOSH training needs for AMEG consisted of the knowledge and skills that were specified by internal and external training requirements and identified by supervisors as required to perform the work and that the employees had not acquired.

Step 1. Identify the Applicable Regulations and Requirements

This step identified (a) the AMEG activities that may be subject to internal and external training requirements and (b) the training requirements that apply to AMEG operations. These requirements included:

- Regulations issued by the USDOL Occupational Safety and Health Administration (OSHA). U.S. Environmental Protection Agency (USEPA), the USDOT Pipeline and Hazardous Materials Safety Administration (PHMSA), and the Oklahoma Department of Environmental Quality and sister agencies in Alaska, California, Georgia, Michigan, and New Jersey
- National consensus standards (e.g., National Fire Protection Association's National Fire Code and the Compressed Gas Association's Pamphlet P-1, Safe Handling of Compressed Gases)
- Agency training requirements, including those issued by the FAA and the Office of Facility Management at the Mike Monroney Aeronautical Center
- Requirements established by the Flight Inspection Service's (FIS) Environmental Management System
- The results of safety, health, and environmental hazard analyses and risk assessments performed by AMEG and FIS EOSH technical professionals
- "Competencies," as defined by the FIS Environmental Management System

The synthesis of these regulations and requirements revealed a total of eighty-two different training requirements that potentially applied to AMEG operations and activities.

Step 2. Collect Information from Supervisors

AMEG supervisors were queried to determine which of the eighty-two training requirements were necessary for each job. Their comprehensive understanding of AMEG operations and activities was essential to finalizing the assessment. A form was developed to collect interview/survey information from each supervisor in the organization. The form included a list of identified training requirements and descriptions of the courses that would meet each requirement, plus the learning objectives for each course.

The data-collection form was distributed to supervisors. Some supervisors chose to complete and return the form, while Wood completed the form for others using telephone or personal interviews.

Step 3. Collect Data from Employee Training Records

Employees' training records were downloaded from the enterprise's learning management system (eLMS).

Step 4: Analyze the Data

This phase involved compiling the data that were collected in Steps 1 and 2 of Phase 2 into a series of Excel spreadsheets, carefully examining and analyzing the data, and developing nine profiles that identified the EOSH training required for specific groups of jobs. One profile identified the courses required for all AMEG employees. Each of the other eight profiles identified courses for specific functional groups. Three sample profiles are shown in Figure 8.3. Note that the number of required training courses for each profile ranged from two to twenty-nine.

Profile 1. All AMEG employees (six applicable courses)

AME EOSH Orientation
ATO Employee General EOSH Awareness–Rights and Responsibilities
ATO Employee General EOSH Awareness–Safety Orientation
Emergency Response
Environmental Awareness
Flight Line Access Safety and Security

Profile 2. Administrative and office personnel (two courses)

Office Ergonomics
Office Safety

Profile 3. Managers and supervisors (six courses)

Managers and Supervisors EOSH Awareness
Accident Investigation
SMIS Awareness Training
OSHA 300 Recordkeeping
Office Ergonomics
Office Safety

FIGURE 8.3 *Sample EOSH Training Profiles, Showing the Training Required for Three Groups of AMEG Employees*

Step 5. Identify Training Gaps

The data collected from employee training records in Step 3 also were transferred to an Excel spreadsheet and were compared with the training profiles that were developed in Step 4. The training records were used to determine the extent to which the required EOSH training had already been completed by various personnel within each training profile and the organization as a whole.

Step 6. Create the Strategic Plan for EOSH Training

The training gaps identified in Step 5 were analyzed and compared with the information that had been collected in Step 1 of the needs assessment, the applicable EOSH regulations, and company requirements. This analysis was combined with the information collected in the other needs assessment steps to create a strategic plan for EOSH training. It included the training profiles, statistical and summary information about the training gaps, and an eighteen-month plan for completing the training. (An example of the EOSH Strategic Plan Training Schedule is shown in Figure 8.4.)

Profile and Courses	2013									2014										
	Apr	May	June	July	Aug	Sept	Oct	Nov	Dec	Jan	Feb	Mar	Apr	May	June	July	Aug	Sept	Oct	Nov
ALL AMEG EMPLOYEES																				
Environmental Awareness		▓																		
ATO Rights and Responsibilities			▓																	
ATO Safety Orientation				▓																
Emergency Response	TBD																			
AMEG EOSH Orientation	NA																			
Flight Line Access Safety and Security	NA																			

Profile and Courses	2013									2014										
	Apr	May	June	July	Aug	Sept	Oct	Nov	Dec	Jan	Feb	Mar	Apr	May	June	July	Aug	Sept	Oct	Nov
ADMINISTRATIVE AND OFFICE EMP																				
Office Ergonomics		▓																		
Office Safety			▓																	

Profile and Courses	2013									2014										
	Apr	May	June	July	Aug	Sept	Oct	Nov	Dec	Jan	Feb	Mar	Apr	May	June	July	Aug	Sept	Oct	Nov
SUPPLY TECHNICIANS																				
Fire Extinguisher Training		▓												▓						
Manual Material Handling				▓																
Personal Protective Equipment					▓															
Chemical Spill and Response, Part 1							▓												▓	
HazMat Shipping Awareness								▓												▓
Waste Management								▓												
Compressed Gas Safety										▓										
Hazard Communication	TBD																			
Powered Industrial Vehicle Part 1	Supvsr																			
Forklift Operator Training	Supvsr																			

FIGURE 8.4 *Example of an EOSH Strategic Plan Training Schedule*

225

Step 7: Prepare and Report Results

Upon completion, the EOSH strategic training plan was distributed to the director of maintenance and all second-level managers within AMEG. With the data analyzed and organized, Wood also prepared and submitted an updated EOSH training program, which established the AMEG EOSH training curriculum to be used going forward.

Phase 3: Conduct Post–Assessment Activities

Despite the significant commitment of resources necessary to implement the EOSH strategic training plan, it was approved and implemented. The organization's training team was assigned responsibility for executing the plan, and time markers were established for monitoring its progress. As the plan was implemented, a model for evaluating both the plan and its course components was being formulated and was set to be fully developed within the first sixty days.

Lessons Learned

While the needs assessment initially focused only on regulatory compliance, the data and the analysis led to changes in perspective. Ensuring compliance became a secondary goal of the needs assessment, and the decision-makers, the analyst, and the needs assessment committee concurred that the primary goal became improving both individual knowledge and skills and enhancing overall organizational safety performance.

CONCLUSION

This chapter described the three phases of the complex needs assessment approach: (1) conduct the pre-assessment, (2) conduct the needs assessment, and (3) conduct the post-assessment. Three case studies showed how the complex needs approach has been used to assess the needs in actual organizations. In each case, the pre-assessment activities were critical to the eventual success of the project.

A complex needs assessment is the appropriate approach when the needs cannot be determined solely by analyzing the knowledge and skills required to perform the work, the jobs and tasks, the competencies that are required to perform jobs, or the strategic needs. A complex needs assessment is especially appropriate when systemic or non-training needs must be determined.

III

Managing a Needs Assessment

NINE Writing Proposals and Reports

PURPOSE

This chapter will enable you to accomplish the following:

- Explore the process of contracting a needs assessment.
- Review the purposes of a needs assessment proposal.
- Consider practical tips for writing a needs assessment proposal.
- Use the needs assessment checklist.
- Learn how to use the needs assessment proposal, the in-process reports, and the final report to manage the needs assessment.
- Learn how to manage needs assessment documents.

RELATED TOOLKIT JOB AIDS

The following job aids for use with the material in this chapter are available in the Needs Assessment Toolkit, which can be found in Section Four of this book:

- Needs Assessment Checklist
- Needs Assessment Proposal Template
- Needs Assessment Interim Report Template

OVERVIEW

Managing a needs assessment project begins with the first client meeting and ends when the client accepts the final report. With practical project-management skills, a needs assessment can be completed efficiently and in a way that builds goodwill among those who participate. Regardless of which needs assessment approach or model you select, you should consider how you will contract the needs assessment, manage documents, and report progress.

> **Tip**
>
> Working on a poorly managed needs assessment feels like following a runaway train. You may not know where the train is going, but you sure can monitor its progress by following the billowing steam, hot air, damage, and destruction.

CONTRACTING A NEEDS ASSESSMENT

Contracting is the first and most critical step in the consulting process. It includes meeting with the client for the first time, writing the proposal, and obtaining the contract. A needs assessment contract is an agreement for a project that specifies the desired outcomes or processes, the timeline, what each party will do, and the budget.

Block (2011) defined a consultant as someone who has "some influence over an individual, a group, or an organization but has no direct power to make changes or implement programs" (p. 2). Most analysts, whether they are hired from outside or work internally in an organization, are consultants. They report to a client or decision-maker who has the authority to address the sensed need.

During their first meeting, the analyst and the client size each other up. They decide whether they really want to work together, and they consider the best ways to accomplish the needs assessment. Indeed, this meeting is like a job interview. Usually, the first meeting between the analyst and the client centers on the following concerns:

- The nature of the sensed problem

- The context surrounding the problem

- The resources that various stakeholders, including the client and the analyst, bring to the project

- The timeframe for the effort

The client wants to know whether the analyst has a strong work ethic, a track record of producing the expected results in similar situations, the competencies required to complete the project, ethical standards, and the skills to limit the costs by applying efficient methods. Implementing an effective needs assessment requires many competencies (International Board of Standards for Training, Performance, and Instruction®, 2005; King, 1998; Rothwell, 1996), including the following:

- Knowledge about the organization or community environment

- Knowledge about performance improvement, management, and systems thinking

- Skill in consulting, problem-solving, negotiating, and advocating for change

- Skill in collecting data using such methods as focus groups, interviews, observation, surveys, and archival data

- Skill in analyzing qualitative and quantitative data

- Skill in exchanging information in informal oral communications, in writing, and in presentations

- Ability to collaborate effectively with the client and the project stakeholders

- Knowledge and skills in applying relevant needs assessment theories and models

- Ability to manage the needs assessment project effectively

- Ability to negotiate outcomes that maximize performance and learning

- Knowledge of ethical standards and skills in following these standards

The analyst wants to know the purpose of the needs assessment. Royse, Staton-Tindall, Badger, and Webster (2009) noted that the purpose can be crystal clear or somewhat vague. They also suggested asking questions, such as the ones below, if the expectations for the needs assessment are unclear:

- Why is the needs assessment being planned at this point in time? (What is the driving motivation behind the needs assessment? Has a particular problem or issue arisen that is the catalyst?)
- What is the purpose of the needs assessment?
- Who will use the needs assessment? (Who must be convinced? What data are needed?)
- How will the needs assessment be used?
- What do we hope to accomplish with the needs assessment?
- When is the report needed? (How much urgency is there?) (p. 28).

The analyst also must consider whether the needs assessment is likely to be successful. Key questions that the analyst should answer before agreeing to implement a needs assessment include the following:

- Can the project use his or her knowledge, skills, and abilities?
- Does the client seek information for making decisions and taking action, or is the needs assessment window dressing for decisions that have already been made?
- Does the decision-maker have the power to take action based on needs assessment information?
- Do those who have a critical stake in the needs assessment, such as the decision-makers, customers, or influential community members, support the project?

- What are the expectations of the client and project stakeholders regarding ongoing communications?
- Do the client and project stakeholders act ethically?
- Are sufficient resources available to complete the project?

When answers to any of these questions reveal that issues exist, consider ways to address them before agreeing to conduct the needs assessment. Some additional potential obstacles and tips for overcoming them are shown in Figure 9.1.

If possible, avoid conducting a needs assessment when there are insufficient resources, the timeline is too short, the decision-maker lacks the authority to take action based on the project findings, or unethical behaviors are promoted. If you cannot avoid the project, check out the consulting strategies suggested by Block (2011) and McNamara (2005) for ways to minimize the problems.

Following are some potential needs assessment obstacles ("O") and their suggested solutions ("S").

O   Lack of consensus about goals.
S   Gain consensus by obtaining the commitment of the decision-maker(s) and communicating that commitment throughout the organization.
S   Gain consensus by convening an advisory group consisting of a senior leader, a mid-level manager, and members of the target group.
S   Revisit the goals of the organization and ensure that the assessment ties in with one or more goals.

O   Senior management supports the effort, but line managers or supervisors do not.
S   Obtain buy-in from a line manager or supervisor who can influence other managers.
S   Seek the intervention of senior management and make the assessment a priority for middle managers.

FIGURE 9.1 *Potential Needs Assessment Obstacles and Tips for Overcoming Them*

O   Lack of a sponsor with authority.
S   Seek the support of someone in a higher position.
S   Create a needs assessment committee comprised of influential people who have a stake in the needs assessment process and results.

O   Too much background information to review in a reasonable time.
S   Revisit the goals of the assessment, establish priorities, and discard information that is not relevant to the assessment.
S   Enlist one or more groups within the organization to summarize the critical information for you.
S   Enlist the needs assessment committee to help prioritize and summarize the critical information.
S   In a community, contact other social service agencies and find out whether they previously sponsored a needs assessment on the issue.

O   Conflict about types of data that must be collected.
S   Revisit the goals of the assessment.
S   Convene a needs assessment committee, as described earlier, to review the data-collection plan and resolve the conflicts.

O   Bias in favor of a particular instrument.
S   Show the benefits of other instruments.

O   Resistance to questioning (such as from middle management or special interest groups).
S   Promote awareness about the benefits of the assessment through informational meetings.
S   Ask senior leaders to intervene and make the needs assessment a priority.
S   Explain the needs assessment process and how the results will be used.

O   Lack of access to those working night shifts or people assigned to restricted work areas.
S   Find alternative personnel.
S   Obtain special permission to gather data.

FIGURE 9.1 *Potential Needs Assessment Obstacles and Tips for Overcoming Them* (continued)

O Disagreement among team members about the methods for collecting or analyzing data.
S Seek the opinion of a third party, such as the decision-maker, the needs assessment committee, or a specialized expert (for example, a statistician).

O Lack of willingness on the part of people to change when implementing a new system or technology.
S Create a change readiness program.
S Engage leaders as spokespersons indicating the need for the new system or technology.

O Attitude of "Who has the time to complete another survey?"
S Obtain buy-in by having the decision-maker(s) endorse the process.
S Explain benefits to users.
S Share the project timeline, which shows the dates for sharing survey results and taking actions.
S Offer incentives for completing the instrument.

O Lack of buy-in to needs assessment results (especially negative or controversial findings).
S Present the positive findings first and emphasize the need to reinforce strengths and address issues.
S Present alternatives to overcome negative or controversial findings.
S Present "negative" findings as opportunities for improvement.

FIGURE 9.1 *Potential Needs Assessment Obstacles and Tips for Overcoming Them* (continued)

Tip

When contracting, if your gut feels queasy or the hair on the back of your neck stands up, consider whether you want to be involved in the needs assessment and whether the planned action is really appropriate, and at the same time, check the ethical guidelines in Chapter Ten.

During the first client meeting, the analyst gathers information to use in drafting a written proposal. For example, the analyst records precisely the client's description of the need, including the words and phrases that the client uses to describe the context, the stakeholders' roles, and the problems or opportunities. After the analyst and the client decide that a written proposal is warranted, the analyst may request copies of organization documents that are relevant to the project, including the mission statement, the strategic plan, marketing materials, organization charts, annual reports, project descriptions, and financial information. These documents can provide insights into the ideas, language, and initiatives that are important in the organization. The information in the documents that is relative to the needs assessment can be summarized and included in the proposal.

The client and analyst also share expectations regarding how communications and updates will occur during the needs assessment. Our recommendation is that the process and results of each phase of the project be shared with the client and appropriate stakeholders as soon as the phase is complete. Some clients prefer that the information be shared in person, and some prefer that the information be shared using a combination of email and phone.

Some clients prefer that the needs assessment be billed at an hourly rate, while others prefer that the consultant quote a cost for the entire project in the proposal. In the latter case, the consultant should carefully consider specifics about what will be required to complete the project. Toolkit Form 9.1 is a checklist for thinking about the important aspects of gathering preliminary data, planning the needs assessment, collecting data, analyzing the information, preparing the report, and making the presentation. Figure 9.2 lists four of the questions appearing in the Toolkit form.

Tip

To obtain written records that show the correct spellings of stakeholders' names and their current titles, exchange business cards. You can encourage others to share their business cards by passing out your own card when introducing yourself.

Gather Preliminary Data
1. Have you had preliminary meetings to gather information from your client and other key people?
2. Have you considered the ethical issues that may arise while gathering preliminary data and the ethical standards that can guide your actions?
3. Have you obtained senior management's perspectives about the goals of the assessment?
4. Have you identified the attitudes of learners and other stakeholders toward the needs assessment and the new program, process system, training, or technology?

FIGURE 9.2 *Some Questions from Toolkit Form 9.1: Needs Assessment Checklist*

THE NEEDS ASSESSMENT PROPOSAL

The needs assessment proposal documents the consultant's insights on the project's purpose, phases, processes, expected outcomes, timeline, and expenses. At the beginning of a needs assessment, the proposal frames an ambiguous situation to some extent and presents a plan of action for completing the proposed project. It also establishes the tone of the project—for example, that the project will be a collaborative effort among the client, the analyst, and the stakeholders—and clarifies responsibilities. Figure 9.3 shows a sample needs assessment proposal. (See Toolkit Form 9.2 for the template.)

After the proposal is drafted, the client and the analyst review it together to ensure that the analyst has accurately understood the sensed problem and the context, and that the planned process for completing the needs assessment is appropriate and achievable.

During the meeting, the analyst revises the initial proposal to reflect decisions on how the needs assessment will be implemented. Most misunderstandings at this point can be negotiated. This review may occur in person, by telephone, or online. Once the proposal is approved by the client, it may serve as a written contract.

Draft Proposal:
Needs Assessment for T & J Marine Products

Submitted to: Tom Sloboth
Plant Manager
T & J Marine Products
Street
City, State, Zip
Phone number/email address

Submitted by: Sally Burns
Human Resource Development Consultant
Address
City, State, Zip
Phone number/email address

Date: XX/XX/XXXX

Version 1

FIGURE 9.3 *Draft Needs Assessment Proposal: T & J Marine Products*

Purpose

T & J Marine Products (T & J's) manufactures and markets products for water sports and pleasure boating. The plant is not meeting its strategic goals of increasing market leadership in two areas: developing new products and implementing new product distribution systems. The plant manager believes that a lack of supervisory knowledge and skills contribute to the failure.

The needs assessment will accomplish the following:

1. Determine if, when, where, and how the lack of supervisory knowledge and skills affects workplace performance.
2. Prioritize the supervisory training that is needed to meet the strategic goals.

The needs assessment has five phases. The table on the next page shows each project phase, the purpose of the phase, the process for completing the phase, the expected outcomes, and the projected due date. Upon completion of each phase, the analyst and the plant manager will review an interim report that details the phase's process and outcomes. They will also review the proposed processes for completing the remainder of the project, especially the next phase. All data collection will be completed on-site; however, all data analysis and report writing will be completed off-site. The analyst will group the data; no individual data will be reported. Note that this needs assessment focuses on knowledge and skill needs. Consequently, if Phase 1 of the project, Gather preliminary data about the sensed needs, reveals that a lack of knowledge and skills does not contribute significantly to the performance problem, the needs assessment will be redesigned or discontinued.

Staffing

Sally Burns, the consultant for this project, is a certified performance technologist. She has worked with many organizations to address their learning and performance needs. She subscribes to the ethical guidelines of ISPI and the Academy of Human Resource Development. She recognizes that training and non-training solutions can contribute to improved performance. She also values participation in the needs assessment by all those who may be affected by the solutions.

Cost

The costs are $150 per hour. The firm will reimburse the analyst for such agreed-upon expenses as travel and copying. The firm will also provide administrative assistance for scheduling interviews and observations and a work station for the duration of the project. This contract may be renegotiated at any time as needed.

Version 1

FIGURE 9.3 *Draft Needs Assessment Proposal: T & J Marine Products* (continued)

Overview of the Needs Assessment

	Phase 1: Gather preliminary data about the sensed needs	Phase 2: Plan the needs assessment	Phase 3: Analyze knowledge and skill requirements	Phase 4: Analyze the data	Phase 5: Prepare the final report
Purpose	• Establish goals • Determine whether and how the lack of supervisory knowledge and skills affects T & J	• Develop a work plan to ensure that the assessment stays on target	• Develop the assessment tools and collect the assessment data	• Interpret the collected data using systematic and useful processes	• Document the needs assessment process and outcomes
Process	• Review organization, performance, and industry data • Interview two managers, two supervisors, and the human resource development director • Summarize each interview and review the summary document with the interviewee	• Review the process for this phase and revise if needed • Determine what types of data must be collected and the sources of data • Determine the types of data-collection tools that will be used • Determine the types of analyses that must be performed • Decide how data will be collected and managed	• Review the process for this phase and revise if needed • Develop each assessment tool • Validate, pilot-test, and obtain approval for each tool from the HRD director and the plant manager • Review the draft data-collection process with those who will be involved in it and revise the process based on their feedback • Collect the data • Monitor the data-collection process • Organize the data	• Review the process for this phase and revise if needed • Compile the qualitative data (e.g., the stories) • Compile the quantitative data (e.g., survey results) • Meet with supervisors to report the needs assessment results • Draft the training priorities • Review the draft analysis and training priorities with the plant manager • Meet with those who will be affected to review the draft analysis and training priorities	• Review the process for this phase and revise if needed • Combine information from all phases of the needs assessment • Meet with management to report the needs assessment results

Out-come	A draft report that (1) summarizes the archival data reviewed and the interviews, (2) establishes goals for the assessment, and (3) describes whether and how lack of supervisory skills affects T & J's performance and whether the solution should include training, and (4) identifies non-training solutions that could contribute to performance improvement	A draft report that recommends (1) the type of data to be collected, (2) the data sources, (3) the types of data-collection tools to be used, (4) the types of analysis to be performed, and (5) how the collected data will be managed	A draft report that (1) documents the needs assessment tools and describes the validation, pilot testing, and approval processes, (2) describes the meeting to review the data-collection process with stakeholders and any revisions to the process, and (3) describes how data were collected, monitored, and organized for analysis	A draft report of the analyzed data and training priorities that is disseminated to those who are involved in the process with a request for their feedback	The final needs assessment report
Due Date	April 3	April 19	May 17	June 2	June 9

Version 1

FIGURE 9.3 *Draft Needs Assessment Proposal: T & J Marine Products* (continued)

243

> **Tip**
>
> Before reviewing the draft proposal with a client, the analyst can state that changes in the document are expected. Normally, the client and analyst together identify a few terms or steps in the process that require clarification. The client's revisions to the proposal indicate his or her commitment to the project. When the draft proposal is revised, be sure to include these edits.

Ways to Use the Needs Assessment Proposal

A written needs assessment proposal serves many purposes. As previously described, it initially frames the project and, once approved, serves as a written contract for the needs assessment. As such it serves as the benchmark for interim and final reports and for renegotiating the needs assessment, if necessary. The proposal is not written in stone; it should be renegotiated as expectations shift. Of course, such renegotiations may affect the project's outcomes, costs, and timeline.

The table in the proposal, the Overview of the Needs Assessment, can be used as a standalone document to prevent project creep or project shrink. **Project creep** occurs when the scope of a project keeps growing. **Project shrink** occurs when the scope of the project keeps getting smaller. To prevent either situation, use the table to guide the implementation of your needs assessment. Complete the needs assessment in phases as specified on the table. At the end of each phase, provide the client an interim report that documents the processes and outcomes for the phase. Before moving to the next phase, meet with the client to review the interim report, obtain the approval for the completed work, and use the Overview of Needs Assessment to confirm that the expectations for the next phase. As conditions change in organizations, such reviews can prevent wasted efforts. When changes do occur, you and the client can document them using the table, thus creating a record for the needs assessment.

You also can use the Overview of the Needs Assessment as a visual map of the project. When meeting with stakeholders, interviewees, and those who will provide documents or be observed, share a copy of the table. It enables others to quickly understand the project phases and the ways in which individual efforts contribute to the larger needs assessment project.

Finally, the Overview of the Needs Assessment serves as an organizer for the final report. We describe this nifty use of the table later in the chapter.

Practical Tips for Writing a Needs Assessment Proposal

Following are some practical tips for writing a needs assessment proposal:

- The cover page should contain the project name, the client's name and contact information, the analyst's name and contact information, and the date. If you ever have dug through a pile of papers on your desk to find important information about a project, you will realize the importance and convenience of having contact information on the cover page.

- Check and double-check spellings, especially names, proper nouns, and organization-specific terms.

- Write the proposal in business language. Use organization-specific language and keep to the point. Most needs assessment proposals for business are three to six pages, but there are times when a longer proposal is needed. Typically, proposals for government agencies are longer, so check with your client about the proposal format, length, and content.

- In the purpose section, remind the reader why the project is important and the value of the expected accomplishment.

- Because most problems require both training and non-training solutions, consider addressing both in the needs assessment proposal. Do so in a way that considers the analyst's skills and that is appropriate for the client and the organization. (*Note:* this often requires conferring with the client.)

- Verify budgetary constraints so that recommendations are reasonable and on target.

- Place the cost section at the end of the document so the client sees it after he or she understands the way in which the needs assessment is framed and the plans for completing it.

- Document each revision to the needs assessment proposal in writing, update the version number, and date the document. (The revised document can be referenced if a new client joins the project or if any disagreement later arises about the project.)

- Number the pages of the proposal, and staple or bind the proposal if sending a paper copy.

In business, a proposal that is accepted or approved by the client usually becomes the contract for the needs assessment. In a government agency, the contracting office often refers to the proposal in the official contract. To protect both the client and the analyst, it is usually best to document the contract in writing. With the contract in place, the analyst can focus on completing the phases of the needs assessment.

MANAGING NEEDS ASSESSMENT DOCUMENTS

A quick review of Figure 9.3, the draft needs assessment proposal, reveals that every phase involves collecting, analyzing, and synthesizing data. Consequently, the number of documents that the analyst uses and creates can become overwhelming unless they are organized and well managed, especially in a large needs assessment. To avoid losing information that is irreplaceable or wasting time thumbing through documents to find just the right one, analysts create a project management system and routinely organize needs assessment information as it is collected.

Most needs assessment projects include digital documents (such as electronic reports and files) and printed documents (such as company brochures and business cards), so the project management systems should accommodate both online and printed documents. A project management system can include a physical folder for each of the following elements:

- Contact information (such as business cards)
- Background information
- Each phase of the project
- Project notes
- Budget and cost information
- Miscellaneous information
- Copies of project documents

An inexpensive file box works well for storing such materials: it keeps everything organized in one place and does not take up much space in the office. Furthermore, it is portable, so project materials can be available at meetings.

The project management system also usually includes electronic folders for online documents, such as background materials, reports, collected data, and analyzed data. Having prearranged locations for all needs assessment materials and reports and back-up copies of computer files makes it easier to write reports and can save hours of work.

Reports

A needs assessment project typically includes interim reports and a final report. An interim report documents the purpose, process, outcomes, and timeline for one phase of the needs assessment. Toolkit Form 9.2 is a template for an interim needs assessment report. Such reports, which are reviewed with the client at the completion of each needs assessment phase, are a key to successfully completing the needs assessment as proposed.

With a government contract, there may be the need for reports that are produced on a quarterly basis and not necessarily linked to a phase of the project. Also, check with your client about whether the final report can consist of a compilation of the proposal and all the interim reports, together with a brief introduction or if another format will be needed. (Alternative forms of reporting can be found in Torres, Preskill, & Piontek, 2005.)

Each report typically begins with an Executive Summary that briefly summarizes the report and is positioned between the report's cover page and the other report sections. The Executive Summary provides a framework for understanding the larger report. It is especially important that the Executive Summary be clear and concise and that it contain the information to support the needs assessment results. Remember that your audience may read only the executive summary and not the larger report (Watkins, Meiers, & Visser, 2012). Because of its importance, the Executive Summary is typically written after the final report has been completed.

During the needs assessment, the client and other stakeholders review the interim reports and provide feedback that keeps the needs assessment project on track. Equally important, the process of reviewing reports engages stakeholders in the needs assessment, which facilitates later implementation of its solutions.

> **Tip**
>
> A needs assessment report highlights some aspects of a situation and minimizes other aspects. Think carefully about what you highlight and minimize!

To quickly draft an interim report, use the Overview of the Needs Assessment table from the approved proposal. Use your word processing program to copy and paste the column for the current phase into a new document. Revise the text to reflect what actually occurred, add a cover page, format the document, and add the Overview of Needs Assessment as an attachment. (See Toolkit Form 9.3 in Section Four of this book.) Figure 9.4 shows an interim report for Phase 1 of the T & J Marine Products Needs Assessment.

Draft Interim Report
Needs Assessment for T & J Marine Products
Phase 1: Gather preliminary data about the sensed needs

Submitted to: Tom Sloboth
                     Plant Manager
                     T & J Marine Products
                     Street
                     City, State, Zip
                     Phone number/email address

Submitted by: Sally Burns
                     Human Resource Development Consultant
                     Address
                     City, State, Zip
                     Phone number/email address

Date: XX/XX/XXXX

Version 1

FIGURE 9.4 *Phase 1 Interim Report for T & J Marine Products*

Executive Summary

This first phase of the needs assessment gathered preliminary data about the sensed needs. The outcomes of this phase provide the foundation for Phase 2 of the needs assessment. The goals, process, findings, and recommendations for this phase are summarized here.

Goals:

1. Establish goals for the assessment.
2. Determine whether and how the lack of supervisory knowledge and skills affects T & J's performance.

Process:

The needs assessment process for this phase included the following steps:

1. Review organizational, performance, and industry data.
2. Interview two managers, two supervisors, and the human resource director.
3. Summarize each interview and review the document with the interviewee.

Findings

1. The market for water sports and pleasure boating is changing. To compete effectively, T & J must meet its strategic goals.
2. Lack of consistent processes and walking the talk by upper management caused some lack of trust.
3. Interviewees recognized that the boating industry has become more competitive, and they wanted more timely information to use in improving their performance.
4. Some interviewees are competent in telling managers what they want to hear rather than in reporting the actual situation.
5. Supervisors need additional knowledge and skills in people management in order to achieve the strategic goals.
6. Non-training needs that should be addressed to improve performance include improving feedback from managers and improving work processes by eliminating unnecessary process steps.

Recommendations: The Phase 1 results indicate that, for T & J to achieve its strategic goals, the supervisors need additional knowledge and skills in people management. To improve performance most effectively, non-training needs should be addressed at the same time.

Version 1

FIGURE 9.4 *Phase 1 Interim Report for T & J Marine Products* (continued)

Phase 1: Gather preliminary data about the sensed needs

Goal

The goal of this first phase of the project was twofold:

1. Establish goals for the assessment.

2. Obtain a broad understanding of whether and how the lack of supervisory knowledge and skills affects T & J's performance and whether the solution should include training. (See Attachment A: Overview of Needs Assessment.)

Process

Completing this phase of the needs assessment involved the following steps:

1. Review organizational, performance, and industry data.

2. Interview two managers, two supervisors, and the human resource development director.

3. Summarize each interview and review the document with the interviewee.

Step 1: Review organizational, performance, and industry data

To complete this step, the following organizational data were reviewed:

- Strategic plan
- Organization chart
- Marketing reports for product areas
- Product development plan
- Product distribution plan
- T & J's culture survey results for 2011 and 2013

The following performance data were reviewed:

- The performance reports for each unit

The following industry data were reviewed:

For the boating industry:

- Boating Industry (magazine) annual statistical review
- Recreational Boat Building Industry home page: http://www.rbbi.com

For water sports:

- www.roho.co.uk
- www.boothandel.nl
- www.nauticfriend.com

Version 1

FIGURE 9.4 *Phase 1 Interim Report for T & J Marine Products* (continued)

Step 2: Interview a manager, two supervisors, and the human resource director

The analyst conducted these unstructured interviews between April 6 and April 10. The Interview Guide is in Appendix B. The interviewees were chosen based on their key roles in contributing to the organization's strategic goals. The analyst began each interview by describing the purpose of the needs assessment, how the interviewee was chosen to participate in the needs assessment, and how information from the interview would be used. Each interviewee was told that information would be grouped for reporting and that only triangulated information (that is, information that was obtained from more than one person or one data-collection method) would be reported. Notes were taken during each interview, and they were also digitally recorded as a back-up.

Step 3: Summarize each interview and review the document with the interviewee

After the analyst summarized the interviews, each interviewee reviewed the text of his or her interview and noted points of clarification. The interviews were revised to reflect these changes.

Phase 1 Findings

The findings below were obtained from at least two people or by at least two data-collection methods:

1. The market for water sports and pleasure boating is changing. To compete effectively, T & J must meet its strategic goals.

2. Lack of consistent processes and walking the talk by upper management caused some lack of trust.

3. Interviewees recognized that the boating industry has become more competitive, and they wanted more timely information to use in improving their performance.

4. Some interviewees are competent in telling managers what they want to hear rather than in reporting the actual situation.

5. Supervisors need additional knowledge and people management skills in order to achieve the strategic goals.

6. Non-training needs that should be addressed to improve performance include improving feedback from managers and improving work processes by eliminating unnecessary process steps.

Version 1

FIGURE 9.4 *Phase 1 Interim Report for T & J Marine Products* (continued)

Recommendations

Summary: For T & J to achieve its strategic goals, the supervisors need additional knowledge and skills in people management. One example is to motivate and communicate with their teams using strategic performance reports. The outcomes of this phase provide the foundation for Phase 2 of the needs assessment. To improve performance most effectively, non-training needs should be addressed at the same time.

Attachments

A. Overview of Needs Assessment [Note: This section of the proposal could be inserted here.]

B. Interview Guide [Note that the Strategic Issues Worksheet (Toolkit Form 7.1) would be inserted here.]

Version 1

FIGURE 9.4 *Phase 1 Interim Report for T & J Marine Products* (continued)

Most needs assessment projects also require a final report. If you have been providing interim reports and maintaining contact with the client, the final report with its findings and recommendations will not come as a surprise. Below is a list of the sections that are usually found in a formal report, along with suggestions on how to create the sections efficiently.

- Executive Summary (typically a page)

- Purpose (Copy and paste this from the proposal.)

- Process (Suggestion: Here's a nifty use for the proposal's Overview of Needs Assessment. Use it to organize this section and follow it with the executive summaries from the interim reports.)

- Findings (Create this section using all findings from interim reports. Include pie charts, graphs, and diagrams as appropriate to highlight key findings.)

- Recommendations (Create this section based on the findings.)

- Appendix, including supporting instruments and data (Attach the proposal and the interim reports, which should already contain all supporting instruments and data.)

In-Person Oral Reports and Presentations

In-person oral reports and presentations provide an opportunity for the client and other stakeholders to ask questions, discuss the findings, and consider the implications of the needs assessment. In other words, such reports and presentations provide a forum that enables the needs assessment stakeholders to own the results. The focus of discussion during the final needs assessment meeting is on the needs assessment report, which documents both the needs assessment process and findings.

The following are guidelines for these presentations:

- Report the positives that you found in the situation first. Report your findings about potential improvements honestly and in a way that respects all the stakeholders. Identify problem areas cited by multiple sources, and recommend one or more feasible actions.

- Tailor the presentation style to the culture of the organization and to the decision-makers' preferences. Today, many oral presentations rely on PowerPoint slides, but check with the client before preparing the presentation. Avoid the mistake made by the consultant who presented a group of decision-makers in a fast-paced organization with a fifty-page report. That consultant, after spending many hours writing the report, was disappointed when nobody read it.

- Estimate the return on investment (ROI) for the proposed recommendations, when appropriate. Some people are uncomfortable forecasting the value of needs assessment recommendations by estimating ROI. However, as Tobey (2005) pointed out, estimates such as these are used every time people predict the future in business and, moreover, such estimates are useful because they are made by the people who are experts in a particular aspect of the business. Before using the ROI calculation, confirm with the client and key stakeholders that the estimate is reasonable.

Additional information on how to calculate and use cost-benefit analysis can be found in Chapter Two. Also, you can find additional information and examples of ROI calculations in Kaminski and Lopes (2009) and Phillips (2003).

- Structure the meeting to move from the known and easy to the unknown and more difficult. Use the needs assessment proposal to remind everyone about the situation at the start of the needs assessment.

- Recognize that some people may want to edit the report. If their edits are fitting, accept them. If their edits are problematic, you may need to explain why you did not include the ideas in your report.

- Support your recommendations with citations from authorities in the field and your knowledge of industry best practices.

Tip

Hale (2005) pointed out that performance improvement professionals often cram their language and models into the clients' head. While as experts we need to know the professional ideas, language, and models, Hale advised that when we work with clients we should avoid using our jargon and as much as possible talk to clients in their own language.

CONCLUSION

Managing the needs assessment process is essential to completing the project effectively and in a timely manner. Most needs assessments are not implemented exactly as they are proposed and must be modified. For example, an interviewee may be on vacation during the time for data collection or a new decision-maker may join the project and wish to make changes. Manage the needs assessment process to allow for flexibility, stakeholder input, and progress, and thus increase the probability that the client will use the needs assessment findings. The next chapter focuses on ethics, which can also influence how needs assessment projects are conducted and how findings are used.

TEN Dealing with Ethical Issues

PURPOSE

This chapter will enable you to do the following:

- Examine ethical issues relevant to needs assessments.

- Refer to the codes of ethics used by several different professional organizations.

OVERVIEW

In this chapter, we focus on an area where expert-level insights are critical—the ethical issues that can arise during a needs assessment. The chapter begins by presenting some real-life needs assessment issues for you to consider based on your personal ethics. Then it examines the codes of ethics (which are sometimes called guidelines or standards) that have been adopted by various professional organizations. These can serve as invaluable resources for improving your thinking about your own moral values and principles for conduct and for aligning your personal values with accepted professional values.

ETHICS IN NEEDS ASSESSMENT

Most decisions in a needs assessment involve value judgments, and value judgments often lead to ethical issues. Because a needs assessment is built on the trust of everyone who participates, your personal integrity and your ability to negotiate skillfully such issues as confidentiality, conflict of interest, data representation, and so forth are critical to achieving a successful needs assessment and the later implementation of your recommendations.

CASE

Ethical issues in needs assessment are often linked. For example, when the U.S. Centers for Disease Control and Prevention (CDC) collects needs assessment data for HIV-prevention programs, they must protect the confidentiality of individuals who are tested for HIV infection. Simultaneously, the CDC must ensure that the agency collects accurate data for decision making on the rate of HIV transmission. Thus, the needs assessment should be designed to address the ethical issues related to confidentiality, respect for patients' rights, and data accuracy. In this case, CDC must assure accuracy of client data without using client names.

Knowing your personal values before you start a needs assessment is helpful in establishing and managing others' expectations for your actions in specific situations. Figure 10.1 presents examples of issues that have arisen in actual needs assessments. As you read them, consider how well you know your own personal values.

Most needs assessments are by nature political, because they involve either support for or challenges to those who are in power. In such situations, ethics are likely to be important.

Ethical Issues or Not; You Decide.

As you read each of the following real-life scenarios, decide whether ethical issues are involved and what appropriate actions you could take.

- During a random review of organization documents, you discover that a manager has downloaded child pornography from the Internet.

- Your client guesses the name of an interviewee who made negative comments in a confidential interview. She plans to "correct the person's misperceptions."

- A person on the needs assessment team misrepresents the data in hopes of influencing an external agency to fund developmental activities that she believes will be beneficial for the agency.

- A colleague asks to use the job and task data you are collecting to negotiate a higher salary.

- While conducting a competency analysis for a division, the firm's president tells you confidentially that the division will be shut down and that your client (the HR manager), who does not yet know this information, will be laid off.

- The well-known instrument your team uses to determine needs for individual development and education has never been validated (and may be providing erroneous information), but clients really like the results and find them useful.

- You realize that your client's goal for the needs assessment is to provide objective data that will support his department's claim for an increased share of the organization's budget.

- You recognize the questions on an interview guide that your company plans to use, because you saw the questions posted on a vendor's website and noticed that they were copyrighted.

- The company's online employee engagement survey is promoted as collecting information from all employees in the company; however, only a few non-exempt employees have access to a computer at work.

- Executives would like to receive the names of the highest rated employees based on the needs assessment data so that these employees can be recognized.

FIGURE 10.1 *Examples of Needs Assessment Ethical Issues*

Because needs assessment is a type of evaluation, two particularly useful resources for needs assessment practitioners are the Program Evaluation Standards and the Guiding Principles for

Evaluators. We review each of these resources below and then provide links to some additional resources for managing ethical issues in needs assessments.

Joint Committee on Standards for Educational Evaluation (JCSEE), Program Evaluation Standards

In 1975, twelve professional organizations that had concerns about the conduct of evaluations (including needs assessments) formed the Joint Committee on Standards for Educational Evaluation. This committee publishes the Program Evaluation Standards. The third edition of these standards is shown in Figure 10.2 The thirty standards support the following five core attributes of evaluation quality: utility, feasibility, propriety, accuracy, and accountability.

You can find additional information about JCSEE Standards and their applications at the JCSEE website (www.jcsee.org) or in *The Program Evaluation Standards: A Guide for Evaluators and Evaluation Users* (3rd ed.; Yarbrough, Shulha, Hopson, & Caruthers, 2011).

American Evaluation Association, Guiding Principles

Although the Joint Committee's Program Evaluation Standards already existed, members of the American Evaluation Association felt it was important for the organization to develop its own set of principles. The Guiding Principles for Evaluators, which is shown in Figure 10.3 focus on the following five areas:

- Systematic inquiry

- Competence

- Integrity and honesty

- Respect for people

- Responsibilities for the general and public welfare

The Program Evaluation Standards and Statements

Utility Standards

The utility standards are intended to increase the extent to which program stakeholders find evaluation processes and products valuable in meeting their needs.

- **U1. Evaluator Credibility** Evaluations should be conducted by qualified people who establish and maintain credibility in the evaluation context.

- **U2. Attention to Stakeholders** Evaluations should devote attention to the full range of individuals and groups invested in the program and affected by its evaluation.

- **U3. Negotiated Purposes** Evaluation purposes should be identified and continually negotiated based on the needs of stakeholders.

- **U4. Explicit Values** Evaluations should clarify and specify the individual and cultural values underpinning purposes, processes, and judgments.

- **U5. Relevant Information** Evaluation information should serve the identified and emergent needs of stakeholders.

- **U6. Meaningful Processes and Products** Evaluations should construct activities, descriptions, and judgments in ways that encourage participants to rediscover, reinterpret, or revise their understandings and behaviors.

- **U7. Timely and Appropriate Communicating and Reporting** Evaluations should attend to the continuing information needs of their multiple audiences.

- **U8. Concern for Consequences and Influence** Evaluations should promote responsible and adaptive use while guarding against unintended negative consequences and misuse.

Feasibility Standards

The feasibility standards are intended to increase evaluation effectiveness and efficiency.

- **F1. Project Management** Evaluations should use effective project management strategies.

- **F2. Practical Procedures** Evaluation procedures should be practical and responsive to the way the program operates.

- **F3. Contextual Viability** Evaluations should recognize, monitor, and balance the cultural and political interests and needs of individuals and groups.

- **F4. Resource Use** Evaluations should use resources effectively and efficiently.

FIGURE 10.2 *Program Evaluation Standards and Statements*

Source: Joint Committee on Standards for Educational Evaluation.

Propriety Standards

The propriety standards support what is proper, fair, legal, right and just in evaluations.

- **P1. Responsive and Inclusive Orientation** Evaluations should be responsive to stakeholders and their communities.
- **P2. Formal Agreements** Evaluation agreements should be negotiated to make obligations explicit and take into account the needs, expectations, and cultural contexts of clients and other stakeholders.
- **P3. Human Rights and Respect** Evaluations should be designed and conducted to protect human and legal rights and maintain the dignity of participants and other stakeholders.
- **P4. Clarity and Fairness** Evaluations should be understandable and fair in addressing stakeholder needs and purposes.
- **P5. Transparency and Disclosure** Evaluations should provide complete descriptions of findings, limitations, and conclusions to all stakeholders, unless doing so would violate legal and propriety obligations.
- **P6. Conflicts of Interest** Evaluations should openly and honestly identify and address real or perceived conflicts of interests that may compromise the evaluation.
- **P7. Fiscal Responsibility** Evaluations should account for all expended resources and comply with sound fiscal procedures and processes.

Accuracy Standards

The accuracy standards are intended to increase the dependability and truthfulness of evaluation representations, propositions, and findings, especially those that support interpretations and judgments about quality.

- **A1. Justified Conclusions and Decisions** Evaluation conclusions and decisions should be explicitly justified in the cultures and contexts where they have consequences.
- **A2. Valid Information** Evaluation information should serve the intended purposes and support valid interpretations.
- **A3. Reliable Information** Evaluation procedures should yield sufficiently dependable and consistent information for the intended uses.

FIGURE 10.2 *Program Evaluation Standards and Statements* (continued)

Source: Joint Committee on Standards for Educational Evaluation.

- **A4. Explicit Program and Context Descriptions** Evaluations should document programs and their contexts with appropriate detail and scope for the evaluation purposes.

- **A5. Information Management** Evaluations should employ systematic information collection, review, verification, and storage methods.

- **A6. Sound Designs and Analyses** Evaluations should employ technically adequate designs and analyses that are appropriate for the evaluation purposes.

- **A7. Explicit Evaluation Reasoning** Evaluation reasoning leading from information and analyses to findings, interpretations, conclusions, and judgments should be clearly and completely documented.

- **A8. Communication and Reporting** Evaluation communications should have adequate scope and guard against misconceptions, biases, distortions, and errors.

Evaluation Accountability Standards

The evaluation accountability standards encourage adequate documentation of evaluations and a meta-evaluative perspective focused on improvement and accountability for evaluation processes and products.

- **E1. Evaluation Documentation** Evaluations should fully document their negotiated purposes and implemented designs, procedures, data, and outcomes.

- **E2. Internal Meta-Evaluation** Evaluators should use these and other applicable standards to examine the accountability of the evaluation design, procedures employed, information collected, and outcomes.

- **E3. External Meta-Evaluation** Program evaluation sponsors, clients, evaluators, and other stakeholders should encourage the conduct of external meta-evaluations using these and other applicable standards.

FIGURE 10.2 *Program Evaluation Standards and Statements* (continued)

Source: Joint Committee on Standards for Educational Evaluation. www.jcsee.org/program-evaluation-standards/program-evaluation-standards-statements. Used with permission.

American Evaluation Association's Guiding Principles for Evaluators

A. Systematic Inquiry: Evaluators conduct systematic, data-based inquiries.

1. To ensure the accuracy and credibility of the evaluative information they produce, evaluators should adhere to the highest technical standards appropriate to the methods they use.

2. Evaluators should explore with the client the shortcomings and strengths both of the various evaluation questions and the various approaches that might be used for answering those questions.

3. Evaluators should communicate their methods and approaches accurately and in sufficient detail to allow others to understand, interpret and critique their work. They should make clear the limitations of an evaluation and its results. Evaluators should discuss in a contextually appropriate way those values, assumptions, theories, methods, results, and analyses significantly affecting the interpretation of the evaluative findings. These statements apply to all aspects of the evaluation, from its initial conceptualization to the eventual use of findings.

B. Competence: Evaluators provide competent performance to stakeholders.

1. Evaluators should possess (or ensure that the evaluation team possesses) the education, abilities, skills and experience appropriate to undertake the tasks proposed in the evaluation.

2. To ensure recognition, accurate interpretation and respect for diversity, evaluators should ensure that the members of the evaluation team collectively demonstrate cultural competence. Cultural competence would be reflected in evaluators seeking awareness of their own culturally-based assumptions, their understanding of the worldviews of culturally-different participants and stakeholders in the evaluation, and the use of appropriate evaluation strategies and skills in working with culturally different groups. Diversity may be in terms of race, ethnicity, gender, religion, socio-economics, or other factors pertinent to the evaluation context.

3. Evaluators should practice within the limits of their professional training and competence, and should decline to conduct evaluations that fall substantially outside those limits. When declining the commission or request is not feasible or appropriate, evaluators should make clear any significant limitations on the evaluation that might result. Evaluators should make every effort to gain the competence directly or through the assistance of others who possess the required expertise.

FIGURE 10.3 *Guiding Principles for Evaluators*

Source: American Evaluation Association.

4. Evaluators should continually seek to maintain and improve their competencies, in order to provide the highest level of performance in their evaluations. This continuing professional development might include formal coursework and workshops, self-study, evaluations of one's own practice, and working with other evaluators to learn from their skills and expertise.

C. Integrity/Honesty: Evaluators display honesty and integrity in their own behavior, and attempt to ensure the honesty and integrity of the entire evaluation process.

1. Evaluators should negotiate honestly with clients and relevant stakeholders concerning the costs, tasks to be undertaken, limitations of methodology, scope of results likely to be obtained, and uses of data resulting from a specific evaluation. It is primarily the evaluator's responsibility to initiate discussion and clarification of these matters, not the client's.

2. Before accepting an evaluation assignment, evaluators should disclose any roles or relationships they have that might pose a conflict of interest (or appearance of a conflict) with their role as an evaluator. If they proceed with the evaluation, the conflict(s) should be clearly articulated in reports of the evaluation results.

3. Evaluators should record all changes made in the originally negotiated project plans, and the reasons why the changes were made. If those changes would significantly affect the scope and likely results of the evaluation, the evaluator should inform the client and other important stakeholders in a timely fashion (barring good reason to the contrary, before proceeding with further work) of the changes and their likely impact.

4. Evaluators should be explicit about their own, their clients,' and other stakeholders' interests and values concerning the conduct and outcomes of an evaluation.

5. Evaluators should not misrepresent their procedures, data or findings. Within reasonable limits, they should attempt to prevent or correct misuse of their work by others.

6. If evaluators determine that certain procedures or activities are likely to produce misleading evaluative information or conclusions, they have the responsibility to communicate their concerns and the reasons for them. If discussions with the client do not resolve these concerns, the evaluator should decline to conduct the evaluation. If declining the assignment is unfeasible or inappropriate, the evaluator should consult colleagues

FIGURE 10.3 *Guiding Principles for Evaluators* (continued)

Source: American Evaluation Association.

or relevant stakeholders about other proper ways to proceed. (Options might include discussions at a higher level, a dissenting cover letter or appendix, or refusal to sign the final document.)

7. Evaluators should disclose all sources of financial support for an evaluation, and the source of the request for the evaluation.

D. Respect for People: Evaluators respect the security, dignity and self-worth of respondents, program participants, clients, and other evaluation stakeholders.

1. Evaluators should seek a comprehensive understanding of the important contextual elements of the evaluation. Contextual factors that may influence the results of a study include geographic location, timing, political and social climate, economic conditions, and other relevant activities in progress at the same time.

2. Evaluators should abide by current professional ethics, standards, and regulations regarding risks, harms, and burdens that might befall those participating in the evaluation; regarding informed consent for participation in evaluation; and regarding informing participants and clients about the scope and limits of confidentiality.

3. Because justified negative or critical conclusions from an evaluation must be explicitly stated, evaluations sometimes produce results that harm client or stakeholder interests. Under this circumstance, evaluators should seek to maximize the benefits and reduce any unnecessary harms that might occur, provided this will not compromise the integrity of the evaluation findings. Evaluators should carefully judge when the benefits from doing the evaluation or in performing certain evaluation procedures should be foregone because of the risks or harms. To the extent possible, these issues should be anticipated during the negotiation of the evaluation.

4. Knowing that evaluations may negatively affect the interests of some stakeholders, evaluators should conduct the evaluation and communicate its results in a way that clearly respects the stakeholders' dignity and self-worth.

5. Where feasible, evaluators should attempt to foster social equity in evaluation, so that those who give to the evaluation may benefit in return. For example, evaluators should seek to ensure that those who bear the burdens of contributing data and incurring any risks do so willingly, and that they have full knowledge of and opportunity to obtain any benefits of the evaluation. Program participants should be informed that their eligibility to receive services does not hinge on their participation in the evaluation.

FIGURE 10.3 *Guiding Principles for Evaluators* (continued)

Source: American Evaluation Association.

6. Evaluators have the responsibility to understand and respect differences among participants, such as differences in their culture, religion, gender, disability, age, sexual orientation and ethnicity, and to account for potential implications of these differences when planning, conducting, analyzing, and reporting evaluations.

E. Responsibilities for General and Public Welfare: Evaluators articulate and take into account the diversity of general and public interests and values that may be related to the evaluation.

1. When planning and reporting evaluations, evaluators should include relevant perspectives and interests of the full range of stakeholders.

2. Evaluators should consider not only the immediate operations and outcomes of whatever is being evaluated, but also its broad assumptions, implications and potential side-effects.

3. Freedom of information is essential in a democracy. Evaluators should allow all relevant stakeholders access to evaluative information in forms that respect people and honor promises of confidentiality. Evaluators should actively disseminate information to stakeholders as resources allow. Communications that are tailored to a given stakeholder should include all results that may bear on interests of that stakeholder and refer to any other tailored communications to other stakeholders. In all cases, evaluators should strive to present results clearly and simply so that clients and other stakeholders can easily understand the evaluation process and results.

4. Evaluators should maintain a balance between client needs and other needs. Evaluators necessarily have a special relationship with the client who funds or requests the evaluation. By virtue of that relationship, evaluators must strive to meet legitimate client needs whenever it is feasible and appropriate to do so. However, that relationship can also place evaluators in difficult dilemmas when client interests conflict with other interests, or when client interests conflict with the obligation of evaluators for systematic inquiry, competence, integrity, and respect for people. In these cases, evaluators should explicitly identify and discuss the conflicts with the client and relevant stakeholders, resolve them when possible, determine whether continued work on the evaluation is advisable if the conflicts cannot be resolved, and make clear any significant limitations on the evaluation that might result if the conflict is not resolved.

FIGURE 10.3 *Guiding Principles for Evaluators* (continued)

Source: American Evaluation Association.

> **5.** Evaluators have obligations that encompass the public interest and good. These obligations are especially important when evaluators are supported by publicly-generated funds; but clear threats to the public good should never be ignored in any evaluation. Because the public interest and good are rarely the same as the interests of any particular group (including those of the client or funder), evaluators will usually have to go beyond analysis of particular stakeholder interests and consider the welfare of society as a whole.

FIGURE 10.3 *Guiding Principles for Evaluators* (continued)
Source: American Evaluation Association. http://eval.org/Publications/GuidingPrinciples.asp. Used with permission from the American Evaluation Association.

Tip

The table below compares the two ethical codes described above. Use it to see quickly the areas of overlap and the differences in the codes. Notice that the AEA Guiding Principles provide more general statements, while the Joint Committee Standards are more specific and detailed.

AEA Guiding Principles	Program Evaluation Standards
Systematic Inquiry	Accuracy Standards; Accountability Standards
Competence	Utility Standards; Feasibility Standards
Integrity and Honesty	Propriety Standards
Respect for People	Propriety Standards
Responsibilities for the General and Public Welfare	

ADDITIONAL RESOURCES FOR MANAGING ETHICAL ISSUES

Additional resources for identifying and managing ethical issues can be found at the websites listed below.

- International Society for Performance Improvement, Human Performance Technology Code of Ethics: www.ispi.org
- Academy of Human Resource Development, Standards on Ethics and Integrity: www.ahrd.org

- American Psychological Association, Ethical Principles of Psychologists and Code of Conduct: www.apa.org/ethics/

- ASTD Code of Ethics: www.astd.org/About/Mission-and-Vision

- Canadian Evaluation Society Guidelines for Ethical Conduct: www.evaluationcanada.ca/site.cgi?s=5&ss=4&_lang=EN

- Australiasian Evaluation Society Code of Ethical Conduct and Guidelines for the Ethical Conduct of Evaluations: www.aes.asn.au/membership-ethical-guidelines.html

- Standards für Evaluation (DeGEval-Standards): www.degeval.de/degeval-standards

Tip

Skim these resources for addressing ethical issues now, so you know where to find assistance when specific issues arise in a needs assessment.

As you examine these websites, you likely will notice both similarities and differences in their content. For example, ASTD's code of ethics focuses on the moral code for self-managed learning and development professionals. By contrast, the primary goal of the Academy of Human Resource Development Standards on Ethics and Integrity was to "define more clearly a holistic balance among individuals, groups, organizations, communities, and societies whenever conflicting needs arise" (Russ-Eft, Burns, Dean, Hatcher, Otte, & Preskill, 1999, p. ii).

CONCLUSION

This chapter focused on the ethical issues you may confront when conducting a needs assessment. The ethical codes adopted by professional associations and your personal moral issues can provide useful insights for managing difficult ethical issues.

ELEVEN

Answers to Frequently Asked Questions

PURPOSE

This chapter will enable you to learn answers to frequently asked questions about needs assessments.

OVERVIEW

In this chapter we present answers to the questions that are commonly asked about needs assessments. You can use these answers to improve the utility, feasibility, propriety, accuracy, and accountability of your needs assessment projects.

COMMONLY ASKED QUESTIONS AND THEIR ANSWERS

Following are eight commonly asked questions about needs assessments and their answers.

   1. *Some people tell me that reports of previous needs assessments are collecting dust in their offices. How can I make sure the findings from my needs assessment are used?*

Consider the following strategies for increasing the usability of your needs assessments:

- *Select projects carefully.* Before agreeing to work on a project, find out whether the proposed project addresses performance or learning requirements that are important to the project's client and stakeholders. Also determine whether they have the needed authority, visible support for the project, and desire to take action. Determine whether the project is likely to produce findings that are relevant, timely, and useful. Examine the political context, including the level of consensus among key stakeholders. Identify potential obstacles to a successful outcome and work with your client to determine if and how the obstacles can be overcome before agreeing to conduct the needs assessment.

- *Involve the client and stakeholders in the needs assessment process in ways that are meaningful to them.* Involve them in learning and decision making regarding the needs assessment process and facilitate their participation in implementing the findings.

- *Form a needs assessment advisory committee (NAC).* This committee can provide you with advice on how to conduct the needs assessment and how to use the results (Baizerman, Fink, & Roholt, 2012). Such committees can offer technical and ethical advice, legitimacy, political power, credibility and/or prestige. Committee members also may serve as champions for using the needs assessment results as part of their normal activities and interactions with other needs assessment stakeholders, including individuals from the funding source, the target program or organization, and the larger community.

- *Realize that the seemingly logical process of implementing a needs assessment may actually modify the situation.* That is, the needs assessment is an intervention. During an effective needs assessment, the client and stakeholders adjust their perceptions and gain new insights. The interpersonal dynamics in a situation often change during the data-collection and analysis process. These adjustments in perceptions, values, and power dynamics are often as powerful as the needs assessment findings that are documented in the final report.

- *Implement the needs assessment in phases and use the findings from each phase as the basis for action in the next phase,* as was illustrated in the sample needs assessment proposal in Chapter Nine.

- *Keep the needs assessment focused on the agreed-upon purpose.* Conduct regular meetings with the client and stakeholders to review the needs assessment purpose and the current progress toward that purpose. Negotiate any proposed changes in the purpose with the client and stakeholders. Be sure to document any changes in writing. Also, do not allow the needs assessment process to be subverted for personal gain.

- *If the needs assessment findings were not used, explore the reasons for this decision with the client.* Determine if some of these reasons can be overcome, and ascertain whether some parts of the recommendations can be implemented.

2. How does successive approximation work in a needs assessment?

Michael Allen (2003) described a problem with using the traditional ADDIE process to develop e-learning—it takes too long. ADDIE is a systematic model of instructional design that was developed in 1975 for the U.S. Army (Clark, 2013). ADDIE's five-phase process to develop instruction or training includes analysis, design, development, implementation, and evaluation. Allen advocated replacing ADDIE with successive approximation.

Allen noted that the ADDIE model requires perfectly executing each phase of the model before turning to the next phase. By contrast, successive approximation relies on improving prototypes through an iterative process of design, creation, and evaluation. The successive approximation process starts with some essential information that is critical to making good decisions. The information need not be complete or entirely correct, but it provides a place to start. Then, the process moves very quickly to rapid prototyping, and "evolves the most promising design into the best application possible within given constraints" (p. 142). Successive approximation is best used when the costs of design, development, and evaluation are low and the level of agreement among stakeholders regarding training needs as a solution is high.

3. How can I avoid having the needs assessment results used for actions that may create long-term problems for the organization, such as inappropriate lay-offs and downsizing?

Needs assessment findings often point to an opportunity for developing people within an organization. However, some organizational leaders may view the findings as an opportunity to remove individuals and reduce costs, even if such behavior negatively affects organizational performance. Here are a few suggestions for avoiding such actions:

- As part of the proposal and contracting process, learn whether the project addresses important performance requirements and discuss alternatives for addressing those requirements. Be alert for discussions of actions you consider problematic and be prepared to dissuade such actions or surface them to the NAC and/or the project's sponsor for discussion.

- Examine previous organizational experiences with needs assessments and determine how the results were used. If previous needs assessments led to inappropriate actions, discuss these with the client before deciding whether or not to proceed with the proposed project.

- Examine the political situation, including the views of key stakeholders. Determine, in advance, the possibilities for misuse of the findings.

- Keep the needs assessment focused on its stated purpose and objectives. This may be best achieved by conducting regular meetings with the client and stakeholders to review the purpose and the current progress.

- If you are conducting the needs assessment in a for-profit company, recognize that layoffs and downsizing may be necessary for the firm to stay in business or to make the desired level of profits. Alternatively, decision-makers may think that cost-cutting is the best way to compete. If the latter is the case, you can share recent research. A statistical study of companies based on their performance (that is, return on assets) revealed the three choices that the exceptional companies made: (1) they competed on differentiators rather than price, (2) they prioritized increasing revenue over reducing costs, and (3) they changed whatever had to be changed to follow rules 1 and 2 (Raynor & Ahmed, 2013).

4. *This book emphasizes stakeholder involvement, but how do I deal with multiple stakeholders at various levels throughout the organization?*

This is a very common situation, particularly in large and complex organizations. One tip is to recognize that stakeholders can participate in various ways throughout the needs assessment process. The case below describes an actual needs assessment that was provided by Kelly M. Hannum and Emily R. Hoole, Center for Creative Leadership. Globious (a pseudonym) is a global health care solutions provider with operations in close to 150 countries.

The case shows how the analysts involved many stakeholders who were at different organizational levels and geographic locations by using a survey, interviews, and focus groups. For more information on the data-collection instruments that were used in this case, check out Example Data-Collection Instruments from Globius Case Study (Toolkit Form 11.1 on the website for this book).

CASE

WHY THE NEEDS ASSESSMENT WAS CONDUCTED

Globious had recently established an Asia Corporate University to provide leadership development for leaders at all levels regionally and at a lower cost. A target audience for the university is mid-level leaders at or below the country manager level. The Asia Pacific region is an area of high growth for the company, so the quality and quantity of leaders who can effectively execute the strategy and continue to achieve the challenging business targets are of critical importance to the continued success of the business. In order to design appropriate and effective leadership development, additional information about the organizational needs for leadership development were required.

The core questions to be addressed included:

- What is the organization trying to accomplish through leadership development?
- Which outcomes matter to the different stakeholder groups?
- What competencies and capabilities are most important for leadership effectiveness?

WHO CONDUCTED THE NEEDS ASSESSMENT

The Center for Creative Leadership was engaged as the vendor to conduct the needs assessment in service of designing and delivering leadership development.

WHO SPONSORED THE NEEDS ASSESSMENT

The head of the Asia Corporate University who is also in a global learning and development role helped to co-design and sponsor the work.

THE NEEDS ASSESSMENT PROCESS

A needs assessment process was designed to gather information addressing the core questions (listed above). The needs assessment process focused on gathering three types of data: Leadership Gap Indicator (LGI) assessment data and qualitative data from interviews and focus groups. These components are described in detail below.

Assessment data were gathered to determine the leadership strengths and gaps of the target population from the perspectives of senior leaders and leaders at the target level. This was accomplished by administering the Leadership Gap Indicator (LGI) assessment, customized using the Globious leadership competencies to understand which leadership competencies are most important now and which competencies will be more important in the future, along with ratings of current levels of performance. The assessment process was designed to allow for disaggregation of data by organizational divisions, countries of operation, and other relevant demographic variables (based on sufficient sample size). These data were used to empirically investigate whether training needs clustered into groups based on strengths and weaknesses.

In-depth exploration of the specific challenges and needs of leaders within Globious was accomplished through interviews and focus groups, which examined the following questions:

- What are the specific challenges this level of leaders experience in their role, division, country, and region?
- What is the unique value proposition of this level to the organization in relation to the business strategy for the next five to seven years in emerging and established markets in the region?
- What is this group's perception of the leadership culture within Globious, along with understanding the developmental climate and expectations for developmental programs?

Interviews and focus groups were conducted in three countries and with multiple divisions within the region:

- Thirty interviews were conducted with a sample of senior leaders and leaders at the target level.
- Interviews with the managers of the target leaders were conducted to get the perspective of the most strategic leaders working directly with the target audience. This included all relevant division heads.
- Focus groups were conducted with Globious employees who report to the targeted leaders (direct reports and others at lower organizational levels) to gain a broader perspective and increase the depth of understanding to uncover challenges and issues for this level which would not be captured in interviews or LGI assessment.

INTERESTING CHALLENGES OR ISSUES

While the response rate for the LGI assessment was acceptable at close to 70 percent, senior leaders in the region were disappointed in the level of participation. The design clearly demonstrated the value of combining the survey with interviews and focus groups as a number of the gaps identified in the survey were not the same as those surfaced during the interview and focus group processes. A much stronger picture of the context and gaps relevant to the external environment, country culture, and division emerged when triangulated across the three data sources.

The sponsor of the work had good relationships with the senior leaders, and most people were aware of the work, the purpose of it, and the need for it. This was helpful when it came to scheduling interviews and focus groups.

Analysis of the multiple sources of data was complex, because it required examining and interpreting information across leader levels (senior/target), the three countries, and three divisions.

However, that level of detail was meaningful and helpful to the organization.

THE OUTCOMES

A number of profiles were developed for use by senior leaders in the region as well as for the design of development experiences for the target leader levels, including the following:

- Profile of an exceptional leader in the region
- Profile of current leaders—identifying gaps between this current state and the exceptional leader profile
- Derailment profile of current leaders by country and division
- Profile of the external and business environment for these leaders by country and division
- Leadership challenges at this level by country and division
- Developmental climate profile for the organization by country and division

HOW THE OUTCOMES WERE USED

Senior leaders in the region had the opportunity to collaboratively process the results of the needs assessment in combination with a recent regional study on leadership and talent practices conducted by a global consulting firm. By combining the internal Globious data with the external study, these leaders were able to make decisions and recommendations for the development of key talent for the region to guide the work of the Asia Corporate University.

LESSONS LEARNED

It is essential to have information from a variety of sources, because you cannot always depend on survey data to provide the contextual information needed, and interviews and focus groups may provide too small of a sample to generalize.

We also had a diversity of nationalities on the team, including members from China, Singapore, India, and the United States, and this was helpful as the leaders we interviewed were also very diverse. The company uses global job rotation heavily, so the leaders we interviewed were most often not from the country we were in. Using female interviewers allowed us to gain the trust of female leaders who were interviewed and gather more insightful data. Male leaders were comfortable sharing as well.

Interestingly, it appeared from the data we gathered that company culture trumped country culture for the most part. There was strong consistency across the countries in the values, but the ways in which these values were constructed within the countries varied. For example, achievement was highly valued in all countries, and it was clear that means achieving the challenging business targets, but for one country an 80 percent solution or 80 percent effort was deemed acceptable, whereas the leaders are trying to get 110 percent effort. So the cultural differences are important in how values are constructed and enacted.

5. *This book emphasizes stakeholder participation in the needs assessment project, but should I involve people who do not want to participate?*

If the needs assessment is conducted by one person and the findings and decisions that result affect only that person, then little collaboration is required. However, we know of few such situations. More commonly, needs assessments involve multiple participants, shared decision making, and shared responsibility for ensuring that the findings of the needs assessment are implemented to produce the expected results.

Learning why the stakeholders do not want to participate is a starting point for action. Consider obtaining answers to the following questions:

• Does the individual understand the purpose and expectations for the needs assessment?

- Does the individual expect the needs assessment to result in a loss of personal power or power of a favored group?

- Is a larger social drama unfolding with increasing tension between the forces for change and the forces against change?

- Is the individual concerned that the needs assessment process may not produce accurate and appropriate findings?

- Does the individual feel that his or her opinions and insights will be ignored or used to cause personal harm or harm to others?

- Does the individual feel respected (or not respected) by the other stakeholders?

Once you know an individual's reasons for noninvolvement, you may address the issues by using the following tactics:

- Schedule a short meeting between you and the individual to clarify misunderstandings and highlight the benefits of collaboration.

- Consider discussing the noninvolvement with his or her supervisor to determine whether that person can support your work.

If the above tactics seem unsuccessful and the individual's collaboration is important to the needs assessment or to implementing its findings, discuss the issue with your client and develop a solution. For example, you may consider whether to let the individual excuse him- or herself or whether other changes can be made in the needs assessment process that would encourage participation. If you decide to let individuals excuse themselves, consider how this will impact the needs assessment findings and follow-up actions.

6. *Some authors describe needs assessment as a type of evaluation, and others describe needs assessment and evaluation as distinct processes. What is the relationship between needs assessment and evaluation?*

The purpose of evaluation is to determine the merit, worth, or value of something. There are many types of evaluation (for example, formative evaluation, summative evaluation, and needs assessment). *Needs assessment is a type of evaluation,* because it relies on data to determine the "merit, worth, or value" (Scriven, 1991, p. 139) of various needs in a situation and to negotiate the most effective way to address those needs.

Some people also use the term *evaluation* to describe the measurement of how something was done, the efficiency and effectiveness of actions, or the degree to which the solution produced the desired results. Thus, many HRD or HPT models show the needs assessment phase occurring at the beginning of a process and the evaluation phase occurring after an intervention has been designed, developed, and implemented. The term evaluation used this way can refer to measuring the entire intervention process or a phase in the process (such as the needs assessment phase). In the latter case, the evaluation could focus on the needs assessment process and outcomes to determine the efficiency and effectiveness of actions and the degree to which the process and results of the needs assessment matched the desired results.

7. *What additional resources could be especially helpful when conducting a needs assessment?*

Many good needs assessment resources are available. Figure 11.1 shows our favorites. We turn to such resources when working on a complex needs assessment or one that has high stakes for individuals or organizations. One cautionary note: authors define their terms, such as needs assessment, needs analysis, and performance analysis, in different ways.

8. *This book describes formal needs assessments. Are informal needs assessments ever useful?*

Yes! Informal assessments are an unspoken, natural part of communication. For example, two people meet in the hallway. One person assesses the situation, notices that the other is carrying a large stack of papers, and decides to submit an important report later. Below are a few additional common examples of questions that start an informal needs assessment:

- How is everything going in your group?
- Do you have all the tools you need for the next job?
- What is happening to slow down the project?

When assessments are shared informally with other group or organizational members, they become explicit (Jordan & Putz, 2004). The dialogue that results from sharing informal assessments can raise awareness of issues, produce information, provide support for individuals, and create the groundwork for future action.

Informal assessments are unlikely to provide the accurate facts and figures needed for evaluating future actions when they are based on flawed data collection or analysis. For example, a group of employees who discussed their unit's needs for change during their afternoon break may not realize that only those who agreed with the leader (and represented a small minority of the unit) voiced their opinions.

Another caution when using informal needs assessments is that they may lack stakeholder participation at the level required for future action. For example, three like-minded managers decided their direct reports would comply with a new procedure. They were surprised when their employees, who were angry with the decision, made sure that the new procedure was ineffective.

Situations that are highly politicized, complex, or resource-intensive usually require precise thinking, extensive negotiation, and documentation. A formal needs assessment is the right tool in such situations, because it prescribes a systematic process, documents one or more characteristics of the situation, and involves collaboration. However, in situations where there is high agreement and low costs, consider using an informal needs assessment. Also consider using informal needs assessment to get participation from stakeholders in a low-cost way.

Both formal and informal assessments are useful for investigating needs, identifying the causes of current performance, finding appropriate solutions, and building a momentum for action. Decide whether your situation requires an informal or formal needs assessment or a combination of both.

The case study below, which describes an informal needs assessment for executive officers from multiple organizations, was submitted by Cathy McCullough of McCullough Group (www.MLeadershipGroup.com).

CASE

In the world of needs assessments, there are two sides: informal and formal. The situation and the specified desired outcomes (as defined by the client) are keys to determining which type of analysis to use. Indeed, there are times when an informal (yet structured) needs assessment can produce very valid and validating results. In this case, an informal yet structured approach was used to guide executives in understanding the common leadership challenges they faced.

Seventy executive officers from different organizations were invited to participate in a roundtable discussion for the purpose of identifying common issues and challenges, if any. The seventy executives were all key decision-makers within their organizations (CEOs, COOs, CFOs, CTOs, GMs, etc.). They were from industries of all sizes and multiple sectors (manufacturing, technology, service, financial, and health care).

Prior to the meeting, each executive officer entered the room and selected a seat at any table. The only requirement was that two executives from the same company could not sit at the same table. Each table was set up for five people.

The session began with a brief general presentation by the facilitator. This presentation ended with the facilitator asking participants to individually list the top five challenges they faced as executive officers in their organizations. Once time was given for this individual activity, each table of executives was asked to have a discussion about their lists, noting any commonalities and/or major differences. Each table was asked to combine their lists into one master list of the top three challenges agreed upon by those at each table. Each table reported out to the larger group, and a master list of key challenges facing each group was recorded on a flip chart by the facilitator.

As each group shared their discussion with the larger group, trends began to emerge as to what the common challenges were for executive officers from industries of all sizes and all sectors (in no particular order):

- Streamlining processes
- How to cascade (communicate) a corporate strategy
- Attracting great people
- Dealing with difficult people
- Getting people to do what you need them to do
- Mysteries around how to motivate people toward higher levels of performance

KEY INSIGHTS

To the amazement of the executive officers in the room:

1. The challenges noted by the seventy executive officers all fell within one of these six categories.
2. The identified challenges had little to do with specific hard-core "technical" skills. Instead, their challenges were more around issues of organization development, leadership, and creating high-performance organizational cultures for growing into the future.

END RESULT

Twenty-two members of this larger group were later pulled together into an executive officer network. The members of this network met once per month in a confidential setting to create a platform for mutual problem solving around these (and other) common issues and challenges, as well as to share best practices relative to formal leadership within an organization. The facilitator of this network also provided outside perspectives and insights to each monthly discussion. One-on-one consultations were also provided to each member as requested.

1. **Resources with information on framing a needs assessment and data-collection and analysis techniques**. *Figuring Things Out* by Zemke and Kramlinger (1982) is a golden oldie that offers practical tactics for implementing a needs assessment, such as, "Start the study as high in the organization as possible and work your way down" (p. 8). It also describes how to implement data-collection techniques, including the popular ones (for example, observation and interview) and such techniques as consensus groups, fault tree analysis, and behavioral frequency counts.

Analysis for Improving Performance by Swanson (2007) provides tools for diagnosing organizational performance and tools for documenting four kinds of expertise: procedural, knowledge-based, and systems-based, and process-based. The synthesis tools that are described in the knowledge-based section are particularly helpful.

In *First Things Fast* (Rossett, 2009) describes how to accelerate a performance analysis, overcome organizational obstacles, and use technology in your analysis. In addition, this book contains many practical tips and examples that are down-to-earth and useable.

A Guide to Assessing Needs (2012) by Watkins, Meiers, and Visser describes how to conduct needs assessments that can provide the basis for justifiable decisions. The book also provides guidance, tools, and techniques for collecting data and for using data to make decisions. You can download the book for free at www.gapsinresults.com/.

The Needs Assessment Kit (Altschuld, 2010) includes five books:
- *Needs Assessment: An Overview*
- *Phase 1, Preassessment (Getting the Process Started)*
- *Phase 2, Assessment (Collecting Data)*
- *Phase 2, Assessment (Analysis and Prioritization)*
- *Phase 3, Post Assessment (Planning for Action and Evaluating the Needs Assessment)*

These books, contain a wealth of needs assessment experience that can be useful as a resource for especially complex needs assessments.

Needs Assessment for Organizational Success by Guerra-Lopez and Kaufman (2013) uses the framework of the Organizational Elements Model (OEM). The OEM has four levels of needs assessment, and each level has a unique focus:

FIGURE 11.1 *Additional Needs Assessment Resources*

- Mega-level: outcomes (societal results and consequences)
- Macro-level: outputs (organizational results)
- Micro-level: products
- Quasi needs: processes and inputs

2. **A research-based model for implementing a knowledge and skills assessment.** The Performance Analysis for Training (PAT) Model (Kunneman & Sleezer, 2000; Sleezer, 1990) can be a useful resource for a knowledge and skill assessment. The PAT model includes a set of worksheets that detail the phases, steps, and activities involved in determining the training needs in an organization. This model needs assessment has been researched and validated.

3. **Models of the human performance technology process.** The Performance Improvement/HPT Model (Van Tiem, Moseley, & Dessinger, 2012) shows the relationships among performance analysis; cause analysis; intervention selection, design, and development; intervention implementation and change; and evaluation.

4. **Books that describe HRD and HPT.** Two resources that discuss needs assessment as part of systematic approaches to HRD and HPT are *Handbook of Human Performance Technology* (Pershing, 2006) and *Foundations of Human Resource Development* (Swanson & Holton, 2009). If you are facing a complex situation, these resources may be especially helpful.

5. **Books that present various approaches to and tools for evaluation, including needs assessment.** *Evaluation in Organizations: A Systematic Approach to Enhancing Learning, Performance, and Change* (Russ-Eft & Preskill, 2009) describes various approaches to evaluation, along with a step-by-step process for designing and implementing such projects. *Building Evaluation Capacity: 72 Activities for Teaching and Training* (Preskill & Russ-Eft, 2005) elaborates the ideas from the previous book and provides worksheets and activities that can be used to engage stakeholders.

7. **Conferences sponsored by professional associations that have expert presentations on needs assessment.** The conferences that are sponsored by ASTD (www.ASTD.org) and the International Society for Performance Improvement (www.ispi.org) are good places to learn about cutting-edge practices. The Academy of Human Resource Development (www.ahrd.org) conferences are good places to learn about needs assessment research and scholarship and the ways in which they affect practice. The conference of the American Evaluation Association (www.eval.org) is a good place to learn about advances in needs assessment as part of evaluation.

FIGURE 11.1 *Additional Needs Assessment Resources* (continued)

CONCLUSION

This chapter provided answers to commonly asked questions. It also identified resources that you can use to extend your knowledge of needs assessment.

HRD, HPT, community development, and international development professionals who conduct needs assessments to improve learning and performance now work in challenging times. Learning and performance improvement has become more important than ever before for individuals, groups, organizations, communities, countries, and international groups. Moreover, new strategies offer more choices than ever before for collecting and analyzing data and reporting results; new research findings present fresh insights into how to improve learning and performance; new technologies provide innovations in communication and data management.

The information presented in this chapter, in combination with information from earlier chapters on needs assessment ideas, models, and approaches, data-collection and analysis strategies, and managing a needs assessment, can help you plan a needs assessment and also deal with issues as they arise. In addition, Part Four of this book contains Toolkit Forms to help you get started.

The assumptions and choices that you make at the beginning of learning, training, and performance improvement initiatives set their direction. This book highlights ways to use data to inform needs assessments, describes various choices that are available when planning and implementing a needs assessment, and provides a toolkit with ready-to-use templates, worksheets, and resources. Given the importance of needs assessment to HRD, HPT, community development, and international development initiatives, using this information to inform practice and improve the efficiency and effectiveness of needs assessments is well worth the effort.

IV
Needs Assessment Toolkit

TOOLKIT FORM 2.1 *Tools and Strategies for Assessing Systems*

Directions: Review the first column and identify the type of system pattern for your situation. Then consider the various assessment strategies and tools for that pattern that are listed in the second column.

Types of System Patterns	Assessment Strategies and Tools
Visible patterns that are easily measured	Identify the visible patterns using such complexity metaphors as the butterfly effect and edge of chaos.
	Distinguish among linear, nonlinear, and random; systemic and nonsystemic patterns.
	Use mathematical models (such as the Balanced Scorecard) to track mutually causal factors.
	Use the 15 percent concept. Gareth Morgan (2006) states that in a work situation, a person has only about 15 percent control, because 85 percent of the control is shaped by the structures, systems, events, and culture in which they operate. The same is true for organizations. Morgan recommends not trying to change the 85 percent that is out of control, but instead knowing where the influence lies and where it can be exercised.
Patterns that are only partially visible or invisible, but easily measured	Become knowledgeable about the focus issue from the literature and practice, so you know where and how to look for these patterns.
	Describe or model the subtle relationships and structures that shape human system dynamics.
	Influence the self-organizing process in human systems by shifting components that are visible and that influence the nonlinear dynamics.
	Use mathematical tools to represent the subtle, nonlinear dynamics of a human system.
	Diagram a network by using network analysis as described in *Linked: The New Science of Networks* by Barabasi (2002). Software can be used to diagram networks.

A Practical Guide to Needs Assessment, Third Edition. Copyright © 2014 John Wiley & Sons, Inc. Reproduced by permission of Wiley. www.wiley.com

TOOLKIT FORM 2.1 *Tools and Strategies for Assessing Systems* (continued)

Types of System Patterns	Assessment Strategies and Tools
	Use social network analysis tools to map and measure the informal relationships between people. These tools can reveal key value creators and informal knowledge communities that drive performance.
Patterns that are invisible and not easily measured	Use facilitated individual and group reflections to identify nonlinear dynamics. Use mathematical models (such as data mining, computer simulation, and artificial intelligence) to make visible the emerging patterns that are deeply embedded in the phenomena.

Note: The information in this table was adapted from Eoyang, G. (2004). Practitioner's landscape. *Emergence: Complexity & Organization, 6*(1, 2), 55–60.

 A Practical Guide to Needs Assessment, Third Edition. Copyright © 2014 John Wiley & Sons, Inc. Reproduced by permission of Wiley. www.wiley.com

TOOLKIT FORM 2.2 *Advances Over Time in Our Knowledge About Learning, Training, and Performance*

To prepare for a planning meeting with a client, skim the material in the following table, which summarizes various ideas about learning, training, and performance in the workplace. Such ideas inform instruction, organization development, and performance improvement practices. While the table is not exhaustive, it highlights some key ideas and shows when they initially affected organizations.

As you skim the table, notice how our understandings of learning, training, and performance changed over time and were influenced by technological advances and other historic events.

Spend some extra time on the jargon, which is italicized, so that you are prepared in case the client uses one of these terms. Consider using the additional resources for this tool that are in the References section of the book or searching the Internet to further explore the specific ideas that might be relevant for your upcoming needs assessment.

Because learning and training are so closely related, they are grouped together in the table. Learning focuses on the acquisition of knowledge and skills; training focuses on the presentation of knowledge and skill

A Practical Guide to Needs Assessment, Third Edition. Copyright © 2014 John Wiley & Sons, Inc. Reproduced by permission of Wiley. www.wiley.com

TOOLKIT FORM 2.2 *Advances over Time in Our Knowledge About Learning, Training, and Performance* (continued)

Stone Age Through Industrial Revolution

	Stone Age	500 BC to 500 AD	300 to 1300 (Middle Ages)	1400 to 1700 (The Renaissance)	1760–1850 Industrial Revolution
Technological Advances and Historical Events	People began amassing knowledge and developing tools. Survival depended on hunting, collecting, and farming.	The Greek and Roman influence included law and philosophy.	The first universities were established in the Arab world. During feudal times in Europe, communities formed around the lord or master. Children were apprenticed to craftsmen to learn specialized skills. Merchant guilds and craft guilds provided mutual protection.	The printing press was invented, and books were written in a language that people could understand. Scientific inquiry was important.	New manufacturing processes were introduced that relied on machines rather than hand production. The factory system of work was introduced.
Performance	Tools were developed.		Merchant guilds and craft guilds controlled the quality of work.		The following economic concepts were introduced: Workers were paid based on their production. *Division of labor* where workers focused on specific subtasks and became skilled and proficient on them.
Learning/ Training	Technical skills were passed from generation to generation.	Skills such as agriculture and construction were taught through *on-the-job training* (OJT) and *apprenticeships*. Education, logic, and reasoning were valued.	Merchant and craft *guilds* controlled the transmission of technical expertise. The following learning concepts were introduced: The teacher arranges the *learning environment* and stimulates students to think. True learning is an active process. *Scholasticism* dominated teaching. This method relies on debate, discussion, and inferences to resolve contradictions	The *scientific method* required observing and describing phenomena, hypothesizing an explanation of the phenomena, and using experiments to test the hypotheses.	Classrooms were created within factories. *Vestibule training* was introduced that combines OJT and *classroom training*. In vestibule training, classrooms are located close to the job site. In addition, training simulates the workplace and uses the same machines that are used on the job.

A Practical Guide to Needs Assessment, Third Edition. Copyright © 2014 John Wiley & Sons, Inc. Reproduced by permission of Wiley. www.wiley.com

TOOLKIT FORM 2.2 *Advances Over Time in Our Knowledge About Learning, Training, and Performance* (continued)

1900s to 1940s

	1900s	1910s (World War I)	1920s	1930s	1940s (World War II)
Technological Advances and Historical Events	Advances in the science of psychology and management occurred.	Increased industry production to support the war effort.	Radio and movies with sound and color were developed.	The Great Depression affected employment worldwide.	Television became available.
Performance	*Scientific management* was introduced, relying on observing and studying tasks as the basis for optimizing work processes. Binet-Simon test was introduced to measure intelligence of children.	Mahatma Gandhi began his *non-violent resistance* movement against British rule.		Studies of workforce productivity were popular. The U.S. government used computers for the census counts and military strategy.	*General systems theory:* A way to think about entities that are composed of nested and inter-connected parts (e.g., teams, organizations, training programs, etc.). *Action research:* a problem-solving approach that involves using a systematic process to investigate and resolve an issue. Those who affect and are affected by the issue participate in the process. Seminal research on overcoming resistance to organizational change involved people in the changes that affected them. *Sociotechnical systems theory:* identifies the interactions of social and technical factors create the conditions for successful (and unsuccessful) job performance. *Critical incident technique* was developed to identify effective and ineffective work behaviors.

A Practical Guide to Needs Assessment, Third Edition. Copyright © 2014 John Wiley & Sons, Inc. Reproduced by permission of Wiley. www.wiley.com

TOOLKIT FORM 2.2 *Advances Over Time in Our Knowledge About Learning, Training, and Performance* (continued)

	1900s	1910s (World War I)	1920s	1930s	1940s (World War II)
Learning/ Training	*Classical conditioning* examined the learning process that occurs through association.	The *Four-Step Job Instruction Training Method (JIT)* was developed that relies on (1) show, (2) tell, (3) do, and (4) check.	Advances were made in *behaviorism*, a school of psychology that focused on observable behaviors and how to manipulate them by changing the environment.	*Behaviorism* continued as a dominant theory in psychology.	*Programmed instruction:* Learners advance at their own rate, test their answers, and advance to new content based on correct answers. The U.S. military relied on training and testing. To support the war effort, the U.S. military funded *Training Within Industry (TWI)*. *Instructional systems design (ISD)*, the systematic process of creating instruction, originated. Audiovisual technology was introduced into the classroom. *Sensitivity training, or T-groups* involved participants reflecting on their group experience using human behavior theories and group feedback. *The hierarchy of needs* was introduced that defines needs as internal forces that produce tension, which the person is motivated to satisfy and thus reduce the tension.

A Practical Guide to Needs Assessment, Third Edition. Copyright © 2014 John Wiley & Sons, Inc. Reproduced by permission of Wiley. www.wiley.com

TOOLKIT FORM 2.2 *Advances Over Time in Our Knowledge About Learning, Training, and Performance* (continued)

1950s to 1990s

	1950s	1960s	1970s	1980s	1990s
Technological Advances and Historical Events	The microchip was invented. Sputnik was launched. Men returning from WWII replaced women in the workplace. Most American men worked in blue-collar or agriculture jobs; women worked in the home.	The first moon walk took place. China's Cultural Revolution was launched. The precursor to the Internet and the *Knowledge Industry, Arpanet*, was developed.	Work shifted from traditional industries to industries that used computer information.	Space Shuttle Challenger exploded. Personal computers were introduced. Microcomputers were used in instruction.	Academicians identified *management* as the cause of American business problems, and management books proliferated (e.g., *Competitive Strategy, One Minute Manager*, and more).
Performance	The *motivation-hygiene theory* identified workplace factors that satisfy employees and those that dissatisfy employees. *Work life quality and productivity* were studied. Modern management practices were introduced.	*Theory X* (managers view employees as lazy) and *Theory Y* (managers view employees as self-motivated) were introduced.	*Organization development* grew in popularity. The International Board of Standards for Training, Performance, and Instruction (ibstpi®) was established to offer research-based competencies for such roles as instructor, online learner, instructional designer, evaluator, and training manager.		*Benchmarking processes*, which compare an organization's performance measures and processes to other organizations, were popular. The *McKinsey 7S model* assesses organizational skills, style, staff, shared values, strategy, structure, systems.

A Practical Guide to Needs Assessment, Third Edition. Copyright © 2014 John Wiley & Sons, Inc.
Reproduced by permission of Wiley. www.wiley.com

TOOLKIT FORM 2.2 *Advances Over Time in Our Knowledge About Learning, Training, and Performance* (continued)

1950s to 1990s (continued)

	1950s	1960s	1970s	1980s	1990s
Performance (continued)	*Total quality management (TQM)*, which emphasizes process measurement and continuous improvement, was adopted in many countries. Techniques of using surveys for organizational diagnosis were developed.	*Expectancy theory* proposed that people select behaviors based on the value of the rewards and their beliefs that the behaviors will lead to performance and the performance will lead to the rewards. The *managerial grid model* was introduced identifying leadership styles based on concern for production and people. The growth of *career counseling* in the workplace reflected the insight that work should have meaning.	The idea of engineering human competence was introduced.		The *balanced scorecard* assesses whether current organizational performance meets expectations for financial and non-financial measures and the targets for each measure. *Lean manufacturing* is an improvement process that eliminates waste, increases quality, and decreases costs. Lean manufacturing tools include 5S, control charts, and redesign of work cells.
Learning/ Training	Research was published on the *Hawthorne Effect*, which recognizes that people who know they are being studied modify their behaviors. *Bloom's Taxonomy* classified learning objectives using three domains: psychomotor, cognitive, and affective.	Instructional objectives focused on the learners' desired performance at the end of instruction, rather than the learning process. *Instructional system:* A process for training an individual to achieve specific instructional goals.	The *ADDIE* (analyze, design, develop, implement, and evaluate) model of instructional systems design was introduced. *Andragogy* identifies the principles and steps for planning learning experiences for *adult learners*.	*Electronic performance support systems (EPSS)* were developed comprised of computer-based tools that provide support for performing work (e.g., job aids, information, tools, software tutorials, job coaching, and so forth).	*Computer-based instruction (CBI)* and *computer-assisted instruction (CAI)* were popular. The computer could provide each learner with directions, instructional content, and feedback. The computer can also measure learners' achievements.

A Practical Guide to Needs Assessment, Third Edition. Copyright © 2014 John Wiley & Sons, Inc. Reproduced by permission of Wiley. www.wiley.com

TOOLKIT FORM 2.2 *Advances Over Time in Our Knowledge About Learning, Training, and Performance* (continued)

	1950s	1960s	1970s	1980s	1990s
Learning/ Training (continued)	The *Four Level Evaluation Model* for training was introduced: Level 1: *Reaction*, Level 2: *Learning*, Level 3: *Behavior*, Level 4: *Results*	*Implicit learning* occurs incidentally without the individual's awareness. Knowledge, such as riding a bike or playing soccer, is possessed by an individual, but hard to communicate using words and symbols. *Criterion-referenced tests* assess learners on their performance, without comparison to others. *Norm-referenced tests* compare learners' performance on the test. The introduction of learning domains, instructional events, and hierarchal analysis.	*Behavioral modeling* involves demonstrating the desired behaviors to learners who are guided as they imitate the behaviors. *Performance needs* were differentiated based on whether they could be addressed by training or non-training solutions. The *single-loop* and *double-loop* learning models were identified. Single-loop involves repeating a pattern, and double-loop involves changing the goal or the strategy.	*Experiential learning* developed that focuses on acquiring knowledge and skills from experiences that are gained in or outside of a classroom.	.

A Practical Guide to Needs Assessment, Third Edition. Copyright © 2014 John Wiley & Sons, Inc. Reproduced by permission of Wiley. www.wiley.com

TOOLKIT FORM 2.2 *Advances Over Time in Our Knowledge About Learning, Training, and Performance* (continued)

2000s	2000 to Today
Technological Advances and Historical Events	Communications occurred through handheld devices wired to the Internet, truly global, and mobile. Data were captured. Behaviors were shared quickly across the globe.
	The workforce became less hierarchical and more globally dispersed.
	Associations and vendors became adept at creating communities of practice for subscribers to share research, communications, and software-supported learning and performance services.
Performance	*HR scorecards* link learning/HRD initiatives and an organization's business strategy.
	Employee engagement links employee perceptions and organizational productivity, profit, retention, and customer satisfaction.
	The *trust* of employees, customers, stockholders, etc., became important.
	To quantify performance, organizations rely on *analytics* based on statistics, computer programming, and operations research to identify meaningful patterns in organizational data.
	Vendors offer easy-to-use online tools for selection, assessment, competency management, coaching, training, etc.
	Governments optimize workforce skills (e.g., national standards are developed for some professions).
Learning/Training	*Learning management systems (LMS)* rely on software to manage training records, administer online training, manage the instructor-learner communication, etc.
	Learning content management systems (LCMS) rely on a central object repository that authors, instructional designers, developers, subject experts, and others use to create, store, manage, deliver, and reuse training content.
	Inverted-teaching, flipped-teaching: Learners access relevant content via computers before or after a class, allowing more time for interaction during the class.
	Learning often occurs when it is needed on the job and in the community, rather than in a training room.
	Learners can compare information that is posted on the Internet (both fact and fiction) and that often has been rated by others.

A Practical Guide to Needs Assessment, Third Edition. Copyright © 2014 John Wiley & Sons, Inc. Reproduced by permission of Wiley. www.wiley.com

TOOLKIT FORM 4.1 *Knowledge and Skills Assessment Interview Guide*

Name: _____ **Date:** _____

Interviewer: _____ **Interviewee:** _____

General Questions

1. Why do you think training is needed?

_____

_____

_____

_____

_____

2. Describe specific instances of how workplace productivity has been affected by lack of knowledge and skills.

_____

_____

_____

_____

_____

_____

3. Give specific examples of how shortfalls in performance have affected unit goals, overall organization goals, or customer-satisfaction indices. (Add other indicators that are specific to your organization).

_____

_____

_____

_____

_____

A Practical Guide to Needs Assessment, Third Edition. Copyright © 2014 John Wiley & Sons, Inc. Reproduced by permission of Wiley. www.wiley.com

TOOLKIT FORM 4.1 *Knowledge and Skills Assessment Interview Guide*
(continued)

4. What other factors (internal or external) do you think are causing performance problems?

_____

_____

_____

_____

_____

Questions for Client Contact

5. What are the goals of the assessment?

_____

_____

_____

_____

6. What resources (monetary and nonmonetary) will be available for conducting the assessment?

_____

_____

_____

7. Whose approval must be obtained in order to proceed with the assessment?

_____

_____

_____

_____

8. Which groups must buy in to the concept?

_____

_____

_____

_____

A Practical Guide to Needs Assessment, Third Edition. Copyright © 2014 John Wiley & Sons, Inc. Reproduced by permission of Wiley. www.wiley.com

TOOLKIT FORM 4.1 *Knowledge and Skills Assessment Interview Guide*
(continued)

9. What are the most convenient times for collecting data?

_____

_____

_____

_____

10. What is the projected timeline for implementing the solutions?

_____

_____

_____

_____

11. List characteristics of the target audience, such as age, educational level, learning styles, attitudes toward learning, and computer literacy.

_____

_____

_____

_____

12. What is the approximate size of the target audience by position, geographic location, and so forth?

_____

_____

_____

_____

13. Has the target audience received prior training in this area? If so, what type of training?

_____

_____

_____

_____

14. What are the prerequisites for the program or programs?

_____

_____

_____

_____

15. Will certification be required?

_____

_____

_____

_____

16. Who are the internal and external customers of the target audience?

_____

_____

_____

_____

A Practical Guide to Needs Assessment, Third Edition. Copyright © 2014 John Wiley & Sons, Inc.
Reproduced by permission of Wiley. www.wiley.com

TOOLKIT FORM 4.2 *Skills Assessment Survey*

The Human Resources Department is conducting a survey of the job requirements of all [name of job function] at [name of company]. The information collected will be used to prepare a training plan for all [name of job function]. Your input is vital for ensuring the success of this initiative.

Instructions: This survey should take approximately fifteen to twenty minutes to complete. For each of the following items, please circle the appropriate rating. For items that are not applicable, circle "N.A." Please be candid in your responses.

Key:

1 = Very low   2 = Low   3 = Medium   4 = High   5 = Very high   N.A. = Not applicable

Current Level of Proficiency

[Enter skills here]

Example:

1. Obtain product information from customer   1   2   3   4   5   N.A.

[Add questions of your own]

Name: _____   Date: _____

Position/Title: _____   Unit: _____

A Practical Guide to Needs Assessment, Third Edition. Copyright © 2014 John Wiley & Sons, Inc.
Reproduced by permission of Wiley. www.wiley.com

TOOLKIT FORM 4.2 *Skills Assessment Survey* (continued)

Interpretation of Scores

All items that receive a rating of "3" or below indicate a need for training. The assumption is that the desired rating is "4" or above.

To ensure accuracy of responses, because there is a possibility that ratings may be inflated, do the following:

- Conduct follow-up interviews with unit managers to corroborate information obtained from surveys.

- Consider sending anonymous surveys. (The major disadvantage of this method is that individualized training needs cannot be identified.)

A Practical Guide to Needs Assessment, Third Edition. Copyright © 2014 John Wiley & Sons, Inc. Reproduced by permission of Wiley. www.wiley.com

TOOLKIT FORM 4.3 *Customer-Service Knowledge and Skills Assessment Survey*

The Training Department is conducting a customer-service training needs assessment at [name of company]. The information collected will be used to prepare a training plan for all customer-service personnel. Your input is vital for ensuring the success of this initiative.

Instructions: This questionnaire will take approximately fifteen minutes to complete. Please be candid when responding to the questions.

1. What are the five main responsibilities of your job? List the approximate percentage of time you spend on each job responsibility.

   _____

   _____

   _____

   _____

   _____

2. What knowledge and skills do you require to be successful in your job?

   _____

   _____

   _____

   _____

3. What are the critical success factors for effective performance in your job?

   _____

   _____

   _____

   _____

4. What are the main barriers to your success?

   _____

   _____

   _____

   _____

A Practical Guide to Needs Assessment, Third Edition. Copyright © 2014 John Wiley & Sons, Inc. Reproduced by permission of Wiley. www.wiley.com

TOOLKIT FORM 4.3 *Customer-Service Knowledge and Skills Assessment Survey* (continued)

5. What are the most difficult aspects of your job?

_____

_____

_____

_____

_____

6. What should the training priorities for your job function be?

_____

_____

_____

_____

_____

7. What prior customer-service training have you received? List all training received, including in previous jobs.

_____

_____

_____

_____

_____

8. What are your preferred learning styles (self-paced, computer-based, classroom)? Describe any others.

_____

_____

_____

_____

_____

A Practical Guide to Needs Assessment, Third Edition. Copyright © 2014 John Wiley & Sons, Inc. Reproduced by permission of Wiley. www.wiley.com

Note: The following portion of the questionnaire can also be distributed to supervisors and other internal or external customers if the instructions are modified.

9. Please complete the following self-assessment, using the following scale:

1 = Very Poor   2 = Poor   3 = Average   4 = Good   5 = Excellent   N.A. = Not Applicable

a. Knowledge of customer-service standards	1	2	3	4	5	N.A.
b. Knowledge of customer-service phone etiquette	1	2	3	4	5	N.A.
c. Knowledge of products	1	2	3	4	5	N.A.
d. Knowledge of product rules and regulations	1	2	3	4	5	N.A.
e. Ability to handle customer-service calls	1	2	3	4	5	N.A.
f. Ability to respond promptly to requests	1	2	3	4	5	N.A.
g. Ability to handle customer complaints	1	2	3	4	5	N.A.
h. Ability to solve problems quickly	1	2	3	4	5	N.A.
i. Ability to make decisions quickly	1	2	3	4	5	N.A.
j. Ability to negotiate	1	2	3	4	5	N.A.
k. Ability to listen carefully	1	2	3	4	5	N.A.
l. Ability to manage stress	1	2	3	4	5	N.A.

[Add questions of your own.]

Name: _____   Date: _____

Position/Title: _____   Unit: _____

A Practical Guide to Needs Assessment, Third Edition. Copyright © 2014 John Wiley & Sons, Inc. Reproduced by permission of Wiley. www.wiley.com

TOOLKIT FORM 4.4 *Management Knowledge and Skills Assessment Survey*

The Training Department is conducting a company-wide training needs assessment at [name of company]. The information collected will be used to prepare a training plan for all [name of job function] personnel. Your input is vital for ensuring the success of this initiative.

Instructions: This questionnaire will take approximately twenty minutes to complete. Please be candid when responding to the questions.

1. What are the five main responsibilities of your job? List the approximate percentage of time you spend on each job responsibility.

Responsibility   Percentage of Time Spent

_____   _____

_____   _____

_____   _____

_____   _____

2. What knowledge and skills do you require to be successful in your job?

3. What are the critical success factors for your effective performance?

4. What are the main barriers to your success?

A Practical Guide to Needs Assessment, Third Edition. Copyright © 2014 John Wiley & Sons, Inc. Reproduced by permission of Wiley. www.wiley.com

TOOLKIT FORM 4.4 *Management Knowledge and Skills Assessment Survey*
(continued)

5. What are the most difficult aspects of your job?

_____

_____

_____

_____

_____

6. What should the training priorities for your job function be?

_____

_____

_____

_____

_____

7. What prior management training have you received? List all such training received, including in previous jobs.

_____

_____

_____

8. What are your preferred learning styles (self-paced, computer-based, classroom)? Describe any others.

_____

_____

_____

_____

_____

Name: _____   Date: _____

Position/Title: _____   Unit: _____

A Practical Guide to Needs Assessment, Third Edition. Copyright © 2014 John Wiley & Sons, Inc.
Reproduced by permission of Wiley. www.wiley.com

TOOLKIT FORM 4.4 *Management Knowledge and Skills Assessment Survey*
(continued)

Instructions: This survey will take only a short time to complete. Please rate your [managers/subordinates] on the following items, using the key below. Please be candid when responding. Circle your choices.

Key: 1 = Strongly Disagree   2 = Disagree   3 = Somewhat Agree
4 = Agree   5 = Strongly Agree   N.A. = Not Applicable

Leadership

1. They are visionaries. — 1 2 3 4 5 N.A.

2. They serve as mentors. — 1 2 3 4 5 N.A.

3. They encourage teamwork. — 1 2 3 4 5 N.A.

4. They treat employees fairly. — 1 2 3 4 5 N.A.

5. They treat employees with respect. — 1 2 3 4 5 N.A.

6. They project a positive view of the organization to customers. — 1 2 3 4 5 N.A.

Communication

7. They clearly communicate what is expected of me. — 1 2 3 4 5 N.A.

8. They clearly communicate what is expected of my coworkers. — 1 2 3 4 5 N.A.

9. They keep me informed about critical business issues that may have an impact on my job. — 1 2 3 4 5 N.A.

10. They keep me updated about the unit's accomplishments. — 1 2 3 4 5 N.A.

11. They make effective presentations to others. — 1 2 3 4 5 N.A.

12. They establish clear channels of communication between group members. — 1 2 3 4 5 N.A.

13. They establish clear channels of communication between this unit and other units. — 1 2 3 4 5 N.A.

Performance Management

14. They are genuinely concerned about my job performance. — 1 2 3 4 5 N.A.

A Practical Guide to Needs Assessment, Third Edition. Copyright © 2014 John Wiley & Sons, Inc. Reproduced by permission of Wiley. www.wiley.com

TOOLKIT FORM 4.4 *Management Knowledge and Skills Assessment Survey*
(continued)

Key: 1 = Strongly Disagree   2 = Disagree   3 = Somewhat Agree
4 = Agree   5 = Strongly Agree   N.A. = Not Applicable

15. They provide employees with challenging tasks.	1	2	3	4	5	N.A.
16. They provide opportunities for professional growth and development.	1	2	3	4	5	N.A.
17. They conduct effective performance appraisal meetings.	1	2	3	4	5	N.A.
18. They resolve conflicts effectively.	1	2	3	4	5	N.A.
19. They provide feedback at the appropriate time.	1	2	3	4	5	N.A.

Project Management

20. They delegate tasks according to the appropriate skill level of the group members.	1	2	3	4	5	N.A.
21. They effectively forecast the workload of the group.	1	2	3	4	5	N.A.
22. They plan effectively.	1	2	3	4	5	N.A.
23. They take appropriate corrective action when necessary.	1	2	3	4	5	N.A.

Customer Service

24. They understand the needs of our customers.	1	2	3	4	5	N.A.
25. They are responsive to the needs of customers.	1	2	3	4	5	N.A.
26. They continually seek ways to improve customer service.	1	2	3	4	5	N.A.
27. They are aware of industry standards for customer service.	1	2	3	4	5	N.A.

Sales

28. They demonstrate effective negotiation skills.	1	2	3	4	5	N.A.
29. They proactively identify sales opportunities.	1	2	3	4	5	N.A.
30. They forge strong relationships with customers.	1	2	3	4	5	N.A.

TOOLKIT FORM 4.5 *Knowledge and Skills Assessment Curriculum Plan*

	Core Curriculum		
	Year 1	**Year 2**	**Year 3**
Sales Executive			
Sales Manager			
Sales Associate			

 A Practical Guide to Needs Assessment, Third Edition. Copyright © 2014 John Wiley & Sons, Inc. Reproduced by permission of Wiley. www.wiley.com

TOOLKIT FORM 4.5 *Knowledge and Skills Assessment Curriculum Plan* (continued)

	Advanced Curriculum		
	Year 1	**Year 2**	**Year 3**
Sales Executive			
Sales Manager			
Sales Associate			

A Practical Guide to Needs Assessment, Third Edition. Copyright © 2014 John Wiley & Sons, Inc.
Reproduced by permission of Wiley. www.wiley.com

TOOLKIT FORM 5.1 *Job Analysis Questionnaire*

Purpose: The purpose of this questionnaire is to gather information about your job.

Directions: Answer all the questions. Return the survey to [name/ department] by [date].

Name: _____

Sample Questions:

1. List all your major responsibilities. Then prioritize each item by assigning a number to it. For example, assign "1" to the responsibility you consider most important.

   _____

   _____

   _____

   _____

   _____

   _____

   _____

   _____

2. Why are these responsibilities important to your job?

   _____

   _____

   _____

   _____

   _____

   _____

A Practical Guide to Needs Assessment, Third Edition. Copyright © 2014 John Wiley & Sons, Inc. Reproduced by permission of Wiley. www.wiley.com

TOOLKIT FORM 5.1 *Job Analysis Questionnaire* (continued)

3. What equipment and tools do you use in your job?

_____

_____

_____

_____

_____

_____

_____

4. Describe some specific duties or tasks you perform in your job that are related to your major responsibilities. List the responsibilities you mentioned previously. After you indicate the specific duty or task, please state how often you perform this duty or task.

_____

_____

_____

_____

_____

_____

_____

5. What knowledge do you require to perform your job successfully?

_____

_____

_____

_____

_____

_____

_____

TOOLKIT FORM 5.1 *Job Analysis Questionnaire* (continued)

6. What qualities are necessary to make you successful in your job?

_____

_____

_____

_____

_____

_____

7. What prior knowledge, skills and abilities, or attitudes did you bring to your position that helped to make you successful in your job?

_____

_____

_____

_____

_____

_____

8. List any courses, workshops, or training programs you attended in the past that you feel have helped you succeed in your job.

_____

_____

_____

_____

_____

_____

_____

_____

A Practical Guide to Needs Assessment, Third Edition. Copyright © 2014 John Wiley & Sons, Inc. Reproduced by permission of Wiley. www.wiley.com

TOOLKIT FORM 5.1 *Job Analysis Questionnaire* (continued)

9. Describe any other contributing factors you feel have made you successful in your job.

_____

_____

_____

_____

_____

_____

_____

_____

TOOLKIT FORM 5.2 *Job Training and Non-Training Recommendations (Professional/Supervisory/Management)*

Job Title (Professional/Supervisory/Management):
Department:
Location:

Job Responsibility 1 _____
   1. Job Task: _____
   2. Job Task: _____
   3. Job Task: _____
   4. Job Task: _____
   5. Job Task: _____
Competencies: _____
Training Requirements: _____
Non-Training Requirements: _____

Job Responsibility 2 _____
   1. Job Task: _____
   2. Job Task: _____
   3. Job Task: _____
   4. Job Task: _____
   5. Job Task: _____
Competencies: _____
Training Requirements: _____
Non-Training Requirements: _____

Job Responsibility 3 _____
   1. Job Task: _____
   2. Job Task: _____
   3. Job Task: _____
   4. Job Task: _____
   5. Job Task: _____
Competencies: _____
Training Requirements: _____
Non-Training Requirements: _____

 A Practical Guide to Needs Assessment, Third Edition. Copyright © 2014 John Wiley & Sons, Inc. Reproduced by permission of Wiley. www.wiley.com

TOOLKIT FORM 5.2 *Job Training and Non-Training Recommendations (Professional/Supervisory/Management)* (continued)

Job Title (Professional/Supervisory/Management):
Department:
Location:

Job Responsibility 4 _____
   1. Job Task: _____
   2. Job Task: _____
   3. Job Task: _____
   4. Job Task: _____
   5. Job Task: _____
Competencies: _____
Training Requirements: _____
Non-Training Requirements: _____

Job Responsibility 5 _____
   1. Job Task: _____
   2. Job Task: _____
   3. Job Task: _____
   4. Job Task: _____
   5. Job Task: _____
Competencies: _____
Training Requirements: _____
Non-Training Requirements:

Job Responsibility 6 _____
   1. Job Task: _____
   2. Job Task: _____
   3. Job Task: _____
   4. Job Task: _____
   5. Job Task: _____
Competencies: _____
Training Requirements: _____
Non-Training Requirements: _____

A Practical Guide to Needs Assessment, Third Edition. Copyright © 2014 John Wiley & Sons, Inc. Reproduced by permission of Wiley. www.wiley.com

TOOLKIT FORM 5.3 *Job Training and Non-Training Recommendations (Administrative)*

Job Title (Administrative):
Department:
Location:

Job Responsibility 1 _____

  1. Job Task: _____

  2. Job Task: _____

  3. Job Task: _____

  4. Job Task: _____

Knowledge: _____

Skills/Abilities: _____

Attitudes: _____

Behaviors: _____

Standards: _____

Training Requirements: _____

Non-Training Requirements: _____

Job Responsibility 2 _____

  1. Job Task: _____

  2. Job Task: _____

  3. Job Task: _____

  4. Job Task: _____

Knowledge: _____

Skills/Abilities: _____

Attitudes: _____

Behaviors: _____

Standards: _____

Training Requirements: _____

Non-Training Requirements: _____

A Practical Guide to Needs Assessment, Third Edition. Copyright © 2014 John Wiley & Sons, Inc. Reproduced by permission of Wiley. www.wiley.com

TOOLKIT FORM 5.3 *Job Training and Non-Training Recommendations (Administrative)* (continued)

Job Title (Administrative):
Department:
Location:

Job Responsibility 3 _____

  1. Job Task: _____

  2. Job Task: _____

  3. Job Task: _____

  4. Job Task: _____

Knowledge: _____

Skills/Abilities: _____

Attitudes: _____

Behaviors: _____

Standards: _____

Training Requirements: _____

Non-Training Requirements: _____

Job Responsibility 4: _____

  1. Job Task: _____

  2. Job Task: _____

  3. Job Task: _____

  4. Job Task: _____

Knowledge: _____

Skills/Abilities: _____

Attitudes: _____

Behaviors: _____

Standards: _____

Training Requirements: _____

Non-Training Requirements: _____

A Practical Guide to Needs Assessment, Third Edition. Copyright © 2014 John Wiley & Sons, Inc.
Reproduced by permission of Wiley. www.wiley.com

TOOLKIT FORM 5.4 *Job Task Analysis Checklist*

_____   Assemble project team.

_____   Select above-average high performers and/or subject-matter experts who will provide input for the work session.

_____   Notify employees' supervisors.

_____   Conduct briefing if necessary.

_____   Prepare job analysis questionnaire.

_____   Distribute, mail, or email questionnaires.

_____   Summarize questionnaires.

_____   Prepare flip chart or computer presentation for session. List key job responsibilities supplied by all participants.

_____   Prepare agenda for work sessions.

_____   Obtain materials for session.

_____   Prepare meeting room for session.

_____   During session, refine list of job responsibilities.

_____   Create task statements for each job responsibility.

_____   Omit nonessential tasks.

_____   Identify knowledge, skills, and abilities required to perform tasks.

_____   Identify training requirements to perform job tasks.

_____   Prioritize training needs.

_____   Prepare draft of job training plan.

_____   Submit draft of job training plan to supervisors for approval.

_____   Prepare final draft of job training plan.

_____   Distribute copies of final job training plan.

A Practical Guide to Needs Assessment, Third Edition. Copyright © 2014 John Wiley & Sons, Inc. Reproduced by permission of Wiley. www.wiley.com

Instructions: In the first row, replace the initials with those of the project's key players. Also update the key and record project members' names below. Then list each task and indicate with a check mark which key players are involved with the step. When a step is completed, record the date.

Task	NAC	PL	HRM	SM 1	SM 2	C	TP	Completion Date
Subtotal: (Hours)								

Project Members: (Enter names of project members here)

Key: NAC = Needs Assessment PL = Project Liaison   HRM = Human Resource Manager
     Committee
     SM 1 = Sales Manager 1   SM 2 = Sales Manager 2   C = Client
     TP = Training Professional

A Practical Guide to Needs Assessment, Third Edition. Copyright © 2014 John Wiley & Sons, Inc.
Reproduced by permission of Wiley. www.wiley.com

TOOLKIT FORM 6.2 *Competency Interview Worksheet*

Name of Interviewer: _____   Date: _____

I. About the Interviewee

Name: _____   Position: _____

Unit: _____   Highest Degree: _____

Previous Training Received: _____

_____

_____

II. About the Interviewee's Job

Name of Manager: _____   Number of Subordinates: _____

Previous Jobs (Year, Position, Company, Location):

_____

_____

_____

_____

_____

_____

_____

_____

_____

1. What are the five main responsibilities of your job? (Probe for quantifiable results, such as "Meet sales quota every quarter.")

_____

_____

_____

_____

_____

_____

A Practical Guide to Needs Assessment, Third Edition. Copyright © 2014 John Wiley & Sons, Inc. Reproduced by permission of Wiley. www.wiley.com

2. What skills and abilities do you require to accomplish each of the above? (Probe for quantifiable behaviors and actions, such as "Make five new cold calls per month.")

_____

_____

_____

_____

_____

_____

_____

3. What other skills and abilities do you require to be successful in your job? (Probe for behaviors and actions, such as "Be courteous to customers.")

_____

_____

_____

_____

_____

III. About the Interviewee's Work Experiences

4.1. Think about a specific time [in the past week, month, or year] when you or someone else experienced success in [name of job]. What was the context? When did it happen? Who was involved? (Probe for behaviors and actions, such as "Took the initiative, made quick decisions, listened carefully.") What did you think or do?

_____

_____

_____

_____

_____

_____

4.2. What did you feel or think? (Probe for behaviors and actions, such as "I felt empowered and handled the problem myself.")

_____

_____

_____

_____

_____

_____

_____

4.3. What did you say? Why were these actions and words effective? (Probe for behaviors and actions, such as "I took the initiative and authorized the overdue shipment. This pleased the customer.")

_____

_____

_____

_____

_____

_____

4.4. What were the results? What significance does this event have? (Probe for behaviors and actions, such as "I learned that by acting quickly and decisively, I saved the company from losing a customer.")

_____

_____

_____

_____

_____

_____

_____

A Practical Guide to Needs Assessment, Third Edition. Copyright © 2014 John Wiley & Sons, Inc. Reproduced by permission of Wiley. www.wiley.com

5.1. Think about a specific time [in the past week, month, or year] when you or someone else experienced failure as a [name of job]. (Probe for behaviors and actions, such as "Failed to take the initiative, could not decide, did not listen carefully.")

_____

_____

_____

_____

_____

_____

_____

_____

_____

_____

_____

_____

_____

_____

_____

_____

_____

5.2. What did you feel or think? (Probe for behaviors and actions, such as "I felt guilty, disappointed, or angry.")

_____

_____

_____

_____

_____

_____

_____

TOOLKIT FORM 6.2 *Competency Interview Worksheet* (continued)

5.3. What did you say? Why were these actions and words ineffective? (Probe for behaviors and actions, such as "I failed to solve the customer's problem. He became angry and upset.")

_____

_____

_____

_____

_____

_____

5.4. What are some other actions you did not take at the time that could have helped you succeed? (Probe for specifics.)

_____

_____

_____

_____

_____

_____

5.5. What were the results? What significance does this event have? (Probe for behaviors and actions, such as "I lost a good customer.")

_____

_____

_____

_____

_____

A Practical Guide to Needs Assessment, Third Edition. Copyright © 2014 John Wiley & Sons, Inc. Reproduced by permission of Wiley. www.wiley.com

TOOLKIT FORM 6.3 *Competency Dictionary Worksheet*

1.

Core Clusters	Definitions

2.

Core Clusters	Definitions

3.

Core Clusters	Definitions

A Practical Guide to Needs Assessment, Third Edition. Copyright © 2014 John Wiley & Sons, Inc. Reproduced by permission of Wiley. www.wiley.com

4.

Core Clusters	Definitions

5.

Core Clusters	Definitions

6.

Core Clusters	Definitions

A Practical Guide to Needs Assessment, Third Edition. Copyright © 2014 John Wiley & Sons, Inc. Reproduced by permission of Wiley. www.wiley.com

TOOLKIT FORM 6.4 *Competency Model Worksheet*

Dimensions	Competencies/Core Clusters			
	Position 1	Position 2	Position 3	Position 4
1.				
2.				
3.				
4.				
5.				
6.				

A Practical Guide to Needs Assessment, Third Edition. Copyright © 2014 John Wiley & Sons, Inc.
Reproduced by permission of Wiley. www.wiley.com

TOOLKIT FORM 6.5 *Individual Learning Development Plan for* _____ *(Year)*

Employee Name: _____ Position: _____

Business Unit: _____ Manager: _____

Competency to Be Developed	Learning and Development Activities	Internal and External Support and Resources Needed	Success Measures	Completion Date	Review Date

Employee Signature: _____ Date: _____

Manager Signature: _____ Date: _____

334 *A Practical Guide to Needs Assessment, Third Edition.* Copyright © 2014 John Wiley & Sons, Inc. Reproduced by permission of Wiley. www.wiley.com

TOOLKIT FORM 7.1 *Strategic Issues Worksheet*

To examine an existing performance problem

1. What are the key organizational issues that must be addressed?

_____

_____

_____

2. How long have the issues existed?

_____

_____

_____

3. What are the consequences of not addressing these issues?

_____

_____

_____

4. Which business processes are affected by the issues?

_____

_____

_____

5. What are the performance improvement goals?

_____

_____

_____

6. What is preventing these goals from being achieved?

_____

_____

_____

TOOLKIT FORM 7.1 *Strategic Issues Worksheet* (continued)

7. What individuals and groups have a stake in addressing the issues and should participate in the needs assessment?

_____

_____

_____

8. What is the ideal timeline to assess the needs for these issues?

_____

_____

_____

To address a future performance need

1. What are the key strategic issues that must be addressed?

_____

_____

_____

_____

2. Why must these issues be addressed?

_____

_____

_____

_____

3. Which current processes are affected?

_____

_____

_____

_____

A Practical Guide to Needs Assessment, Third Edition. Copyright © 2014 John Wiley & Sons, Inc.
Reproduced by permission of Wiley. www.wiley.com

TOOLKIT FORM 7.1 *Strategic Issues Worksheet* (continued)

4. What are the performance improvement goals?

_____

_____

_____

_____

5. What is preventing these goals from being achieved?

_____

_____

_____

_____

6. What individuals and groups have a stake in addressing the issues and should participate in the needs assessment?

_____

_____

_____

_____

7. What is the ideal timeline to assess the needs for these issues?

_____

_____

_____

_____

A Practical Guide to Needs Assessment, Third Edition. Copyright © 2014 John Wiley & Sons, Inc.
Reproduced by permission of Wiley. www.wiley.com

TOOLKIT FORM 7.2 *Fisher's Models of Organizational Performance Worksheet**

This form describes eight models that can be used to map organizational performance. A brief description introduces each, and space for taking notes follows each. Use these models, individually or in combination, to consider various relationships that exist among aspects of performance, how performance improvements at one level actually combine to create performance improvements at another level, and whether the necessary performance supports are in place.

Models 1 through 4 focus on relationships among aspects of performance at the same hierarchical level within an organization (that is, the individual level, the group level, or the organizational level). Models 5, 6, and 7 focus on how phenomena at one level can affect the performance of interest at another level. Model 8 integrates Models 1, 2, 4, and 5.

Model 1: Organization Level Performance

This model shows processes that occur among the aspects of performance at the highest level in an organization. Each solid arrow in Figure 1 indicates the direction of the process among the aspects of performance. For example, the arrow between the organization's capacity and production process depicts the use of organizational resources to create products or services.

The dotted line represents the organization's permeable boundary. The thick shaded arrows show exchanges with the external resource and product markets. The resource market is the competitive space where the organization obtains land, capital, natural resources, and so forth. The product market is the competitive space where the organization interacts with customers and receives compensation and economic rents for its products and services. Economic rents are the returns received in excess of the cost of creating the product or service.

The organization's capacity includes the resources that were obtained from the resource market or from organizational members and that can be selected to produce a product or service. The organization's accomplishments garner economic rents that flow back into organization capacity and experience that contributes to the learning process. Organizational performance also depends on the processes that occur at the individual and the group levels.

*Note that earlier versions of this information were published in Fisher and Sleezer (2003).

 A Practical Guide to Needs Assessment, Third Edition. Copyright © 2014 John Wiley & Sons, Inc. Reproduced by permission of Wiley. www.wiley.com

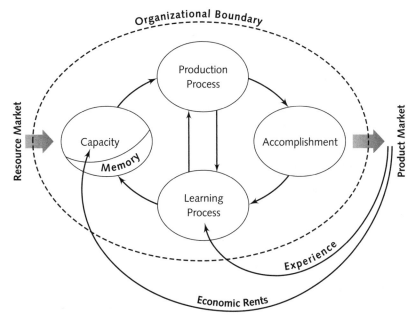

FIGURE 1 *Aspects of Organization Level Performance*

Notes on aspects of organizational level performance:

_____

_____

Model 2: Individual Level Performance

Each individual is a distinct unit, who combines his or her personal resources (individual capacity) with the resources provided by the organization (such as tools, data, and raw materials) to produce value-enhanced accomplishments that are deployed to other parts of the organization. Individual accomplishments become the resources that fuel the production process of other individuals and groups, thus creating a value-added chain. The individual production process adds value to a portion of the final organizational accomplishment that is instrumental to the organization's performance. The overlap of individual and organizational capacity in Figure 2 depicts that when an individual learns by engaging in the production process or by evaluating accomplishments, the initial learning is stored in the individual's memory and contributes to organizational memory if shared. Knowledge held by an individual can be viewed as part of the organization's aggregate capacity (but not necessarily organizational memory, because most of this knowledge is lost to the organization if the individual leaves).

A Practical Guide to Needs Assessment, Third Edition. Copyright © 2014 John Wiley & Sons, Inc.
Reproduced by permission of Wiley. www.wiley.com

FIGURE 2 *Aspects of Individual Level Performance*

Notes on aspects of individual level performance:

_____

_____

Models 3 and 4: Group Level Performance

This level is very complex, as shown in Model 3 (see Figure 3). Each dot represents an individual who operates in the manner described at the individual level. Moreover, the individuals who are represented by the dots could be operating at different speeds and be at different stages in the performance cycle.

The clusters of dots enclosed with dashed lines represent groups. The overlapping clusters show individuals who have multiple relationships.

Model 4 shows the aspects of group-level performance. Performance at the group level also includes the aspects of performance (see in Figure 4). Capacity at the group level includes group member skills, abilities, and knowledge as well as resources provided by the organization. It also includes resources that result from interactions among individuals within the group and that enable the group to produce accomplishments that the same individuals working alone could not attain.

The group production process involves individuals working together in value-enhanced ways that are unavailable to the group's individual members. The group's accomplishments become resources to other parts of the organization, where they lead to further enhancement in a value-adding chain. The group receives feedback from the production processes and from

A Practical Guide to Needs Assessment, Third Edition. Copyright © 2014 John Wiley & Sons, Inc. Reproduced by permission of Wiley. www.wiley.com

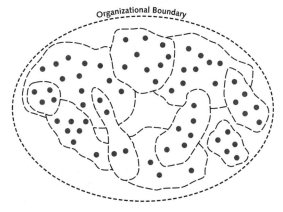

FIGURE 3 *Complexity at the Group Level*

Notes on aspects of complexity:

_____

_____

_____

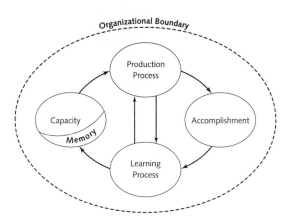

FIGURE 4 *Aspects of Group Level Performance*

Notes on aspects of group level performance:

_____

_____

_____

A Practical Guide to Needs Assessment, Third Edition. Copyright © 2014 John Wiley & Sons, Inc. Reproduced by permission of Wiley. www.wiley.com

comparisons with set standards; this feedback results in new knowledge that may be used to improve group production processes and thus enhance the value of group accomplishments. The new knowledge that a group acquires by evaluating its accomplishment and by reflecting on the feedback from the production process may become organizational memory via sharing and formal documentation.

Model 5: Compositional Links Among Performance Levels

Performance at one level can be combined to create performance at a higher level. For example, a firm's organizational climate for innovation reflects the shared perceptions of all the employees in a firm. Such compositional links occur within the same aspect of performance. As an example, the model in Figure 5 shows the compositional links for the capacity aspect of performance. One arrow shows the link that could occur if individual contributions combine to create organization capacity; another arrow shows the link that could occur if individual contributions combine to create group capacity; and a third arrow shows the link that could occur if group contributions combine to create organization capacity. For more information on compositional links see Klein and Kozlowski (2000).

FIGURE 5 *Compositional Links Among Performance Levels*

Notes on compositional links that are relevant to the need:

_____

_____

_____

A Practical Guide to Needs Assessment, Third Edition. Copyright © 2014 John Wiley & Sons, Inc. Reproduced by permission of Wiley. www.wiley.com

Model 6: Cross-Level, Multi-Aspect Links

Some relationships link both the levels and the aspects of performance. The model in Figure 6 shows a sample of these relationships for two aspects of performance: capacity and process. Individual capacity also may affect group production when individual skills contribute to the group process. Individual capacity also may directly affect organizational production process (such as an expert technician's role). Organization capacity contributes to individual production when the individual uses the organization's pool of resources (such as computers) to do work. Group capacity influences the individual's production process when an individual, as part of a group process, learns skills that he or she then transfers to the individual production process.

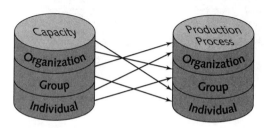

FIGURE 6 *Example of Cross-Level, Multi-Aspect Links*

Notes on cross-level, multi-aspect links:

_____

_____

_____

Model 7: Hybrid Relationships

This model (see Figure 7) introduces the notion of hybrid relationships. In such cases, performance at one level affects performance at another level, which in turn affects a process. For example, an individual can share an idea that modifies a group's production process. As another example, a group can brainstorm ideas that modify the organization's production process. Closer inspection shows that hybrid links are actually combinations of the compositional and intralevel links described earlier. In each example, the sharing of resources with others is at the core of the relationship.

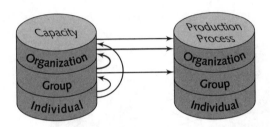

FIGURE 7 *Example of Hybrid Links*

Notes on hybrid links:

_____

_____

_____

Model 8: Intralevel and Compositional Relationships

Model 8 shows the intralevel and compositional relationships described in Models 1, 2, 4, and 5 (see Figure 8). Note that to keep the figure legible, the relationships between top management and the product and resource markets are not shown. The arrows between the aspects of performance depict process transfers at all three levels.

A Practical Guide to Needs Assessment, Third Edition. Copyright © 2014 John Wiley & Sons, Inc. Reproduced by permission of Wiley. www.wiley.com

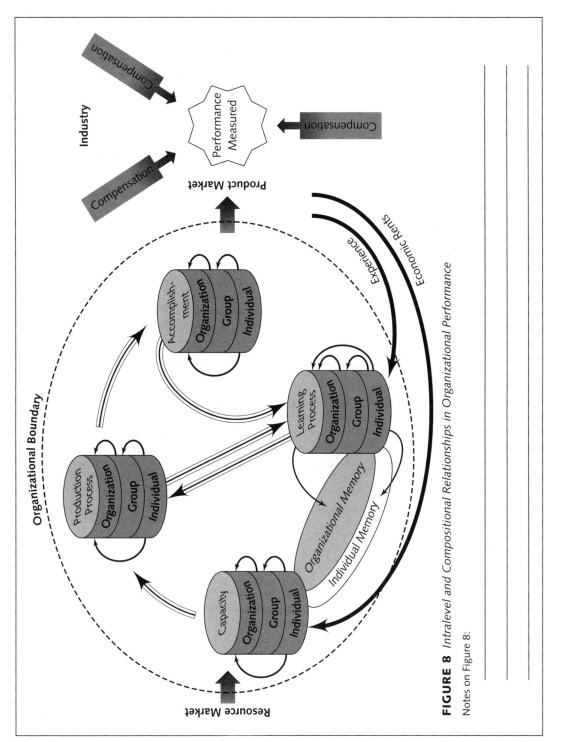

FIGURE 8 *Intralevel and Compositional Relationships in Organizational Performance*

Notes on Figure 8:

A Practical Guide to Needs Assessment, Third Edition. Copyright © 2014 John Wiley & Sons, Inc.
Reproduced by permission of Wiley. www.wiley.com

TOOLKIT FORM 7.3 *Process Map Worksheet*

A process map uses graphic symbols to show the steps of a process. It also shows where a process begins and ends. Following are the graphic symbols to use:

Instructions

1. To show information received from a source OUTSIDE a process boundary, such as a customer, customer request, or another business unit, use a RECTANGLE. ▭

2. To show any activity that is being carried out WITHIN a process, such as completing a form, use an OVAL. ⬭

3. To show the FLOW between activities (INPUTS and OUTPUTS), use an ARROW. ⟶

Tips for Process Mapping

1. Before mapping a process, define the starting and ending points and the level of detail that is needed.

2. Document steps in sequence. Try to restrict your diagram to major steps at first. Do not become bogged down in too much detail.

3. Begin by identifying the output and the input. Then identify the first major process activity, such as processing quotes, as shown in Figure 7.6. Determine the flow of information to and from this process. Use single-pointed arrows for information that flows in one direction. For information that flows back and forth between two units or processes, use two-pointed arrows.

4. Identify the next major process. Document the inputs and outputs to this process.

5. Link all major processes as well as the inputs and outputs.

6. If you cannot define intermediate steps, make notes. Come back to these steps later.

7. When you have finished creating your process map, retrace steps to verify accuracy of the information collected.

8. Review the process map with the project sponsor and other involved stakeholders for verification.

A Practical Guide to Needs Assessment, Third Edition. Copyright © 2014 John Wiley & Sons, Inc. Reproduced by permission of Wiley. www.wiley.com

TOOLKIT FORM 7.3 *Process Map Worksheet*
(continued)

Process: _____

Questions to Ask

1. What is the sequence of activities that must be performed to complete this process?
2. Who performs each activity?
3. How much time does it take to perform each activity or step?
4. What are the external inputs?
5. Where do internal inputs come from?
6. What are the outputs?
7. Where do the outputs go?

Key:

☐ Department or Unit
⬭ Processing Activity
⟶ Flow of Information in One Direction
⟷ Flow of Information in Both Directions

TOOLKIT FORM 7.4 *Gap Analysis Worksheet*

Process	Current Performance Indicators	Gap	Effect

A Practical Guide to Needs Assessment, Third Edition. Copyright © 2014 John Wiley & Sons, Inc.
Reproduced by permission of Wiley. www.wiley.com

TOOLKIT FORM 7.5 *Change Readiness Checklist*

Have clear objectives for the change initiative been established?

Has a leader been assigned to facilitate the change effort?

Are the desired change and its impacts clearly documented and agreed upon by organizational decision-makers?

To what extent does the leader have the requisite authority interpersonal skills, and organization development expertise to facilitate the change initiative?

To what extent are adequate internal resources available for implementing the performance improvement plan?

To what extent are external resources required?

In what ways have reasons for change been communicated to top management?

In what ways has top management committed to implementing the performance improvement plan?

To what extent is top management willing to take risks to implement the performance improvement plan?

A Practical Guide to Needs Assessment, Third Edition. Copyright © 2014 John Wiley & Sons, Inc.
Reproduced by permission of Wiley. www.wiley.com

In what ways have reasons for change been communicated to middle management?

In what ways has middle management committed to implementing the performance improvement plan?

In what ways have reasons for change been communicated to frontline employees?

To what ways are frontline employees committed to implementing the performance improvement plan?

What milestones for celebrating successes have been established?

What strategies have been devised for motivating and reinforcing those involved in the performance improvement initiative?

What kind of follow-up plan to monitor the change initiative has been developed?

A Practical Guide to Needs Assessment, Third Edition. Copyright © 2014 John Wiley & Sons, Inc. Reproduced by permission of Wiley. www.wiley.com

TOOLKIT FORM 7.6 *Performance Improvement Planner*

Project Identification Number: _____

Project Description: _____

Project Sponsor (Name/Business Unit): _____

Performance Improvement Goal: _____

_____

_____

Critical Success Factors: _____

_____

_____

_____

Obstacles to Success: _____

_____

_____

_____

Prerequisites for Starting the Project: _____

_____

_____

Project Structure: _____

_____

_____

Team Requirements: _____

_____

Resources: _____

_____

Expected Cost: _____

_____

Expected Benefits:_____

_____

_____

_____

TOOLKIT FORM 7.6 *Performance Improvement Planner* (continued)

Timeline

Milestone	Expected Start Date	Expected Completion Date
1. _____	_____	_____
2. _____	_____	_____
3. _____	_____	_____
4. _____	_____	_____
5. _____	_____	_____
6. _____	_____	_____

Completed By: _____   Approved By: _____

Date: _____   Date: _____

A Practical Guide to Needs Assessment, Third Edition. Copyright © 2014 John Wiley & Sons, Inc. Reproduced by permission of Wiley. www.wiley.com

TOOLKIT FORM 8.1 *Complex Needs Assessment Planning Template*

Title of the Complex Needs Assessment: _____

Date: _____

Needs Assessment Committee Members: _____

Phase 1: Conduct the pre-assessment. (Activities in this phase include getting organized, forming a needs assessment committee, specifying the boundaries for the needs assessment, and planning the data collection, analysis, and reporting processes).

Planned Activities

_____

_____

_____

_____

_____

_____

Phase 2: Conduct the needs assessment. (Activities in this phase include collecting and analyzing data on *what* is and *what should be*, prioritizing needs based on the data, identifying solution criteria and potential solutions, and reporting results).

Planned Activities

_____

_____

_____

_____

_____

_____

Phase 3: Conduct the post-assessment. (Activities in this phase include supporting the client and stakeholders in developing action plans to address the needs).

Planned Activities

_____

_____

_____

_____

_____

_____

_____

_____

A Practical Guide to Needs Assessment, Third Edition. Copyright © 2014 John Wiley & Sons, Inc. Reproduced by permission of Wiley. www.wiley.com

TOOLKIT FORM 9.1 *Needs Assessment Checklist*

The following checklist can be used for a variety of needs assessments, including the five approaches presented in this book. Because the assessment requirements for each situation differ, use the items that are most applicable to your organization's needs. Also, note that some needs assessments have additional steps that are not included in this checklist.

Gather Preliminary Data

	1. Have you had preliminary meetings to gather information from your client and other key people?
	2. Have you considered the ethical issues that may arise while gathering preliminary data and the ethical codes that can guide your actions?
	3. Have you obtained senior management's perspectives about the goals of the assessment?
	4. Have you identified the attitudes of learners and other stakeholders toward the needs assessment and the new program, process, system, training, or technology?
	5. Is there consensus about the goals of the needs assessment among those involved?
	6. Do you have a holistic perspective about the project, the organization, and its larger environment?
	• How does this project fit with other organizational efforts?
	• How do the organization's systems, culture, and politics support the project?
	• Have you identified any factors that are likely to impede the needs assessment or the project?
	• Have you identified the prerequisites for installing, developing, using, revising, or updating the program, system, process, training, or technology?
	• Have you identified any needed organizational changes that are complementary to the effort you are working on (for example, changes in work design, rewards, tools, culture, training, or environment)?

A Practical Guide to Needs Assessment, Third Edition. Copyright © 2014 John Wiley & Sons, Inc. Reproduced by permission of Wiley. www.wiley.com

TOOLKIT FORM 9.1 *Needs Assessment Checklist* (continued)

	• If complementary changes are occurring, do you know who is responsible for implementing and monitoring the changes?
	• Have you identified the educational level of the target audience?
	• Have you determined learners' preferred learning styles?
	• Have you identified the computer literacy levels of the target audience?
	7. Have you determined what testing or evaluation strategies will be used to measure success?
	8. Have you determined whether certification will be required?
	9. Have you identified resources that are available to conduct and implement the assessment?
	10. Do you require the assistance of external sources, such as subject-matter experts or consultants?
	11. Have you reviewed records, reports, and other pertinent extant data?
	12. Have you obtained input from all other pertinent sources, such as archives and internal or external sources?
	13. Have you determined what kind of needs assessment you will conduct (that is, job and task, knowledge and skill, competency, or strategic or complex needs analysis)?
Plan the Assessment	
	14. Have you established a project plan?
	15. Have you established a system for managing the needs assessment?
	16. Have you determined what types of data must be collected?
	17. Have you identified multiple sources of data?
	18. Have you identified multiple data-collection methods that will be effective?

A Practical Guide to Needs Assessment, Third Edition. Copyright © 2014 John Wiley & Sons, Inc. Reproduced by permission of Wiley. www.wiley.com

TOOLKIT FORM 9.1 *Needs Assessment Checklist* (continued)

	19. Have you designed the process or processes for collecting and storing data?
	20. Have you established a mechanism for tabulating and analyzing results?
	21. Have you developed a plan for having the appropriate people review the draft data analysis?
	22. Have you considered the ethical guidelines that should be followed when planning and implementing this plan?
	23. Have you notified the appropriate people about the assessment?
	24. Have you obtained approval to proceed with the assessment?

Data Collection

	25. Have you developed the needs assessment tools?
	26. Have you validated the needs assessment tools?
	27. Have you pilot-tested the needs assessment tools?
	28. Do you have a system for managing the collected data?
	29. Have you scheduled the data collection?
	30. Have you communicated the purpose and process of the data collection with those who will participate in it?

Analyze Data

	31. Have you compiled results?
	32. Have you identified patterns and deviations in data?
	33. Have you organized the data for review by the client and stakeholders?
	34. Have you briefed your client and key stakeholders about the draft results of the assessment?

A Practical Guide to Needs Assessment, Third Edition. Copyright © 2014 John Wiley & Sons, Inc. Reproduced by permission of Wiley. www.wiley.com

TOOLKIT FORM 9.1 *Needs Assessment Checklist* (continued)

Prepare Final Report and Presentation

	35. Have you established priorities for implementing the solutions identified by the needs assessment?
	36. Have you estimated the projected costs, benefits, and ROI for implementing each solution?
	37. Does the report contain all the relevant information?
	38. Is the report accurate, precise, and concise?
	39. Is the report format appropriate for the audience and organization?
	40. Have you included all the appropriate supporting documents in the appendix?

A Practical Guide to Needs Assessment, Third Edition. Copyright © 2014 John Wiley & Sons, Inc. Reproduced by permission of Wiley. www.wiley.com

TOOLKIT FORM 9.2 *Needs Assessment Proposal Template*

Replace the information in the brackets with information specific to your project.

Proposal: [Title of the needs assessment]

Submitted to: [Client's name]
[Client's title]
[Client's address]
[Client's phone number/email address]

Submitted by: [Analyst's name]
[Analyst's title]
[Analyst's address]
[Analyst's phone number/email address]

Date: [Date proposal is submitted to client]
[Name of Proposal] Page 2

Version [insert number here]

A Practical Guide to Needs Assessment, Third Edition. Copyright © 2014 John Wiley & Sons, Inc. Reproduced by permission of Wiley. www.wiley.com

Purpose

[Insert one to two paragraphs with background information about the organization and the reason for conducting the needs assessment.]

[Insert one paragraph that overviews the needs assessment, describes how it will accomplish the purpose, and refers to the table on the next page.]

Staffing

The analyst for this project, [insert analyst's name], has [insert brief description of the analyst's experience/education/certification in needs assessment].

Cost

The costs for the needs assessment are [insert per hour costs or total project costs]. In addition, the organization will pay for such agreed-upon expenses as [specify expenses the organization will pay]. The organization will also provide the analyst with [specify the services that the organization will provide for the needs assessment, such as transportation, copying, mailing, and printing]. [Specify the work that the analyst will do at the organization] will be done on-site; however, [specify the needs assessment work that will not be completed at the worksite] will be completed off-site. This contract can be renegotiated at any time as needed.

Version [insert number here]

A Practical Guide to Needs Assessment, Third Edition. Copyright © 2014 John Wiley & Sons, Inc. Reproduced by permission of Wiley. www.wiley.com

Projected Needs Assessment Phases, Outcomes, and Timelines

	Phase 1: [title]	Phase 2: [title]	Phase 3: [title]	Phase 4: [title]	Phase 5: [title]
Purpose	[Insert the purpose of the phase.]	[Insert the purpose of the phase.]	[Insert the purpose of the phase.]	[Insert the purpose of the phase.]	[Insert the purpose of the phase.]
Process	[Insert the steps required to complete the phase.]	[Insert the steps required to complete the phase.]	[Insert the steps required to complete the phase.]	[Insert the steps required to complete the phase.]	[Insert the steps required to complete the phase.]
Outcome	[Insert the expected outcome or outcomes.]	[Insert the expected outcome or outcomes.]	[Insert the expected outcome or outcomes.]	[Insert the expected outcome or outcomes.]	[Insert the expected outcome or outcomes.]
Projected Due Date	[Insert the expected completion date for the phase.]	[Insert the expected completion date for the phase.]	[Insert the expected completion date for the phase.]	[Insert the expected completion date for the phase.]	[Insert the expected completion date for the phase.]

Version [insert number here]

A Practical Guide to Needs Assessment, Third Edition. Copyright © 2014 John Wiley & Sons, Inc. Reproduced by permission of Wiley. www.wiley.com

TOOLKIT FORM 9.3 *Needs Assessment Interim Report Template*

Directions: Replace the information in the brackets with information specific to your project.

Report Title: [for example, Phase I Report, Phase II Report, etc.]

Submitted to: [Client's name]
[Client's title]
[Client's address]
[Client's phone number/email address]

Submitted by: [Analyst's name]
[Analyst's title]
[Analyst's address]
[Analyst's phone number/email address]

Date: [Date proposal is submitted to client]

Version [insert number here]

362   *A Practical Guide to Needs Assessment, Third Edition.* Copyright © 2014 John Wiley & Sons, Inc. Reproduced by permission of Wiley. www.wiley.com

TOOLKIT FORM 9.3 *Needs Assessment Interim Report Template* (continued)

Executive Summary

[Insert one or two sentences that overview what was accomplished in this reporting period.] [Insert one sentence stating why this accomplishment is important for the project and organization.] The following sections summarize the goals, process, findings, and recommendations for this phase.

Goals

1. [List a goal for the project or phase here.]
2. [List another goal for the project or phase here.]
3. [Continue listing project goals.]

Process

1. [List a process step for the project or phase.]
2. [List another process step for the project or phase.]
3. [Continue listing process steps and writing descriptions as needed.

Findings

1. [List a finding for the project or phase here.]
2. [List another finding for the project or phase here.]
3. [Continue listing findings as needed.]

Recommendations

[Summarize the recommendations for the phase and project, which are based on the findings, in one or two paragraphs.]

Attachments

[Attach the Overview of Needs Assessment and all supporting instruments and data.]

Version [insert number here]

A Practical Guide to Needs Assessment, Third Edition. Copyright © 2014 John Wiley & Sons, Inc. Reproduced by permission of Wiley. www.wiley.com

TOOLKIT FORM 9.3 *Needs Assessment Interim Report Template* (continued)

[Title of the phase or project]

Goal

The goals of this phase were:
1. [List a goal here.]
2. [List another goal here.]

(See Attachment A: Projected Needs Assessment Phases, Processes, Outcomes, and Timelines.)

Process

Completing this phase of the needs assessment involved [summarize the process steps that were used to complete this phase. These should match the steps that are listed in Attachment A.]

Findings

[Summarize all findings here.]

Recommendations

[Report all recommendations here.]

Attachments

Version [insert number here]

A Practical Guide to Needs Assessment, Third Edition. Copyright © 2014 John Wiley & Sons, Inc. Reproduced by permission of Wiley. www.wiley.com

Attachment A: Overview of the Needs Assessment

	Phase 1: [title]	Phase 2: [title]	Phase 3: [title]	Phase 4: [title]	Phase 5: [title]
Purpose	[Insert the purpose of the phase.]	[Insert the purpose of the phase.]	[Insert the purpose of the phase.]	[Insert the purpose of the phase.]	[Insert the purpose of the phase.]
Process	[Insert the steps required to complete the phase.]	[Insert the steps required to complete the phase.]	[Insert the steps required to complete the phase.]	[Insert the steps required to complete the phase.]	[Insert the steps required to complete the phase.]
Outcome	[Insert the expected outcome or outcomes.]	[Insert the expected outcome or outcomes.]	[Insert the expected outcome or outcomes.]	[Insert the expected outcome or outcomes.]	[Insert the expected outcome or outcomes.]
Due Date	[Insert the expected completion date for the phase.]	[Insert the expected completion date for the phase.]	[Insert the expected completion date for the phase.]	[Insert the expected completion date for the phase.]	[Insert the expected completion date for the phase.]

Version [insert number here]

A Practical Guide to Needs Assessment, Third Edition. Copyright © 2014 John Wiley & Sons, Inc. Reproduced by permission of Wiley. www.wiley.com

Glossary

Accomplishments	The outputs resulting from certain actions and behaviors.
Actuals	Current performance or knowledge (Rossett, 1987).
Anonymity	Characteristic of information such that its source (the author or the person who generated it) is not known to the analyst(s) or to any others.
Anticipated needs	Needs that are expected to prevail in the future.
Behavior	Actions of a person, or what people do (Harless, 1970).
Behavior Engineering Model (BEM)	A classic model for analyzing relationships among behaviors, accomplishments, and performance; identifies six variables that can be manipulated to change performance.
Behavioral interviews	A data-collection method that obtains information about what high performers do that makes them successful and what low performers do that makes them fail. (See also Critical Incident.)

Brainstorming	A method of problem solving in which group members contribute ideas spontaneously, and these ideas are not initially judged.
Business goal	A statement describing a measure or target for an organization or a business unit that will be achieved during a certain period of time.
Business process	A series of activities that provide products, deliver services, or manage resources.
Business strategy	The set of policies, plans, and directions that the organization uses to achieve its business goals and achieve its mission; has a long-term focus.
Business unit	A department or function within an organization.
Client	A person, work unit, or organization that uses the professional services of an analyst.
Closed-ended question	A question containing specific options from which a respondent must choose, such as a multiple-choice question.
Community	A group of people who share common characteristics, such as governance, locality, culture.
Comparative needs	Needs occurring among two or more entities with similar characteristics.
Competency	A knowledge, skill, or attitude that enables a person to perform effectively the activities of a given occupation or to function to the standards expected in employment (International Board of Standards for Training, Performance, and Instruction, 2005).
Competency dictionary	An organized list of definitions for individual competencies.

Competency model

A composite picture or conceptual framework of the competencies necessary for people to be successful in a job function.

Complex needs assessment

An approach to needs assessment used in multifaceted situations; use when a single approach (the knowledge and skills assessment, the job and task analysis, the competency-based assessment, or the strategic needs assessment) by itself is not appropriate.

Confidentiality

When only the analyst(s) can identify the responses of individual subjects and no others can connect individuals with their responses. Confidential individual data usually are aggregated for reporting.

Conflict of interest

A clash between one's personal interests and one's professional position.

Consultant

Someone who has influence in a situation but does not have the power to make changes or implement programs directly (Block, 2000).

Core cluster

Competencies grouped together under a broad dimension.

Cost/benefit analysis

A comparison of the costs and the benefits for one or more options.

Critical incident

Process of collecting information about important (critical) performance in special situations (incidents) (Flanagan, 1954, 1974).

Critical-incident needs

Needs that become apparent after system failures.

Curriculum

An overall plan containing the objectives, course modules, content outline, and delivery strategies for training or educational programs.

Deficiency How a situation deviates (in a negative direction) from the ideal (Harless, 1970).

Domain A cluster of related competencies grouped together under a broad dimension.

Downsizing A reduction in the number of personnel within an organization; also called a reduction in force or RIF.

Environment Conditions surrounding performance, such as the work environment, equipment, tools, or machinery used in performing tasks (Harless, 1970).

Ethics A set of principles or values, in this case the principles guiding the conduct of professionals undertaking needs assessments.

Expressed needs Needs that are evident (e.g., demands for a product or service exceed supply).

Evaluation A process for determining and reporting on the merit, worth, or value of needs or of a program, process, or product (Scriven, 1991).

Formative evaluation An evaluation whose purpose is to identify possible modifications for improving a program, process, or product.

Needs assessment A process for figuring out the gap between the current condition and the desired condition (called a need) and how to address the need and close the gap.

Summative evaluation An evaluation whose purpose is to make a final judgment on the merit, worth, or value of a program, process, or product.

Extant data	A term given to quantitative and qualitative data that already exist.
Felt needs	Needs that reflect what people think they need.
Fill-in-the-blank question	An open-ended question that limits the length of responses
Focus group	A data-collection method in which the opinions of five to eight people who share similar expertise (such as operations staff) are sought at the same time.
Gap	Difference between what is and what should be, between an actual state (what results are) and a desired state (what results should be) (Kaufman, Rojas, & Mayer, 1993).
High performers	People who consistently exceed expectations and are informally labeled "masters" or experts by their peers and managers.
Human system dynamics	The field that explores the underlying forces that shape the ever-emerging and dynamic patterns of human systems of all sizes.
Individual learning development plan	A learning blueprint that is developed for a person and shows the learning activities, support and resources, success indicators, and measures for improving performance.
Inter-rater reliability	The level of agreement among raters.
Interval scales	A series of marks used to record information. Can come from a closed-ended question. Possesses the following characteristics: (1) the points on the scale appear in an increasing (or decreasing) order and (2) there exists an equal distance between points on the scale.

Interventions	Activities that interfere so as to modify a process or situation. For example, organization development consultants use such interventions as team building and culture change to modify the process or situation in the client's context.
Interviews	A data-collection method used with individuals that can be conducted in person, by phone, or by computer technology (such as online cameras and videoconferencing).
Semi-structured interviews	A list of objectives with corresponding questions initially guides the interview; interviewer spontaneously asks supplemental questions to further explore areas of interest.
Structured interviews	A list of objectives, a corresponding list of questions, and in some cases, a corresponding list of responses to questions that guide the interview process.
Unstructured interviews	Questions are not listed in advance of the interviews; rather, a list of objectives and the topics to be covered guide the interview.
Job analysis	A process of gathering, organizing, evaluating, and reporting work-related information.
Job function expert	Someone within or outside the organization who is considered an expert or highly skilled in a particular job task.
Job responsibility	The scope of activities for a job function or job position, such as operations manager.
Job task	What must be done in order to fulfill a responsibility—usually four to six tasks for each responsibility.

Job task statement   The what, why, and how of a job.

Knowledge   The body of facts about a subject matter and the understanding that a person acquires through study or experience. What people must know, such as subject matter, concepts, or facts, in order to do a job.

Learning   The gaining of knowledge, understanding, skills, and abilities; is not observable; only resulting behavior is observable.

Learning channel   A way of acquiring knowledge, understanding, skills, and abilities.

Likert-type scale   A scale on which respondents are asked to rate values or attitudes (Likert, 1932).

Mission   A broad statement describing an organization's future plans and directions.

Multiple-choice question   A type of closed-ended question that includes a list of three or more options from which respondents select one or more responses.

Need   A learning or performance gap that exists between the current condition and the desired condition.

Needs assessment   A diagnostic process that relies on data collection, collaboration, and negotiation to identify and understand gaps in learning and performance and to determine future actions.

Needs assessment committee   A group of influential people who have a stake in the needs assessment; they provide such resources as technical and ethical advice, legitimacy, political power, credibility and/or prestige.

Needs assessment proposal	Document that specifies the project's purpose, proposal phases, processes, expected outcomes, timeline, and expenses. When approved, the proposal serves as a contract.
Network	A complex, interconnected group or system.
Nominal scale	A series of marks that is used to record information (e.g., north, south, east, west; or hospital a, hospital b, hospital c, and so forth), with no specific ordering.
Normative needs	Needs that arise when an individual or group is not meeting one or more established standards.
Observation	A type of data collection that involves the watching, inspecting, and taking note of behaviors and the environment.
Open-ended question	A question that a respondent answers in his or her own words.
Optimals	Desired knowledge or performance (Rossett, 1987).
Ordinal scale	A series of marks that are ordered, but the intervals between the marks are not the same (such as a Fahrenheit scale).
Organizations	People working together to accomplish something, examples include government agencies, businesses, communities, community groups, inter-organizational groups.
Organizational Elements Model	An organization assessment model that can be used to determine quasi-needs and needs based on the gaps between what is and what should be in an organization's inputs, processes, products, outputs, and outcomes.

Performance	Behaviors and their resulting accomplishments and capacities; performance, unlike learning, is observable.
Performance improvement planner	A blueprint that documents all the performance improvement projects that must be undertaken to improve the overall effectiveness of an organization.
Performance statement	An explanation or elaboration of the activities that constitute a competency statement and provide specific details about a competency.
Pilot test	A trial run in which an object, such as a data-collection instrument, is tested for problems or "bugs."
Position training plan	A matrix showing how the knowledge, skills, and abilities needed for an individual to perform a job can be acquired.
Process boundary	An arbitrary "line" that shows where a business process begins or ends.
Process map	A graphical illustration of the steps or activities that are performed in a business.
Project creep	Expansion of or increase in a project that occurs when the scope of a project keeps growing.
Project shrink	Contraction of or reduction in a project that occurs when the scope of the project keeps getting smaller.
Qualitative data	Data that are not numeric; can be words, diagrams, or pictures.

Quantitative data	Data that can be expressed in numeric form, such as indices, sales averages, or number of word-processing programs used.
Ratio scale	A series of marks that are ordered, have the same intervals between marks, and have a zero value as part of the scale (such as height or weight).
Reliability	The level of consistency in the item or the data; reflects the level of error in the measurement.
Return on investment (ROI)	A performance measure for comparing the costs and benefits of an investment; often used to compare several proposed interventions.
Root cause analysis	A systematic procedure for identifying the most probable cause of problems so organizational leaders can eliminate them rather than continue to deal with their symptoms. Involves continuing to ask "Why?" until the pattern becomes evident and the causes of the problem obvious.
Self-organization	The tendency for complex adaptive systems to generate new organizational forms spontaneously when pushed far from equilibrium.
Silo model	An organizational model in which the functions or departments operate as though they were independent of the other organizational functions or departments, or as separate silos.
Skills or abilities	Knowledge that one proficiently applies in appropriate situations; what people must do in order to perform a job.

Social network theory   Analysis technique that depicts social relationships using nodes and ties. Nodes are the individual entities within a network; ties are the relationships between the entities. A social network maps all the relevant ties between the nodes that are being studied. A social network analysis can provide both a visual and a mathematical analysis of human relationships.

Sponsor   The person, work unit, or organization that pays for the needs assessment; the person with ultimate responsibility for something (such as a needs assessment).

Stakeholders   People who have a financial, emotional, social or other involvement in the outcomes of a needs assessment; the findings and recommendations may affect them or their work.

Standard   A criterion that specifies how a task should be performed.

Survey   A data-collection method typically used to gather data from many people at one time; can be mailed, emailed, or offered online.

Systems theory   The view of an entity, such as an organization, as being comprised of interdependent and nested components; includes the inputs, processes, outputs, feedback, markets, and customers.

Task analysis   A method of determining the knowledge, skills, tools, conditions, and requirements needed to perform a job.

Training	A process that supports individual learning (a gain in knowledge and skills) through specialized instruction and practice.
Trustworthiness	The level of confidence that we can trust particular data (typically qualitative) to provide insight into "truth" or "reality." The procedures used to collect and analyze data affect trustworthiness of the data. For example, data that are collected and analyzed using sloppy procedures are not trustworthy.
Two-choice question	A closed-ended question the answer to which can be either one thing or the other (e.g., yes/no, true/false), and the responses are mutually exclusive.
Validity	The level of confidence we can have that specific data provide insight into "truth" or "reality." The instrument or test design as well as the content and the procedures used to collect and statistically analyze data (typically quantitative) affect the validity of the resulting data.
Want	Something the client would like to have even though it does not contribute to the learning or performance goal.
World view	Can be thought of as a value or belief system about how the world operates including who should make decisions, and the rules that govern society (Beck & Cowen, 2006).
Worthy performance	The ratio of valuable accomplishments to costly behaviors (Gilbert, 1978).

References

INTRODUCTION

Hodgins, W. (2009a). Designers 'R us!? Unpublished paper presented at Learning 2009, Orlando, Florida.

Hodgins, W. (2009b). Designers 'R us!? [PowerPoint slides]. Retrieved from www.slideshare.net/WayneH/presentations.

Miniwatts Marketing Group. (2012). Internet world stats. Retrieved from www.internetworldstats.com/stats.html. World Stats.

Porter, M. E. (1980). Competitive strategy. New York, NY: The Free Press.

CHAPTER ONE

Mathews, B. P., Ueno, A., Kekale, T., Repka, M., Pereira, Z., & Silva, G. (2001). Quality training: Needs and evaluation-findings from a European survey. *Total Quality Management, 12*(4), 483–490.

Preskill, H., & Russ-Eft, D. (2003). A framework for reframing HRD evaluation practice and research (pp. 199–257). In A. M. Gilley, L. Bierema, & J. Callahan (Eds.), *Critical issues in HRD.* Cambridge, MA: Perseus.

Russ-Eft, D., & Preskill, H. (2005). In search of the holy grail: ROI evaluation in HRD. *Advances in Developing Human Resources, 7*(1), 71–85.

Russ-Eft, D., & Preskill, H. (2009). Evaluation in organizations: A systematic approach to enhancing learning, performance, and change (2nd ed.). New York, NY: Basic Books.

Scriven, M. (1991). *Evaluation thesaurus* (4th ed.). Thousand Oaks, CA: Sage.

Stufflebeam, D. L., McCormick, C. H. Brinkerhoff, R. O., & Nelson, C. O. (1985). *Conducting educational needs assessments.* (Evaluation in Education and Human Services Vol. 10). Boston, MA: Kluwer-Nijhof.

Watkins, R., Meiers, M. W., & Visser, Y. L. (2012). *A guide to assessing needs.* Washington, DC: The World Bank.

CHAPTER TWO

Beck, D. E., & Cowan, C. C. (2006). *Spiral dynamics: Mastering values, leadership, and change.* Malden, MA: Blackwell Publishing.

Eoyang, G. (2004). Practitioner's landscape. *Emergence: Complexity & Organization, 6*(1, 2), 55–60.

Gilbert, T. J. (1978). *Human competence: Engineering worthy performance.* New York, NY: McGraw-Hill.

Guerra-Lopez, I., & Kaufman, R. (2013). *Needs assessment for organizational success.* Alexandria, VA: ASTD

Harless, J. (1970). *An ounce of analysis (is worth a pound of objectives).* Newman, GA: Harless Performance Guild.

Kaufman, R. (1992). *Strategic planning plus: An organizational guide.* Thousand Oaks, CA: Sage.

Kaufman, R. (2005). Defining and delivering measurable value: A mega thinking and planning primer. *Performance Improvement Quarterly, 18*(3), 6–16.

Mager, R. F., & Pipe, P. (1984). *Analyzing performance problems; Or, you really oughta wanna* (2nd ed.). Belmont, CA: Pitman Management and Training.

Phillips, J. J., & Phillips, P. P. (2005). *Measuring return on investment (ROI) basics.* Alexandria, VA: ASTD.

Rummler, G. A., & Brache, A. P. (1995). *Improving performance: How to manage the white space in the organization chart.* San Francisco, CA: Jossey-Bass.

Swanson, R. A., & Gradous, D. B. (1990). *Forecasting the financial benefits of human resource development.* San Francisco, CA: Jossey-Bass.

CHAPTER THREE

Altschuld, J. W., & White, J. L. (2010). *Needs assessment analysis and prioritization.* Thousand Oaks, CA: Sage.

Callahan, M. (1985, February). Be a better needs analyst. *Info-line 8502.* Alexandria, VA: ASTD.

Centers for Disease Control and Prevention. (2010). Community Health Assessment and Group Evaluation (CHANGE) action guide: Building a foundation of knowledge to prioritize community needs. Atlanta, GA: U.S. Department of Health and Human Services. Retrieved from www.cdc.gov/healthycommunitiesprogram/tools/change/pdf/changeactionguide.pdf.

Dillman, D. A. (2000). *Mail and internet surveys: The tailored design method* (2nd ed.). Hoboken, NJ: John Wiley & Sons.

Dillman, D. A., Smyth, J. D., & Christian, L. M. (2009). *Internet, mail, and mixed mode surveys.* Hoboken, NJ: John Wiley & Sons.

Guba, E. G., & Lincoln, Y. S. (1981). *Effective evaluation: Improving the usefulness of evaluation results through responsive and naturalistic approaches.* San Francisco, CA: Jossey-Bass.

Krueger, R. A., & Casey, M. A. (2000). *Focus groups* (3rd ed.). Thousand Oaks, CA: Sage.

Likert, R. (1932). A technique for the measurement of attitudes. *Archives of Psychology, 140*, 1–55.

Paul, K., & Bracken, D. (1995, January). Everything you always wanted to know about employee surveys. *Training and Development, 49*(1), 47.

Phillips, J. J., & Holton, E. F., III. (Eds.) (1995). *In action: Conducting needs assessment.* Alexandria, VA: ASTD.

Robinson, D. G., & Robinson, J. C. (1989). *Training for impact.* San Francisco, CA: Jossey-Bass.

Rossett, A. (1987). *Training needs assessment.* Englewood Cliffs, NJ: Educational Technology Publications.

Ruona, W.E.A. (2005). Analyzing qualitative data. In R. A. Swanson & E. F. Holton III (Eds.), *Research in organizations: Foundations and methods of inquiry* (pp. 233–263). San Francisco, CA: Berrett-Koehler.

Russ-Eft, D., & Preskill, H. (2009). *Evaluation in organizations: A systematic approach to enhancing learning, performance, and change* (2nd ed.). New York, NY: Basic Books.

Schwarz, R. (1995, May). Hiring good facilitators. *Training and Development, 49*(5), 67.

Swanson, R. A. (2007). *Analysis for improving performance* (2nd ed.). San Francisco, CA: Berrett-Koehler.

Watkins, R., Meiers, M. W., & Visser, Y. L. (2012). *A guide to assessing needs*. Washington, DC: The World Bank.

CHAPTER FOUR

McLean, G. N. (2005). *Organization development: Principles, processes, performance*. San Francisco, CA: Berrett-Koehler.

Phillips, J. J., & Holton, E. F., III (Eds.) (1995). *In action: Conducting needs assessment*. Alexandria, VA: ASTD.

Robinson, D. G., & Robinson, J. C. (1995). *Performance consulting: Moving beyond training*. San Francisco, CA: Berrett-Koehler.

Russ-Eft, D., & Preskill, H. (2009). *Evaluation in organizations: A systematic approach to enhancing learning, performance, and change* (2nd ed.). New York, NY: Basic Books.

Torres, R. T., Preskill, H. S., & Piontek, M. E. (2005). *Evaluation strategies for communicating and reporting: Enhancing learning in organizations* (2nd ed.). Thousand Oaks, CA: Sage.

CHAPTER FIVE

Brannick, M. T., & Levine, E. L. (2002). *Job analysis: Methods, research, and applications for human resource management in the new millennium*. Thousand Oaks, CA: Sage.

Butruille, S. (1989, March). Be a better job analyst. *Info-line 8903*. Alexandria, VA: ASTD.

Callahan, M. (1985, March). Be a better task analyst. *Info-line 8503*. Alexandria, VA: ASTD.

Fine, S. A., & Cronshaw, S. F. (1999). *Functional job analysis: A foundation for human resources management*. Mahwah, NJ: Lawrence Erlbaum Associates.

Shepherd, A. (2001). *Hierarchical task analysis*. New York, NY: Taylor & Francis.

Swanson, R. A. (2007). *Analysis for improving performance. Tools for diagnosing organizations and documenting workplace expertise* (2nd ed.). San Francisco. CA: Berrett-Koehler.

CHAPTER SIX

Bergmann, H., Hurson, K., & Russ-Eft, D. (1999). *Everyone a leader: A grassroots model for the new workplace*. Hoboken, NJ: John Wiley & Sons.

Boyatzis, R. (1982). *The competent manager*. Hoboken, NJ: John Wiley & Sons.

Flanagan, J. C. (1954). The critical incident technique. *Psychological Bulletin, 51,* 327–358.

Flanagan, J. C. (1974). *Measuring human performance*. Palo Alto, CA: American Institutes for Research.

Griffiths, B. (1997, February). Constructing and validating a competency model. Unpublished manuscript.

Gupta, K., Sleezer, C. M., & Russ-Eft,, D. F. (2007). *A practical guide to needs assessment* (2nd ed., updated and expanded). San Francisco, CA: Pfeiffer.

International Board of Standards for Training, Performance, and Instruction® (2005). Glossary of terms. Retrieved from ttp://www.ibstpi.org.

Klein, J. D., Spector, J. M., Grabowski, B. L,, & de la Teja, I. (2004). *Instructor competencies: Standards for face-to-face, online, and blended settings* (3rd ed.). Greenwich, CT: Information Age.

Koszalka, T. A., Reiser, R., & Russ-Eft, D. (2013). *Instructional designer competencies: The standards* (4th ed.). Charlotte, NC: Information Age.

Marrelli, A. F. (1998). An introduction to competency analysis and modeling. *Performance Improvement, 37*(5), 8–17.

McClelland, D. C. (1973). Testing for competence rather than for "intelligence." *American Psychologist, 28*, 1–14.

McLagan, P. (1980, December). Competency models. *Training and Development, 34*(12), 23.

Richey, R. C., Fields, D. C., & Foxon, M. (2001). *Instructional design competencies: The standards.* Syracuse, NY: ERIC Clearinghouse on Information & Technology, Syracuse University.

Rothwell, W. J. (1996). *ASTD models for human performance improvement: Roles, competencies, and outputs.* Alexandria, VA: ASTD.

Russ-Eft, D. (2004). Customer service competencies: A global look. *Human Resource Development International, 7*, 211–231.

Russ-Eft, D., Bober, M. J., de la Teja, I., Foxon, M. J., & Koszalka, T. A. (2008). *Evaluator competencies: Standards for the practice of evaluation in organizations.* San Francisco, CA: Jossey-Bass.

Spencer, L. M., & Spencer, S. M. (1993). *Competence at work: Models for superior performance.* Hoboken, NJ: John Wiley & Sons.

White, R. W. (1959). Motivation reconsidered: The concept of competence. *Psychological Review, 66*, 297–333.

CHAPTER SEVEN

Fisher, S. R. (2000). A multilevel theory of organizational performance. Doctoral dissertation, Oklahoma State University, Stillwater.

Fisher, S. R., & Sleezer, C. M. (2003). An overview of a multilevel theory of organizational performance. Paper presented at Institute of Behavioral and Applied Management conference, Tampa, Florida.

Gephart, M. A., & Van Buren, M. E. (1996, October). Building synergy: The power of high-performance work systems. *Training & Development, 50*(10), 21–36.

Mankins, M. C., & Steele, R. (2005, July/August). Turning great strategy into great performance. *Harvard Business Review, 83*(7/8), 64–72.

Porter, M. E. (1980). *Competitive strategy*. New York, NY: The Free Press.

Porter, M. E. (2008). The five competitive forces that shape strategy. *Harvard Business Review, 86*(1), 25–40.

Rummler, G. A., & Brache, A. P. (1995). *Improving performance: How to manage the white space in the organization chart*. San Francisco, CA: Jossey-Bass.

Swanson, R. A. (2007). *Analysis for improving performance*. (2nd ed.). San Francisco, CA: Berrett-Koehler.

CHAPTER EIGHT

Altschuld, J. W., & Kumar, D. D. (2010). *Needs assessment: An overview*. Thousand Oaks, CA: Sage.

Buckingham, M., & Coffman, C. (1999). *First break all the rules*. New York, NY: Simon and Schuster.

Denison (n.d.). Retrieved from www.denisonconsulting.com/ model-surveys/denison-surveys/organizational-culture.

Everything DiSC® (n.d.). Retrieved from www.everythingdisc.com.

The five dysfunctions of a team. (n.d.). Retrieved from www.tablegroup. com/dysfunctions/,

Gallup. (2013). Q12® Meta-Analysis. Retrieved from www.gallup.com/ strategicconsulting/126806/Q12-Meta-Analysis.aspx.

MBTI instrument for life®. (n.d.). Retrieved from www.myersbriggs.org.

Witkin, B. R. (1984). *Assessing needs in educational and social programs: Using information to make decisions, set priorities, and allocate resources*. San Francisco, CA Jossey-Bass.

CHAPTER NINE

Block, P. (2011). *Flawless consulting* (3rd ed.). San Francisco, CA: Pfeiffer.

International Board of Standards for Training, Performance, and Instruction. (2005). Evaluator competencies. Retrieved from www.ibstpi.org.

Hale, J. A. (2005). The future of ISD: Death if we keep killing it. Paper presented at International Society for Performance Improvement conference, Dallas, Texas.

Kaminski, K., & Lopes, T. (2009). Return on investment: Training and development. SHRM Education Resources for HR Educators Module. Retrieved from www.shrm.org/Education/hreducation/Pages/ReturnonInvestmentTrainingandDevelopment.aspx.

King, S. B. (1998). Practitioner verification of the human performance improvement analyst competencies and outputs. Doctoral dissertation, Pennsylvania State University. Digital Dissertations, AAT 9915873.

McNamara, C. (2005). *Field guide to consulting and organizational development with nonprofits.* Minneapolis, MN: Authenticity Consulting, LLC.

Phillips, J. J. (2003). *Return on investment in training and performance improvement programs* (2nd ed.). Burlington: MA: Butterworth-Heinemann.

Rothwell, W. J. (1996). *ASTD models for human performance improvement: Roles, competencies, and outputs.* Alexandria, VA: ASTD.

Royse, D., Staton-Tindall, M., Badger, K., & Webster, J. M., (2009). *Needs assessment pocket guides to social work research methods.* New York, NY: Oxford University Press.

Tobey, D. ((2005). *Needs assessment basics.* Alexandria, VA: ASTD.

Torres, R. T., Preskill, H., & Piontek, M. (2005). *Evaluation strategies for communicating and reporting: Enhancing learning in organizations* (2nd ed.). Thousand Oaks, CA: Sage.

Watkins, R., Meiers, M. W., & Visser, Y. L. (2012). *A guide to assessing needs: Essential tools for collecting information, making decisions, and achieving development results.* Washington, DC: The World Bank.

CHAPTER TEN

American Evaluation Association. (2004). Guiding principles for evaluators. Retrieved from www.eval.org/Publications/Guiding Principles.asp.

International Society for Performance Improvement. (2002). Code of ethics. Retrieved from www.ispi.org.

JCSEE (2013). Program evaluation standards. Retrieved from www. JCSEE.

Joint Committee on Standards for Educational Evaluation. (2013). The program evaluation standard statements. Retrieved from www.jcsee .org/program-evaluation-standards/program-evaluation-standards-statements.

Russ-Eft, D., Burns, J. Z., Dean, P. J., Hatcher, T. G., Otte, F. L., & Preskill, H. S. (1999). Academy of Human Resource Development Standards on Ethics and Integrity. Bowling Green, OH: AHRD. Retrieved from www.ahrd.org.

Yarbrough, D. B., Shulha, L. M., Hopson, R. K, & Caruthers, F. A. (2011). *The program evaluation standards: A guide for evaluators and evaluation users* (3rd ed.). Thousand Oaks, CA: Sage.

CHAPTER ELEVEN

AHRD (2013). Events calendar. Retrieved from www.ahrd.org.

American Evaluation Association. (n.d.). Learning. Retrieved from www .eval.org.

ASTD. (2012). ASTD events. Retrieved from www.astd.org.

Allen, M. W. (2003). *Michael Allen's guide to e-learning*. Hoboken, NJ: John Wiley & Sons.

Altschuld, J. W. (Ed.). (2010). *Needs assessment kit* (Vols. 1–5). Thousand Oaks, CA: Sage.

Baizerman, M. L., Fink, A., & Roholt, R. V. (2012). From consilium to advice: A review of the evaluation and related literature on advisory structures and processes. In R. Velure Roholt & M. L. Baizerman (Eds), Evaluation advisory groups. *New Directions for Evaluation, 136,* 5–29.

Clark, D. (August 24, 2013). ADDIE Timeline. In Big and Little Dog's Performance Juxtaposition. Retrieved from www.nwlink. com/~donclark/history_isd/addie.html.

Guerra-Lopez, I., & Kaufman, R. (2013). *Needs assessment for organizational success.* Alexandria, VA: ASTD.

ISPI. (2013). Education. Retrieved from www.ispi.org.

Jordan, B., & Putz, P. (2004). Assessment as practice: Notes on measures, tests, and targets. *Human Organization, 63*(3), 346–358.

Kunneman, D. E., & Sleezer, C. M. (2000). Using performance analysis for training in an organization implementing ISO-9000 manufacturing practices: A case study. *Performance Improvement Quarterly, 13*(4), 47–66.

Pershing, J. A. (2006). *Handbook of human performance technology* (3rd ed.). San Francisco, CA: Pfeiffer.

Preskill, H., & Russ-Eft, D. (2005). Building evaluation capacity: 72 activities for teaching and training. Thousand Oaks, CA: Sage.

Raynor, M. E., & Ahmed, M. (2013). Three rules for making a company truly great. *Harvard Business Review, 91*(4), 108–117.

Rossett, A. (2009). *First things fast.* San Francisco, CA: Pfeiffer.

Russ-Eft, D., & Preskill, H. (2009). *Evaluation in organizations: A systematic approach to enhancing learning, performance, and change* (2nd ed.). New York, NY: Basic Books.

Scriven, M. (1991). *Evaluation thesaurus* (4th ed.). Thousand Oaks, CA: Sage.

Sleezer, C. M. (1990). The development and validation of a performance analysis for training model (vols. 1–3). Doctoral dissertation, University of Minnesota. Digital Dissertations, AAT 9100979.

Swanson, R. A. (2007). *Analysis for improving performance* (2nd ed.). San Francisco, CA: Berrett-Koehler.

Swanson, R. A., & Holton, E. F., III. (2009). *Foundations of human resource development* (2nd ed.). San Francisco, CA: Berrett-Koehler.

Van Tiem, D. M., Moseley, J. M., & Dessinger, J. C. (2012). Performance improvement/HPT model. Retrieved from www.ispi.org/images/HPT-Model-2012.jpg.

Watkins, R., Meiers, M. W., & Visser, Y. L. (2012). *A guide to assessing needs.* Washington, DC: The World Bank.

Zemke, R., & Kramlinger, T. (1982). *Figuring things out: A trainer's guide to needs and task analysis* (4th ed.). Reading, MA: Addison-Wesley.

TOOLKIT FORMS

Barabasi, A. (2002). *Linked: The new science of networks*. Cambridge, MA: Perseus.

Fisher, S. R., & Sleezer, C. M. (2003). An overview of a multilevel theory of organizational performance. Paper presented at Institute of Behavioral and Applied Management Conference, Tampa, Florida.

Klein, K. J., & Kozlowski, S.W.J. (2000). *Multilevel theory, research, and methods in organizations: Foundations, extensions, and new directions*. San Francisco, CA: Jossey-Bass.

Morgan, G. (2006). Provocative ideas: The 15% concept. Retrieved from www.imaginiz.com/.

ADDITIONAL RESOURCES FOR TOOLKIT 2.2

Bandura, A. (1977). *Social learning theory*. New York, NY: General Learning Press.

Becker, B. E., Huselid, M. A., & Ulrich, D. (2001). *The HR scorecard: Linking people, strategy, and performance*. Boston, MA: Harvard Business School Press.

Bee, F., & Bee, R. (1997). *Training needs analysis and evaluation*. London, UK: Chartered Institute of Personnel & Development.

Chow, I. H-S. (1995) .Management education in Hong Kong: needs and challenges. *International Journal of Educational Management, 9*(5), 10–15.

Clark, D. (2013). Performance, learning, leadership, & knowledge. Retrieved from www.nwlink.com/~donclark/

Ferond, C. (2006). The origin and evolution of performance technology. In J. Pershing (Ed.), *Handbook of human performance technology* (3rd ed.). San Francisco, CA: Pfeiffer.

Flanagan, J. C. (1954). The critical incident technique. *Psychological Bulletin, 51*(4). Retrieved from www.analytictech.com/mb870/Readings/flanagan.pdf.

Gilbert, T. J. (1978). *Human competence: Engineering worthy performance.* New York, NY: McGraw-Hill.

Harless, J. (1970). *An ounce of analysis (is worth a pound of objectives).* Newman: GA: Harless Performance Guild.

Honey, P., & Mumford, A. (1986), ,*Using your learning styles.* Maidenhead, UK: Peter Honey Publications.

Kaplan, R. S., & Norton, D. P. (1993, September/October). Putting the balanced scorecard to work. *Harvard Business Review*, pp. 134–147.

Kaufman, R. (1991). *Strategic planning plus: An organizational guide.* Thousand Oaks, CA: Sage.

Lee, W. W., & Roadman, K. H. (1991). Linking needs assessment to performance based evaluation. *Performance and Improvement, 30*(6), 4–6.

Mager, R. F., & Pipe, P. (1970). *Analyzing performance problems; or, you really oughta wanna.* Belmont, CA: Fearon Pitman.

McGehee, W., & Thayer, P. W. (1961). *Training in business and industry.* Hoboken, NJ: John Wiley & Sons.

Miller, V. A. (1967). The history of training. In R. L. Craig (Ed.), *Training and development handbook.* New York, NY: McGraw-Hill.

Montagna, J. A. (2006). The industrial revolution. Retrieved from www.yale.edu/ynhti/curriculum/units/1981/2/81.02.06.x.html.

National Vocational Qualifications. www.management-standards.org/

Nobel Foundation. (2006). Retrieved from http://nobelprize.org/medicine/laureates/1904/pavlov-bio.html.

Parasuraman, A., Zeithaml, V., & Berry, L. L. (1985, Autumn). A conceptual model of service quality and its implications for future research. *Journal of Marketing*, 49, 41–50.

Parasuraman, A., Zeithaml, V., & Berry, L. L. (1991). Refinement and reassessment of the SERVQUAL scale. *Journal of Retailing, 67*(4), 420-450.

Prahalad, C. K., & Hamel, G. (1990), The core competence of the corporation. *Harvard Business Review, 68*(3), 79–91.

Reiser, R. A. (2001). History of instructional design and technology: Part II: A history of instructional design. *ETR&D, 49*(2), 57–67. Retrieved from www.speakeasydesigns.com/SDSU/student/SAGE/compsprep/History_of_Instructional_Design.pdf.

Rossett, A. (1987). *Training needs assessment.* Englewood Cliffs, NJ: Educational Technology.

Rossett, A. (1999). *First things fast.* San Francisco, CA: Pfeiffer.

Rummler, G. A., & Brache, A. P. (1995). *Improving performance: How to manage the white space on the organization chart* (2nd ed.). San Francisco, CA: Jossey-Bass.

Sadler-Smith, E. (1996). Learning styles: a holistic approach. *Journal of European Industrial Training, 20*(7), 29–36.

Scriven, M. (1991). *Evaluation thesaurus* (4th ed.). Thousand Oaks, CA: Sage.

Sleight, D. A. (1993). A developmental history of training in the United States and Europe. www.msu.edu/□~sleightd/trainhst.html.

Swanson, R. A., & Torraco, R. J. (1995). The history of technical training. In L. Kelly (Ed.), *Technical and skills training handbook of the American Society for Training and Development* (pp. 1–47). New York, NY: McGraw-Hill.

Taylor, F. W. (2006, January 24-26). http://en.wikipedia.org/wiki/Frederick_Winslow_Taylor.

The Industrial Society. (2000, April). Training evaluation. *Managing Best Practice, 70.*

The Myers and Briggs Foundation. www.myersbriggs.org/

Van Tiem, D. M., Moseley, J. M., & Dessinger, J. C. (2004). *Fundamentals of performance technology* (2nd ed.). Silver Spring, MD: ISPI.

Waterman, R., Peters, T., & Phillips, J. J. (1991). The seven-S framework. In H. Mintzberg & J. Quinn (Eds.), *The strategy process: Concepts, contexts, cases.* Englewood Cliffs, NJ: Prentice Hall.

Zemke, R., & Kramlinger, T. (1982). *Figuring things out: A trainer's guide to needs and task analysis* (4th ed.). Reading, MA: Addison-Wesley.

GLOSSARY

Beck, D. E., & Cowan, C. C. (2006). *Spiral dynamics: Mastering values, leadership, and change.* Malden, MA: Blackwell.

Block, P. (2000). *Flawless consulting* (2nd ed.). San Francisco, CA: Jossey-Bass.

Flanagan, J. C. (1954). The critical incident technique. *Psychological Bulletin, 51*, 327–358.

Flanagan, J. C. (1974). *Measuring human performance.* Palo Alto, CA: American Institutes for Research.

Gilbert, T. J. (1978). *Human competence: Engineering worthy performance.* New York, NY: McGraw-Hill.

Harless, J. (1970). *An ounce of analysis (is worth a pound of objectives).* Newman, GA: Harless Performance Guild.

International Board of Standards for Training, Performance, and Instruction. (2005). Glossary of terms. Retrieved from www.ibstpi.org.

Kaufman, R., Rojas, A. M., & Mayer, H. (1993). *Needs assessment: A user's guide.* Englewood Cliffs, NJ: Educational Technology Publications.

Likert, R. (1932). A technique for the measurement of attitudes. *Archives of Psychology, 140*, 1–55.

Rossett, A. (1987). *Training needs assessment.* Englewood Cliffs, NJ: Educational Technology Publications.

Scriven, M. (1991). *Evaluation thesaurus* (4th ed.). Thousand Oaks, CA: Sage.

Index

Page references followed by *fig* indicate an illustrated figure.

About the Authors

CATHERINE (CATHY) M. SLEEZER, PH.D., works with employee training and performance improvement specialists to provide consulting services on human resources for private, public, and government sector organizations. She has held roles in managing human resource projects for a large international organization (Baker Hughes). She has also held roles in academia (professor of HRD at Oklahoma State University, assistant professor at Penn State, where she taught HRD and research courses). She also served as director of the Training and Development Research Center at Penn State, where she led applied research projects in collaboration with organizations. She is a certified performance technologist. She is a former president of the International Board of Standards for Training, Performance, and Instruction (ibstpi), former board member of the Academy of Human Resource Development, and a former member of the ASTD Research Committee. She has many research publications in the areas of needs assessment, evaluation, training, and performance improvement. Her co-authored books include *Human Resources Development Review: Research and Implications* (Sage), *Human Resource Development and Information Technology: Making Global Connections* (Kluwer), and *Improving Human Resource Development Through Measurement* (ASTD), and *Fieldbook of ibstpi Evaluator Competencies* (Information Age). She also co-authored the ASTD course Measuring Training and Performance: A Course in Human Performance Improvement.

DARLENE F. RUSS-EFT, PH.D., is a professor of adult education and higher education leadership in the College of Education at Oregon State University, where she teaches master's and doctoral courses in research, program evaluation, and learning theory. Prior to joining Oregon State University, she was director of research for AchieveGlobal and Zenger-Miller. She is a current director of the International Board of Standards for Training, Performance, and Instruction, the AHRD past president, a past editor of *Human Resource Development Quarterly*, a past member of the American Evaluation Association Board, and a past chair of the ASTD research committee. Her previous books include *Human Resources Development Review: Research and Implications* (Sage), *Evaluator Competencies: Standards for the Practice of Evaluation in Organizations* (Jossey-Bass), *Building Evaluation Capacity: 72 Activities for Teaching and Training* (Sage), *Evaluation in Organizations: A Systematic Approach to Enhancing Learning, Performance, and Change* (Perseus Press), *Instructional Designer Competencies: The Standards* (Information Age), and *Fieldbook of ibstpi Evaluator Competencies* (Information Age).

KAVITA GUPTA is a community volunteer leader who has chaired or co-chaired more than twenty-five committees for the University of Southern California, Children's Hospital of Wisconsin, the American Cancer Society Midwest Division, and private and public schools. She has managed fund-raising initiatives totaling over $300k and overseen hundreds of volunteers. Kavita also writes book reviews for the National Association for College Admission Counseling. Prior to this, Kavita worked as a consultant and corporate trainer. She started her career with Citicorp and later worked with clients and conducted workshops on needs assessment and how to design training programs for managers, professionals and line employees from the public and private sector, as an adjunct faculty member of the University of New Hampshire and Maine Continuing Education Division. She also served on professional boards and committees for the American Society for Training and Development and presented at trade conferences. Kavita holds an M.S. in instructional systems technology from Indiana University and an M.A. in sociology and B.A. in economics from a university in India.